Dear Reader,

For me, discovering a plant-based diet was a gift. I lost 20 pounds, lowered my cholesterol by 40 points, reversed the heart palpitations that were plaguing me, and stopped arthritis in its tracks, all without medication!

I now feel passionate about **helping you discover** the greatest wealth on earth—your health. We didn't evolve on this planet eating the sugary, salty, oily food that's so prevalent today. Unfortunately, we're paying the price because, according to the American Medical Association, diet is now our number one killer. Despite this unfortunate situation, adopting this **wholesome way of eating** can help you restore your well-being.

That's why I'm so excited to share with you these plant-based meal **prep tips and delicious recipes**. Inside, you'll not only discover what a plant-based diet looks like, you'll also get clarification on the science, find tasty new foods, learn which convenience foods you can eat, and much more. In addition, you'll learn tips for meal prepping that will make this lifestyle quick and efficient to start. Plus, you'll enjoy the food!

Congratulations on taking your health into your own hands. We don't have a minute to waste.

Diane K. Smith

Welcome to the Everything® Series!

These handy, accessible books give you all you need to tackle a difficult project, gain a new hobby, comprehend a fascinating topic, prepare for an exam, or even brush up on something you learned back in school but have since forgotten.

You can choose to read an Everything® book from cover to cover or just pick out the information you want from our four useful boxes: Questions, Facts, Alerts, and Essentials. We give you everything you need to know on the subject, but throw in a lot of fun stuff along the way too.

question	fact
Answers to common questions.	Important snippets of information.

alert	essential
Urgent warnings.	Quick handy tips.

We now have more than 600 Everything® books in print, spanning such wide-ranging categories as cooking, health, parenting, personal finance, wedding planning, word puzzles, and so much more. When you're done reading them all, you can finally say you know Everything®!

PUBLISHER Karen Cooper

MANAGING EDITOR Lisa Laing

COPY CHIEF Casey Ebert

PRODUCTION EDITOR Jo-Anne Duhamel

ACQUISITIONS EDITOR Julia Jacques

DEVELOPMENT EDITOR Laura Daly

EVERYTHING® SERIES COVER DESIGNER Erin Alexander

THE

EVERYTHING®

PLANT-BASED
MEAL PREP
COOKBOOK

DIANE K. SMITH

**200 EASY, MAKE-AHEAD RECIPES
FEATURING PLANT-BASED INGREDIENTS**

ADAMS MEDIA

NEW YORK   LONDON   TORONTO   SYDNEY   NEW DELHI

Adams Media
An Imprint of Simon & Schuster, Inc.
57 Littlefield Street
Avon, Massachusetts 02322

An Everything® Series Book.
Everything® and everything.com® are registered trademarks of Simon & Schuster, Inc.

First Adams Media trade paperback edition November 2020

ADAMS MEDIA and colophon are trademarks of Simon & Schuster.

For information about special discounts for bulk purchases, please contact Simon & Schuster Special Sales at 1-866-506-1949 or business@simonandschuster.com.

The Simon & Schuster Speakers Bureau can bring authors to your live event. For more information or to book an event contact the Simon & Schuster Speakers Bureau at 1-866-248-3049 or visit our website at www.simonspeakers.com.

Interior design by Colleen Cunningham
Photographs by James Stefiuk

Manufactured in the United States of America

2 2021

Library of Congress Cataloging-in-Publication Data has been applied for.

ISBN 978-1-5072-1422-0
ISBN 978-1-5072-1423-7 (ebook)

Always follow safety and commonsense cooking protocols while using kitchen utensils, operating ovens and stoves, and handling uncooked food. If children are assisting in the preparation of any recipe, they should always be supervised by an adult.

This book is intended as general information only, and should not be used to diagnose or treat any health condition. In light of the complex, individual, and specific nature of health problems, this book is not intended to replace professional medical advice. The ideas, procedures, and suggestions in this book are intended to supplement, not replace, the advice of a trained medical professional. Consult your physician before adopting any of the suggestions in this book, as well as about any condition that may require diagnosis or medical attention. The author and publisher disclaim any liability arising directly or indirectly from the use of this book.

Contents

10: DESSERTS **239**

2-WEEK PLANT-BASED MEAL PLAN **264**

STANDARD US/METRIC MEASUREMENT CONVERSIONS **268**

INDEX **269**

Introduction

According to a 2020 *US News & World Report* study, a plant-based eating plan is one of the healthiest diets you can choose. Plant-based meals can help you avoid the chronic health issues that arise from consuming too much highly processed, sugar-laden, oil-saturated, and high-sodium foods. But how will you keep track of which fresh ingredients to purchase and then use them while they're still fresh? With meal planning and prep!

If you're new to eating a plant-based diet, transitioning away from meat and dairy might feel a bit overwhelming at first, but meal planning will help you stay organized and on track. If you're already eating a plant-based diet, the ideas and recipes in this book will give you hundreds of new recipe ideas to make each meal of the day something you'll look forward to. Planning ahead will also help you avoid giving in to unhealthy temptations and cravings—you'll already have a refrigerator full of meals and snacks ready to go. You can also now find shortcuts at your local grocery store, such as prechopped vegetables, to make plant-based meal prep even faster and easier.

Plant-based meals are not only healthy, they're also mouthwateringly delicious. You'll be piling your plate with colorful vegetables, juicy fruits, and plant-based proteins to keep you full. The fruits and vegetables that form the foundation of this eating plan provide loads of antioxidants, deliver key vitamins and minerals, and promote healthy levels of cholesterol and blood sugar. From hearty breakfasts like Pumpkin Pancakes to protein-packed lunches like the Roasted Vegetable–Quinoa Bowl to scrumptious dinners like Roasted Vegetable Tacos to sweet treats like Avocado Brownies, you're sure to find crowd-pleasing dishes the whole family will enjoy.

The Everything® Plant-Based Meal Prep Cookbook outlines all the key information you need, including how to create a plant-based diet that fills all your nutritional needs and ways to mix and match ingredients so that nothing goes to waste. The two hundred recipes feature easy-to-find ingredients and storage and reheating instructions so your leftovers will taste like they were just cooked! You'll also find a two-week sample meal plan that includes full days of food choices—breakfast, lunch, dinner, snacks, and even desserts—to get you started creating your own weekly plans that fit your schedule and taste buds. The longest-lived people in the world eat a mostly plant-based diet, so congratulations on adopting this healthy lifestyle. Meal prepping will help make plant-based eating a simple part of your life in no time!

CHAPTER 1

How to Eat and Meal Prep a Plant-Based Diet

Eating foods grown in nature is the most natural way to eat, but if you're new to this lifestyle, your taste buds might tell you something different at first. Many of us have gotten used to salty, sugary, oily versions of food and don't even realize it. In this chapter, you'll discover how that happened and learn what it means to eat a whole-food, plant-based diet. Implementing new habits can sometimes be a challenge, but meal prepping will help you through it. Let this chapter clear a path toward wholesome whole-food living.

Whole-Food, Plant-Based Diet, Defined

A whole-food, plant-based diet is a lifestyle in which you eat whole foods grown in nature: fruits, vegetables, whole grains, legumes, nuts, and seeds (all of which are rich in fiber, vitamins, phytonutrients, and minerals)—and little to no meat, fish, or dairy.

Is "Plant-Based" the Same As "Vegan"?

The term "plant-based" was originally coined to distinguish it as a healthier version of a vegan diet. Being vegan includes an ethical lifestyle choice that values animals as sentient beings. The vegan philosophy, in addition to eating no meat, dairy, eggs, or fish, dictates that no animals should be harmed. A vegan diet does not technically distinguish between healthy and unhealthy plant foods, so you could still eat French fries, chips, candy, nondairy ice cream, and vegan butter on a vegan diet.

Can I Eat Meat?

The doctors who are leaders in the whole-food, plant-based diet movement recommend you do not eat meat, fish, or dairy except while you're making the transition, especially if you have heart disease. However, if you look at the locations around the world where people are the longest-lived, called the Blue Zones, you'll find that their diets are 95 percent plant-based. Meals are centered around beans and plant-based foods, while meat and dairy are eaten infrequently. If meat comprises 5 percent of your diet, you are still getting the vast majority of the benefits of a plant-based diet.

Health Benefits of a Plant-Based Diet

In short, a plant-based diet is great for your health because it provides all the essential vitamins and nutrients (except for vitamin B_{12}) that your body needs to function—and no unwanted additives and preservatives. Plus, plant foods contain on average 64 times more antioxidants than animal foods.

Your body runs on fuel supplied by the food you eat, in the form of protein, carbs, and fat (macronutrients). But food doesn't just give you energy.

Let's look at just a few of the many ways that science has found that plant-based nutrients benefit our health.

Improves heart health: Beta-glucans in oats, barley, and some fruits (such as pears and apples) help lower cholesterol, reduce blood pressure, and keep arteries clean. Fiber-rich foods such as legumes, broccoli, carrots, beets, and Brussels sprouts have the same beneficial effect, plus they can also lower triglycerides and homocysteine, a compound that can raise heart attack risk.

Supports digestion: The millions of microorganisms and bacteria in your gut, called the microbiome, function best on a high-fiber diet, and they play a big role in digestive health. By eating a plant-based diet, which is high in fiber, you'll be able to keep your digestive system running smoothly.

Boosts immune function: Vitamin C—found in many foods, including citrus, bell peppers, broccoli, tomato, and kale—helps your immune system function at its best by reducing inflammation. Beta-carotene, present in orange vegetables like carrots and sweet potatoes as well as leafy greens, also improves immune function. So does the vitamin D found in mushrooms.

Lowers the risk of type 2 diabetes: Foods high in fat, and especially animal fat, contribute to type 2 diabetes by clogging receptors meant for insulin. While sugary foods are never a good choice for health, by eating more fruits and vegetables, you'll lower fat consumption and possibly even reverse type 2 diabetes. Foods high in fiber, such as beans, also help the body absorb blood sugar more easily.

Reduces the risk of cancer: Contrary to popular opinion, organic, non-GMO soy has been shown to help prevent the resurgence of breast cancer and reduce the chances of getting it in the first place by its unique ability to block human estrogen from causing problems. A diet low in dairy helps to prevent prostate cancer. All fruits and vegetables have a unique ability to prevent small, cancerous blood vessels from growing.

Improves emotional states: Quercetin—found in apples, red onions, leafy greens, broccoli, and grapes—reduces inflammation that has been linked to depression. In addition, plant foods can help restore balance of neurotransmitters in the brain.

Animal Foods Can Have a Negative Impact on Your Health

Overconsumption of animal products, including fish, can lead to the development of chronic disease. The World Health Organization now considers red and processed meats to be carcinogens. Certain types of fish contain mercury, PCBs, and antibiotics, making them potentially hazardous to health, especially when consumed in large amounts. In addition:

- Animal products are also high in calories and saturated fat, which have been implicated in heart disease, type 2 diabetes, high blood pressure, stroke, and other lifestyle diseases.
- Chicken, eggs, and other animal products are high in arachidonic acid, a precursor to inflammation, which is the root cause of many chronic diseases.
- *Scientific American* has linked the heavy use of antibiotics in animals raised on factory farms to the growth of drug-resistant diseases like MRSA. Unfortunately, many of these viruses eventually affect humans.

After decades of research, the science is clear: Eating a whole-food, plant-based diet is a much healthier choice.

The Lowdown on Processed Foods

There's a reason that "whole" is emphasized in a whole-food, plant-based diet. Some foods, while technically plant-based, are more highly processed than others. Processing means that food has been cooked, canned, frozen, packaged, or changed in nutritional composition by fortifying, preserving, or preparing it. Most processed foods come in a box, carton, jar, or bag. There are also various levels of processing. For example, white rice or white bread is more processed than brown rice and whole-grain bread.

It's unrealistic for most of us to avoid *all* processed and packaged foods. So where do you draw the line? This list of processed foods, from least processed to most, provided by www.eatright.org, can help you prioritize:

- Minimally processed foods such as bagged spinach, cut vegetables, and roasted nuts are often simply prepped in advance for convenience.
- Foods processed at their peak of freshness to lock in nutritional quality include canned tomatoes and frozen fruit and vegetables.
- Foods with ingredients such as sweeteners, spices, colors, and preservatives added for flavor and texture include jarred pasta sauce, salad dressing, yogurt, and cake mixes.
- Ready-to-eat foods such as crackers, granola, and deli meat are more heavily processed.
- The most heavily processed foods are premade meals, including frozen pizza and microwaveable dinners.

This list may seem complicated, but here's the good news—you don't have to avoid *all* processed foods. Look for food that is minimally processed at its peak to lock in nutritional quality. This includes frozen fruits and vegetables, bagged items in their fresh natural state (such as salad greens and raw nuts), and foods that have very little added sugar, oil, salt, or other additives.

It's also recommended that you eat very little or no salt on a plant-based diet. Using flavorful herbs and spices really helps you kick the salt habit without losing flavor. Adjust any of the recipes in this book with herbs and/or spices to your liking so that the flavor you like comes through. While salt is used in these recipes, it is purposely kept at a low level.

How to Decide If Packaged Food Is Okay to Eat

In order to decide if processed or packaged food is appropriate to eat on a plant-based diet, it's important to become a label reader. These are the black-and-white boxes shown on food packages that tell you what ingredients the food contains and the nutritional facts about the food. Here are some tips for reading labels:

- The list of ingredients starts with the ingredient in the highest quantity. If the list begins with sugar, it's probably not a healthy food.
- If the list of ingredients is very long or has too many long and complicated-sounding words, avoid that item!
- Foods with high amounts of sodium, sugar, oil, or additives such as food coloring, flavorings, thickeners, or emulsifiers are not good choices.
- Look for foods that say "low sodium" or "high fiber."

- If a packaged food says it's "natural" or "healthy," check out the ingredients and decide for yourself if that's true.

The more you practice reading labels, the easier it will become.

Will I Get Enough Protein?

It's a common misconception that a plant-based diet is deficient in protein. The truth is that most plant foods have some protein, so there is little chance that you'll be deficient.

question

Should I Be Concerned about Eating Soy?

Fears about soy are unfounded. The latest research shows that although soy does contain phytoestrogens, these "plant" estrogens, which are unrelated to human estrogen, actually offer protection from breast cancer and resurgence after diagnosis and treatment. In addition, soy puts little stress on the kidneys, unlike animal protein.

What's not so well known is that there is a plethora of options when it comes to excellent sources of plant-based protein. The most common source of plant protein is from soy and its derivatives, such as edamame, tofu, soy milk, and tempeh (a packaged food made from fermented soybeans with different flavorings). There is also a packaged product called seitan that is made from the protein portion of wheat. Legumes and beans follow close behind as protein powerhouses. Some "pseudograins" are also higher in protein, for example, quinoa and buckwheat (these are technically seeds).

The Recommended Dietary Allowance (RDA) for protein is 0.8 grams of protein per kilogram of body weight or .36 grams per pound. For a 140-pound woman, that's 50 grams of protein, and for a 175-pound man, 63 grams of protein per day. (The RDA is the amount of a nutrient you need to meet your basic nutritional requirements.) This amount of protein is easily met if you're eating a well-rounded plant-based diet with lots of vegetables, whole grains, and legumes, as well as some nuts and seeds.

Are Carbs Bad?

The trend to avoid carbohydrates has been raging on and off for decades. While a high-protein diet devoid of carbs can help you lose weight in the short run, there is nothing wrong with eating nutritionally dense carbs, such as intact whole grains and whole-grain breads and pasta. In fact, according to a 2015 study in *BMC Medicine*, eating whole grains can reduce the risk of death from many diseases, including cancer, by 17 percent.

These types of carbs are very different from the refined carbs found in sugary cereals, white bread, candy, and soda. Avoid highly processed carbs that have little fiber or

nutrition. Instead, look for these whole-grain choices:

- Wheat berries
- Brown rice
- Barley
- Millet
- Farro
- Oats
- Quinoa and buckwheat (considered pseudograins)

It's really the type of carbs that makes the difference, so look for whole-grain choices.

Indulge In Fruits and Vegetables

Fruits and vegetables are packed full of vitamins, minerals, and fiber—in other words, everything your cells need to be nourished and function optimally. If you're worried that plant-based eating will get boring, have no fear. You'll find plenty of deliciously satisfying recipes here in *The Everything® Plant-Based Meal Prep Cookbook*.

Organic

If you can afford it, it's best to eat organic produce. If you have to prioritize which foods to purchase, stick with the Environmental Working Group's "Clean 15" (foods that are okay to purchase in nonorganic varieties) and avoid their "Dirty Dozen" (foods that are most often contaminated with pesticides; it's best to buy organic varieties of these):

Clean Fifteen	*Dirty Dozen*
1. Avocados	1. Strawberries
2. Sweet corn	2. Spinach
3. Pineapple	3. Kale
4. Onions	4. Nectarines
5. Papaya	5. Apples
6. Sweet peas (frozen)	6. Grapes
7. Eggplant	7. Peaches
8. Asparagus	8. Cherries
9. Cauliflower	9. Pears
10. Cantaloupe	10. Tomatoes
11. Broccoli	11. Celery
12. Mushrooms	12. Potatoes
13. Cabbage	
14. Honeydew melon	
15. Kiwi	

Fresh versus Frozen versus Canned

Fruits and vegetables that are frozen, canned, or dried in their natural state without added sugars or preservatives and low in salt are good choices for a plant-based diet. Is there any nutritional advantage to one product over the other? While you might think that fresh produce is the best, it turns out that frozen foods are equal and sometimes even superior in nutritional value, depending on how long "fresh" produce has been on the shelf (fresh produce tends to lose nutrients over time). Frozen food is available year-round, so when peaches are out of season in your area, you can choose frozen and still get all their nutrition, for example. Frozen produce is picked at the peak of ripeness, retains its nutritional value, and is often pre-prepped, making it easier to use for meal prep.

Canned produce undergoes more processing, which can break down essential nutrients. And, unfortunately, many cans are lined with the plastic chemical BPA, BPS, or BPF. However, some produce in cans are a good choice. For example, tomatoes are available year-round, easy to use, and often have a better quality and taste than fresh tomatoes. Tomatoes are also available in glass jars or cardboard Tetra Paks, which avoid the use of chemical linings.

> **question**
>
> **Should I Avoid Fruit Because It's Too Sugary?**
>
> Fruit and other whole-grain carbs will not spike your blood sugar like processed carbs do. Fruit appears to actually benefit blood sugar control, causing it to fall, not rise, because it has a different metabolic effect on your body than the refined carbohydrates found in processed foods.

Eat Your Beans Every Day

Because beans are the cornerstone of every long-lived society in the world, they deserve a special place on your plant-based plate. Dr. Joel Fuhrman recommends eating ½ cup of beans every day. They're a good source of B vitamins, protein, and fiber.

Beans are easy to prepare from scratch, and they're an important part of meal prep. You'll save money if you make them yourself from dry beans, but you also can purchase them canned from the store in low- or no-sodium varieties.

The Lowdown on Nuts and Seeds

Nuts and seeds can be a healthy part of a whole-food, plant-based diet in moderation. Because they are high in fat and calories, 1–2 ounces per day is all that's recommended by some doctors. Dr. Fuhrman's research has shown that nuts and seeds are essential for good health and even weight loss. They help lower cholesterol, minimize inflammation, and reduce the risk of heart disease.

However, other doctors who tout the benefits of the plant-based diet—notably, cardiologist Caldwell Esselstyn—advocate avoiding nuts and seeds altogether, especially if you already have heart disease. Choose what you feel is best for your health when it comes to eating nuts and seeds.

How to Soak Cashews

Raw, unsalted cashews are a part of many plant-based recipes because they add creaminess and take the place of processed oil. If you have a high-powered blender, you may not need to soak them. If you don't or aren't sure, use one of these soaking methods first to soften them before blending.

- If you have time, cover cashews in water and soak 2–3 hours. Drain and rinse. Soaking overnight is not necessary, but also works.

- For a quick soak, cover in boiling water and soak for 10 minutes. Drain and rinse.

What about Oils?

Because oils (such as canola, corn, olive, or soybean) are processed, they should not play much of a role in a plant-based diet. They're very high in calories and fat—119 calories and 14 grams of fat per tablespoon! Some researchers point out the deleterious effect of any processed oil, including olive oil, on endothelial function (the lining of our blood vessels), while others claim that in moderation, oil can be a healthy part of your diet. It's best to talk to your doctor about what is best for you.

> **essential**
>
> Most oils are high in omega-6 fatty acids, which many people get way too much of. However, most people do not eat enough omega-3s. That's why eating nuts and seeds is a better choice. Flaxseeds, hemp seeds, and chia seeds all have omega-3s.

The most significant and healthiest whole-food sources of fat are raw nuts, seeds, and avocado. Some fruits, vegetables, and grains also contain modest amounts of fat.

At all costs, stay away from hydrogenated oil (found in margarine), which contains trans fats. Trans fats have been associated with chronic diseases including heart disease, obesity, cancer, and diabetes. Coconut oil, which is 100 percent fat, is not any better, since about 80–90 percent of it is saturated. Saturated fats are implicated in high cholesterol levels.

Cooking Without Oil

The main thing to remember about including oil in a plant-based diet is to limit its use to very little to none. Most of the recipes in this book use very little or no oil.

Cooking and baking without oil is easier than you think. To sauté or stir-fry, simply substitute a little water, vegetable broth, or wine in place of oil. You can achieve browning, too, if you use a nonstick pan and give it enough time. Roasting in the oven without oil works well. Deep frying is out, of course, but an air fryer will give you the taste of fried food without the use of oil. And baking works too. Check out this article for more details about cooking without oil: www.plant basedcooking.com/cooking-without-oil.

Recipe Substitutions

When embarking on a new plant-based diet, you might be concerned with finding substitutions for your old favorite recipes. Whether it's dairy, eggs, meat, or seafood, don't worry—you have a lot of fantastic options!

Use your label-reading skills to assess your options for vegan mayonnaises, sour creams, cream cheeses, and other cheeses. They usually won't have the healthiest

ingredients, and that's why you'll find many of these recipes right here in *The Everything® Plant-Based Meal Prep Cookbook*.

Substitutions for Meat

Take care when considering the store-bought varieties of meat alternatives. Plant-based meat substitutes have grown by leaps and bounds in recent years. Major fast-food restaurants have gotten on board with fake burgers, chicken, and even "vegan" seafood. Grocery store aisles are full of these fake "meats." For the most part, these items are something you should avoid if you're eating a plant-based diet because they are often full of calories, salt, fat, and additives. No Evil Foods produces meat substitutes without oil, but while these can be a stepping-stone for those who want to cut back on meat, you're better off with homemade options. These plant-based choices are good substitutes for meat:

- **Tofu:** Many types of tofu are available on the market today. In addition to the typical unseasoned soft, firm, extra-firm, and silken varieties that come packaged in water, you'll also find many that are marinated and delicious straight from the package. They're easy to use in a stir-fry, sandwiches, or pasta.

  Many recipes in this book call for tofu to be pressed before using. Pressing removes excess water from the tofu block and makes it sturdier and easier to work with. The easiest way to do this is to use a tofu press, available from many retailers, but you can also press tofu yourself: After draining the tofu, wrap it in a clean kitchen towel or a few layers of paper towel. Place the wrapped tofu block on a plate or baking sheet. Add a second baking sheet or plate, and weigh it down with a stack of heavy plates, a skillet, or other weights. Allow the tofu to drain as long as necessary, usually at least 15 minutes.

- **Tempeh:** Made from fermented soybeans, tempeh is another excellent meat substitute that can be crumbled or used whole, steamed, sautéed, or roasted.
- **Seitan:** Made from the protein portion of wheat. Try making it yourself, as most store-bought versions are too processed. To make 8 servings of a basic recipe, you'll need 2 cups vital wheat gluten flour; 2 teaspoons onion powder; 1 teaspoon garlic powder; 1 teaspoon marjoram; 6 cups water, divided; 2 tablespoons low-sodium tamari; and 2 tablespoons molasses. In a bowl, mix together the wheat gluten flour and spices. Add 2 cups water to the mixture and stir until it becomes a sponge-like dough. This should not be excessively wet. Knead the dough on a floured surface for about two minutes to make the dough come together and more elastic. Let it rest for 10 minutes. If it's too sticky, add a little more wheat gluten and knead again to incorporate. Add 4 cups water, tamari, and molasses to a large saucepan over medium-high heat and bring to a boil then lower the temperature to just under boiling. Cut seitan into 3" × 3" pieces and place into the broth. Cover and simmer for about 45–60 minutes. Drain and use in recipes for stir-fry, sandwiches, stews, and more.
- **Beans:** Any variety of beans, either whole or mashed, are a great main ingredient for things like burritos and sandwiches. You won't get the same texture as meat, but you will get a highly satisfying, nutritious meal.
- **Mushrooms:** Naturally infused with a meaty, savory umami flavor, mushrooms are a great meat substitute.

Substitutions for Dairy Milk and Cheese

There are many plant milk options out there, but try to stick with those that have the fewest ingredients. Look for soy milk made with just beans and water or almond milk made with just almonds and water. Unsweetened almond milk is suggested for most recipes in this book, but any kind of plant milk can be substituted, including soy, cashew, rice, or oat. Keep in mind that soy milk is highest in protein and works best for baking.

When it comes to vegan cheese options, you'll want to again look for varieties that have few ingredients. Unfortunately, most "fake" cheeses are overprocessed and contain oil and additives.

Substitutions for One Egg

There are many choices for substituting eggs, such as:

- Mix 1 tablespoon ground flaxseeds with 3 tablespoons water and let sit 10 minutes before using.
- Mix 1 tablespoon chia seeds with 3 tablespoons water and let sit for 15 minutes before using.
- Use ¼ cup unsweetened applesauce.
- Use ¼ cup mashed peeled banana.
- Use ¼ cup silken tofu.
- Mix 3 tablespoons chickpea flour with 3 tablespoons water.
- Mix 1 tablespoon cornstarch with 3 tablespoons water.

- Mix 2 tablespoons arrowroot powder with 3 tablespoons water.
- Use 3 tablespoons aquafaba (liquid from a can of chickpeas).

Substitutions for Oil and Butter

Because oils and butter are processed and high in calories, you'll want to avoid them. Here are some alternatives:

- **Vegetable broth:** You can sauté vegetables in broth using a couple of tablespoons at a time, being careful not to drown the food. The vegetables should simmer nicely in just enough broth to keep wet. You can also use broth in baked vegetable recipes as a fat replacement—just make sure to keep checking as they're cooking in case you need to add more broth. In a pinch, water can be used in the same way.
- **Bananas:** Bananas are a great replacement in cookies, quick breads, or things like pancakes, but be aware that your recipe will have a banana flavor! Substitute mashed banana for oil in a 1:1 ratio in a recipe. If the batter is too dry, add more in, little by little. It might take some experimenting to get it right.
- **Applesauce:** If you don't want all your baked goods to taste like bananas, applesauce is another good replacement option. It works well for things that are dense, like cakes and muffins. You can do a 1:1 swap of applesauce for a plant-based butter alternative.

- **Prune puree:** To make prune puree, blend pitted prunes in a food processor with water until smooth. (Use 1 tablespoon water for every ounce of prunes that you use.) Prunes work best in chocolate-flavored recipes like brownies; in lighter-flavored foods, the prune flavor will come through. Use an amount of puree equal to the amount of fat that is called for in the recipe.
- **Nut butter:** When baking, you can also use nut butter as a fat replacer. This works especially well in cookie, muffin, and bread recipes. Although you're adding calories to the recipe, you're also adding protein, minerals, and fiber. Swap it out of the recipe cup for cup. Use a creamy variety of whatever nut butter you choose. Expect a denser (but quite lovely) end product.

question

Can I Use Sweeteners?

The healthiest plant-based sweeteners are maple syrup, date sugar (dehydrated ground dates), date syrup, coconut sugar, and molasses, although even some of those are missing nutrition. Date sugar and blackstrap molasses are the only two plant-based sweeteners with any significant nutritional value. If you must use a sugar replacement, stick with stevia or erythritol, two of the better ones.

What Is Plant-Based Meal Prep?

Now it's time to learn more about how meal prepping can make eating a whole-food, plant-based diet quick and easy. Meal prep is simply the idea of planning, shopping for, and then preparing a week's worth (or more) of plant-based meals and proportioning them in storage containers so they can be reheated and eaten throughout the week ahead.

Benefits of Meal Prep

Prepping your meals does require some up-front investment of time and energy, but it's well worth it. Meal prepping helps you:

- Stay on track with your dietary goals
- Create variety in your meals so you don't rotate through the same meals every week
- Be less apt to impulse eat, especially at snack time
- Resist buying fast food, takeout, or processed "convenience" foods
- Save money by buying in bulk
- Save time by prepping ingredients for multiple meals at once
- Feel less stressed about what to make

Organization is the key to meal prep.

Meal Prep Methods

There are a couple of ways to go about organizing your plant-based meal prep:

1. **The "extra portions" method:** This is where you double recipes, such as casseroles, and store portions to use later.
2. **The "free-form" method:** You will batch-cook individual foods such as beans, rice, and roasted vegetables. These can be mixed and matched for versatile meals on the fly. Use your imagination to combine one part protein, one part carb, and one part vegetable (and usually, a lovely sauce to tie them together) into a complete meal.

The extra-portion method is a good choice for when you're getting used to meal prepping. You can advance to the free-form method when you're more experienced. The recipes in *The Everything® Plant-Based Meal Prep Cookbook* have purposely been chosen for crossover ingredients that can be used in different recipes. For example, after making Cashew Cream (see recipe in Chapter 9), you'll have it on hand as a topping for baked apples or as a key ingredient in Creamy Vegetable Noodle Soup (see recipe in Chapter 5).

Writing a Weekly Meal Plan
A weekly meal planner is a list of what you will make for each meal over the course of a seven-day period. The two-week plan featured at the end of the book has ideas for how to build one for yourself.

The first step is to add recipe ideas to a weekly planner. You can use an electronic or paper version—whatever works best for you.

Make sure to mark the days on which you'll eat leftovers and any nights that you won't be eating at home.

> **fact**
>
> Even if you prep and freeze dishes for future weeks, try to plan only one week at a time. Otherwise, you might end up with leftovers that may go bad before you eat them. (Food usually lasts about 4–5 days in the refrigerator.)

The best recipes for meal prep are those that do well in the refrigerator or freezer for several days, such as bowls, soups, stews, sandwich fillings, smoothies, pasta, and burgers.

Useful Kitchen Tools and Appliances for Plant-Based Meal Prep

A few everyday appliances and tools will make your plant-based meal prep and storage a snap.

The Right Equipment
These must-have kitchen tools will save you a lot of time and effort as you prep and cook:

- **Slow cookers and/or Instant Pot®:** If you don't already have an Instant Pot® or a slow cooker like a Crock-Pot, they're definitely worth the investment. An

Instant Pot® will both slow cook and pressure cook and is great for cooking beans and rice, soups and stews, as well as oatmeal or other whole-grain porridge. Just throw your ingredients in before you go to bed and have a healthful, warm breakfast waiting for you when you awaken. If you're slow cooking, start in the morning and have dinner waiting for you when you come home.

- **Blender:** A high-powered blender is great for making smoothies, but it also can be used for making soups, nut milk, salad dressing, oat flour, and recipes that use raw cashews like Cashew Cream and Blender "Cheese" Sauce (see recipes in Chapter 9).
- **Food processor:** Food processors are adept at chopping vegetables and making hummus, bread crumbs, vegetable burgers, gravy, pesto, and nut butter.
- **Knives:** You'll be using knives daily to chop produce, so find a high-quality set, keep them sharp, and learn how to use them properly.
- **Nonstick pans:** These are important for whole-food, plant-based cooking since you will not be sautéing in oil. (See tips for cooking without oil in this chapter.)
- **Parchment paper or Silpat (a silicone mat):** These make for easy cleanup after baking.
- **Steamer basket:** Steaming vegetables helps retain nutrients versus boiling them directly in water.

- **Tofu press:** Although a few recipes use unpressed tofu, most recipes require you to press the liquid out of the block of tofu.

> **fact**
>
> Figuring out portion size, especially for grains, can take a little trial and error. For whole grains, a serving is ½ cup. For bread, it's 1 slice. For cereal, it's ¾–1 cup. Some containers might seem small, but they actually hold a full serving size.

Storage Containers

Invest in a supply of storage containers of varying sizes.

GLASS OR PLASTIC CONTAINERS

There are many storage options these days, including airtight plastic and glass options. Most are stackable and some are divided, making it easy to keep contents separated. Think about what and how much you will store most often, and buy products that match your need.

If you're buying containers for the freezer, use heavy-duty, freezer-grade products to prevent cracking and breakage. They are manufactured with specific materials that handle both high heat and freezing. Glass is preferred over plastic because some plastics contain BPAs and other potentially hazardous chemicals. Plastic is also more difficult to recycle than glass.

PLASTIC BAGS

Quart and gallon-sized are practical for the refrigerator and freezer. Freezer-specific bags do a good job of preventing freezer burn while keeping food fresh. They also have a handy label right on them already. If frozen properly, storage bags can be stacked one on top of another and take up little space. When storing food in sealable bags, be sure to squeeze out as much air as possible before sealing. If you don't want plastic to touch your food, use a sheet of parchment paper to separate the bag and your food.

TIPS FOR USING STORAGE CONTAINERS

These tips will help keep your reheated food safe to eat and tasting great:

- Use small containers for breakfast prep, such as overnight oats or a yogurt parfait, and save your large containers for main meals.
- It's best to let food cool off in the storage container with the top on. This keeps bacteria from getting into the food. The latest USDA guidelines suggest rapidly cooling in the refrigerator.

- If you're freezing food, cool it down in the refrigerator first before placing the container in the freezer. The reverse is also true. When thawing, it's best to place frozen containers in the refrigerator first.
- Never go straight from the freezer to the microwave with glass containers, as the rapid change in temperature can cause them to break.
- When storing food in the freezer using glass or plastic containers, leave about ¾" of space (headroom) for expansion between the top of the food and the top of the container.

Your Meal Prep Game Plan

There is no one right way to tackle meal prep, and you should experiment to see what works best for you. Perhaps you'd like to split it up into two days instead of one, prepping fruits and chopping vegetables one day and cooking recipes the next.

Shop on the day before you plan to meal prep so that it's out of the way and you can concentrate on prepping. To get ready for an entire week, plan for about two to three hours of prepping, including cleanup. Here are some tips for meal prepping common plant-based dishes:

- **Breakfast:** Prep breakfast by cooking double portions of oatmeal or preparing frozen "smoothie packs." You could also prep a tofu scramble that can be used in several ways during the week, such as for a scrambled tofu taco or burrito.
- **Grains and legumes:** Use your slow cooker or Instant Pot® to prepare the whole grains and legumes on your meal plan.
- **Roasted vegetables:** While the beans and grains are cooking, heat your oven and start chopping the vegetables. Roast any vegetables that are required and set aside the rest for other uses.
- **Sauces and dressings:** Make sauces and dressings while the legumes, grains, or vegetables are cooking.

Keep prepping until you have everything you need for the week and your recipe creations and/or meal prepped items are safely stored in the refrigerator.

Reheating a Meal

To reheat a meal, use the microwave, stovetop, or oven, being careful to choose a method suitable for the type of food. Food that's been roasted or baked doesn't do as well if it's reheated in the microwave. In this case, reheat in the oven, toaster oven, or on the stovetop. If you use the broiler, be sure to watch it carefully, as food can burn quickly under it.

Most other foods, such as soups, stews, casseroles, pasta, and grain dishes (except breads) do well in the microwave or stovetop, heated to a temperature of 165°F. Some recipes in this book include specific tips for reheating.

Personalize the Recipes

Use your best judgment when making these recipes. If you're healthy and want to include a little oil, some sugar, or more salt, it shouldn't change the quality of the recipe, but it will, of course, change the nutrition information. If you want to lower or leave out salt or oil altogether, that's an option as well. For example, you could swap out soy or tamari sauce for the lower-sodium choice of coconut aminos.

Your healthy, delicious, whole-food plant-based life is waiting for you. Let's get cooking!

CHAPTER 2

Breakfast

Breakfast Burrito with Tofu Scramble

The classic breakfast burrito just got better, packed with protein and stuffed with tofu, beans, avocados, onions, and fresh salsa.

THE BENEFITS OF TURMERIC

Turmeric is best known for the anti-inflammatory and antioxidant properties of its active compound, curcumin. But it can also help relieve pain, improve liver function, and possibly reduce the risk of cancer. Use turmeric in soups, smoothies, dressings, and sauces for a healthy addition to your diet.

½ cup chopped yellow onion

¼ cup water

1 (14-ounce) container firm organic tofu, drained and rinsed

½ teaspoon ground turmeric

¼ teaspoon salt

¼ teaspoon freshly ground black pepper

1 (15-ounce) can fat-free, low-sodium refried beans

4 (10") whole-grain tortillas

6 medium green onions, trimmed and sliced (including most of the green tops)

2 medium avocados, peeled, seeded, and sliced

½ cup fresh salsa

1 Heat a medium nonstick skillet over medium heat. Add yellow onion and water, and sauté until mostly soft, about 5–7 minutes.

2 Crumble tofu into skillet. Add turmeric, salt, and pepper, and stir to combine. Continue to cook until it's heated through, stirring frequently, about 4–5 minutes.

3 In a small saucepan over medium heat, heat refried beans, stirring constantly, until warmed through.

4 Wrap tortillas in a damp paper towel and microwave on high until softened, about 1 minute.

5 To assemble the burritos, lay 1 tortilla on a plate. Spread 2 tablespoons refried beans down the center of tortilla, leaving about 1" on one end. Top with one-fourth of tofu scramble. Sprinkle on one-fourth of green onions, followed by one-fourth of sliced avocados and 2 tablespoons salsa.

6 Fold up the bottom of tortilla and then fold in the two sides, leaving top open. Repeat with remaining tortillas and fillings.

7 Freeze whole, premade burritos, omitting the green onions, avocado, and salsa. Wrap burritos in paper towel and foil, and freeze in a freezer-safe bag for up to 1 month. When ready to eat, remove foil and microwave in paper towel for 2–4 minutes. Open the burrito and add toppings.

Buckwheat Pancakes

SERVES 3

Per Serving:

Calories	533
Fat	17g
Sodium	579mg
Carbohydrates	86g
Fiber	11g
Sugar	16g
Protein	15g

CAN YOU FREEZE PANCAKES?

Have pancakes whenever you want by cooking a larger batch and freezing. After cooling, place them on a baking sheet lined with parchment paper and freeze for 10 minutes before transferring to an airtight container or freezer-safe bag for up to 2 months. To reheat, simply place on a microwave-safe plate and microwave on high for 1–1½ minutes. Or heat on a baking sheet in a preheated oven at 200°F for 15–20 minutes.

These pancakes are so good topped with fresh fruit and a drizzle of maple syrup. They're also gluten-free, high in fiber and protein, and heart-healthy. You can use fresh or thawed frozen bananas and blueberries.

1 cup buckwheat flour

½ cup cornmeal

½ cup old-fashioned oats

1 teaspoon baking soda

1 teaspoon baking powder

½ teaspoon salt

1 teaspoon cinnamon

1 large banana, peeled and mashed

1 cup unsweetened soy milk (or more to thin)

½ cup unsweetened applesauce

1 teaspoon vanilla extract

1 tablespoon maple syrup

½ cup chopped walnuts

1 cup blueberries

1. In a large bowl, combine flour, cornmeal, oats, baking soda, baking powder, salt, and cinnamon. Stir to mix well.
2. In a medium bowl, add banana, soy milk, applesauce, and vanilla. Whisk to combine.
3. Pour banana mixture into flour mixture, and stir until just combined. Let sit for a minute. Add a little more soy milk if mixture is too thick.
4. Heat a nonstick griddle over medium heat. For each pancake, drop about 2 tablespoons batter onto the griddle. Flip when edges seem dry. Don't overcook, or pancakes may be too dry.
5. Remove to a plate and top with syrup, nuts, and berries.

Chickpea Flour Omelet with Curried Greens

This omelet is unique, thanks to its curried greens and pasta sauce. Make extra filling for topping potatoes or as a side dish (refrigerate in an airtight container for up to 1 week).

SERVES 4

Per Serving:

Calories	330
Fat	17g
Sodium	397mg
Carbohydrates	36g
Fiber	14g
Sugar	9g
Protein	13g

Filling

1 (10-ounce) bag spinach

⅓ cup water

2 cups Basil Marinara (see recipe in Chapter 9)

½ teaspoon curry powder

¼ teaspoon salt

¼ teaspoon freshly ground black pepper

Omelet

1 cup chickpea flour

¼ teaspoon baking powder

½ teaspoon ground turmeric

1 tablespoon dried parsley

2 tablespoons nutritional yeast

1 cup water (or more if needed)

2 medium avocados, peeled, seeded, and sliced

4 medium green onions, trimmed and sliced

HAVE YOU TRIED CHICKPEA FLOUR?

Chickpea flour is made from milled chickpeas and is a versatile substitute that can be used in place of eggs for omelets. It's gluten-free, high in protein, low in calories, and can also be used in baking, substituting for grain flours. In a batter, it produces a light texture.

1 Heat a large skillet over medium-high heat. Add spinach and water. Sauté until wilted and almost tender, about 3–5 minutes.

2 Add Basil Marinara, curry powder, salt, and pepper to the skillet and cook until greens are tender, about 5–7 minutes. Add more water if it's too thick.

3 In a medium bowl, combine chickpea flour, baking powder, turmeric, parsley, and yeast. Add 1 cup water and whisk. It should be the consistency of pancake batter, pourable and not too thick.

4 Heat a nonstick omelet pan over medium-low heat (use nonstick cooking spray if your pan tends to stick). Pour ¼ cup batter into pan and swirl the pan around to move batter to edges. Cover and wait until omelet is slightly brown, about 5 minutes, then turn omelet and cook the other side for 2 minutes.

5 With a spatula, carefully release omelet and place it on a plate. Spoon one-fourth of the curried greens filling on one half of the omelet and fold over the other half. Repeat to make remaining omelets. Top with slices of avocado and green onions.

Country Hash Browns with Sausage Gravy

SERVES 4

Per Serving:

Calories	477
Fat	26g
Sodium	1,382mg
Carbohydrates	48g
Fiber	7g
Sugar	4g
Protein	15g

BROWNING WITHOUT OIL

Oil is not necessary for browning or caramelizing. The best way to achieve this is to sauté vegetables in a hot nonstick skillet. The vegetables release their own water and will eventually start to brown. Turn them in the pan as needed.

Crispy, golden hash browns are easily made without butter or oil because they brown nicely in a nonstick pan.

Gravy

⅓ pound vegan breakfast sausage, cut into small pieces

3 tablespoons whole-wheat all-purpose flour

½ teaspoon onion powder

2 tablespoons nutritional yeast

½ teaspoon salt

½ teaspoon freshly ground black pepper

1 cup One-Pot Vegetable Broth (see recipe in Chapter 5)

1 cup unsweetened almond milk

2 teaspoons low-sodium tamari soy sauce

Hash Browns

1 (16-ounce) bag frozen shredded hash browns (with no added oil)

1 cup diced yellow onion

2 medium cloves garlic, peeled and minced

1 medium bell pepper, any color, seeded and chopped

1 small jalapeño pepper, seeded and thinly sliced

2 tablespoons chopped fresh chives

1 To make the gravy, heat a medium nonstick skillet over medium heat. Add sausage and cook, stirring, until browned, about 3 minutes.

2 Add rest of gravy ingredients and whisk over medium heat until gravy starts to thicken, about 5 minutes. Reduce heat to low and keep warm.

3 Heat a large nonstick skillet over medium heat. Spread frozen hash browns in skillet and cook for 6–10 minutes, then flip and cook until potatoes begin to brown, about 5 minutes more.

4 Stir in onion, garlic, bell pepper, and jalapeño pepper and flatten in an even layer. Continue to flip and brown until they become as crispy as you like.

5 Serve hash browns drizzled with gravy and garnished with chives.

6 Refrigerate leftovers in an airtight container for up to 3 days. To serve, reheat in a skillet over medium heat until heated through.

Homemade Nondairy Nut Milk

Homemade nut milk is easy to make in a high-powered blender. You'll not only enjoy the superior flavor and avoid unhealthy ingredients—you'll also save money. Nut milks are great for break-fast or to add to a soup or casserole for creaminess. You can also make this from cashews or hazelnuts instead of almonds.

1 cup raw unsalted almonds, soaked at least 4 hours or overnight

4 cups water

1 teaspoon vanilla extract

2 medium Medjool dates, pitted

1 Drain and rinse soaked nuts.
2 Add nuts, water, vanilla, and dates to a high-speed blender. (You can use a regular blender, but you may have to blend it longer and it may not be blended as smooth.)
3 Blend on high for several minutes, until mixture becomes smooth and nuts are finely ground. Pour into a nut bag over a large bowl.
4 With your hands, carefully "milk" the bag to release liquid into the bowl until all of it is strained.
5 Carefully transfer to an airtight glass container and refrigerate until well chilled. Stir or shake well before serving.
6 Refrigerate in an airtight glass container for up to 5 days.

SERVES 2

Per Serving:

Calories	130
Fat	11g
Sodium	5mg
Carbohydrates	3g
Fiber	0g
Sugar	1g
Protein	5g

STRAINING NUT MILKS

If you're going to make your own almond milk, having a nut bag helps to strain the milk. Some are made of organic cotton. It's easy to clean, and can be purchased online. Look for one that has strong reinforced seams, so it will last. The pulp can be thrown away or used in other recipes such as crackers, muffins, smoothies, or hummus.

Cinnamon-Apple Crepes

This versatile recipe works for dessert or breakfast. The apple filling is also delicious in the Cinnamon-Apple Yogurt Parfait (see recipe in Chapter 10). Crepes have a tendency to stick to the pan, so a teaspoon of coconut oil or nonstick cooking spray helps.

½ cup oat flour

½ cup whole-wheat all-purpose flour

1¼ cups soy milk

½ medium banana, peeled and mashed

1 tablespoon maple syrup

1 teaspoon vanilla extract

⅛ teaspoon salt

1 teaspoon coconut oil

1 recipe Baked Cinnamon-Apple Slices, without topping (see recipe in Chapter 10)

8 tablespoons unsweetened plain plant yogurt

2 tablespoons confectioners' sugar

SERVES 4	
Per Serving:	
Calories	319
Fat	7g
Sodium	120mg
Carbohydrates	62g
Fiber	8g
Sugar	29g
Protein	7g

1 In a medium bowl, combine oat flour, whole-wheat flour, soy milk, banana, maple syrup, vanilla, and salt; stir to mix well. Refrigerate for 30 minutes.

2 In a small nonstick skillet over medium-high heat, add coconut oil and swirl to coat the skillet. Or, use a metal pan and add a little nonstick cooking spray.

3 Stir batter again before cooking.

4 Place about ¼ cup batter in skillet and swirl to fully coat the bottom. Cook for a minute, then check to see if crepe is set.

5 Using a spatula, carefully flip crepe and heat for 1 more minute. Transfer to a plate. Repeat with remaining batter.

6 Fill each crepe with ¼ cup Baked Cinnamon-Apple Slices, 2 tablespoons yogurt, and a sprinkle of confectioners' sugar.

7 Stack leftover crepes on a plate with wax or parchment paper between each one and cover tightly with plastic wrap. Refrigerate up to 5 days, or freeze in an airtight container for up to 2 months. Thaw in the refrigerator overnight. Reheat in a dry skillet over medium heat.

Pumpkin Cinnamon Nut Granola

MAKES 8 CUPS

Per Serving (½ cup):

Calories	126
Fat	3g
Sodium	10mg
Carbohydrates	24g
Fiber	3g
Sugar	7g
Protein	3g

PSEUDOGRAINS AND CEREAL GRAINS

Quinoa, buckwheat, millet, teff, wild rice, and amaranth are technically not cereal grains. However, they have cereal grain-like qualities and cook just like grains. They're also gluten-free, which makes them a great alternative to wheat. Quinoa is easy to cook, and it's high in complete protein since it contains all nine essential amino acids. Eating grains or pseudograins helps to fill you up and provides energy while keeping you satisfied.

Homemade granola is so much tastier and healthier than store-bought options. You can eat it for breakfast topped with berries, sprinkled over yogurt, or in a quick dessert parfait layered with plant yogurt and berries. If you don't have almonds, walnuts or pistachios would work as well, and you can substitute maple syrup for the date syrup with equally great results.

2 cups old-fashioned oats

2 cups puffed corn

2 cups puffed millet

½ cup sliced almonds

½ cup unsweetened applesauce

¼ cup pumpkin puree

¼ cup date syrup

2 teaspoons cinnamon

1 teaspoon vanilla extract

¾ cup unsweetened dried cranberries

1 Preheat oven to 300°F. Line two rimmed baking sheets in parchment paper.
2 Measure oats, corn, millet, and almonds into a large bowl.
3 In a separate small bowl, mix applesauce, pumpkin, date syrup, cinnamon, and vanilla until combined.
4 Add applesauce mixture to oat mixture and stir to combine.
5 Spread on prepared baking sheets and bake for 30–45 minutes, until lightly browned, turning every 15 minutes. Remove from oven and add cranberries; stir to combine.
6 Cool granola completely before transferring to airtight glass jars. Store in the pantry for up to 3 weeks or up to 3 months in the freezer.

Pumpkin Pancakes

These healthy flapjacks are perfectly spiced and are a delicious way to start your day—or enjoy them as a dessert topped with berries and sweet Cashew Cream (see recipe in Chapter 9). They're especially tasty in the autumn months. Serve with maple syrup, jam, or your favorite fruit and/or nuts.

½ cup old-fashioned oats

¼ cup cornmeal

1¼ cups whole-wheat all-purpose flour

2 teaspoons baking powder

1 teaspoon baking soda

1 teaspoon cinnamon

½ teaspoon ground ginger

½ teaspoon allspice

½ teaspoon salt

½ cup pumpkin puree

1 teaspoon vanilla extract

1 large or 2 small ripe bananas, peeled and mashed

1½ cups unsweetened soy milk

SERVES 4

Per Serving:

Calories	290
Fat	4g
Sodium	823mg
Carbohydrates	57g
Fiber	8g
Sugar	6g
Protein	11g

1 Heat a nonstick griddle over medium heat.

2 In a large bowl, combine oats, cornmeal, flour, baking powder, baking soda, cinnamon, ginger, allspice, and salt. Stir to mix well.

3 In a medium bowl, add pumpkin, vanilla, banana, and soy milk. Whisk until well combined.

4 Pour pumpkin mixture into oat mixture; stir until just moistened.

5 Spray griddle with nonstick cooking spray. For each pancake, drop ¼ cup batter onto griddle. Cook until bubbles start to form around the edges and the bottom is nicely browned, about 5 minutes. Flip and cook the other side for about 3 minutes.

6 To store, cool pancakes completely, place in a sealed container, and refrigerate for up to 7 days. To freeze pancakes, once cooled, place on a baking sheet lined with parchment paper and freeze for 10 minutes. Transfer to an airtight container or freezer-safe bag for up to 2 months. To reheat, place on a microwave-safe plate and microwave on high for 1–1½ minutes. Or heat on a baking sheet in a 200°F oven for 15–20 minutes.

GLUTEN-FREE OPTIONS

It's easy to substitute gluten-free flours for whole-wheat flour in most recipes at a 1:1 ratio. You can find ready-made gluten-free options in most grocery stores. To make a gluten-free version of this recipe, for example, use ½ cup gluten-free oats and substitute 1¼ cups gluten-free flour, such as rice, for the whole-wheat flour.

Raspberry Chocolate Chia Smoothie

SERVES 2

Per Serving:

Calories	229
Fat	7g
Sodium	29mg
Carbohydrates	40g
Fiber	12g
Sugar	14g
Protein	7g

The chia seeds in this smoothie provide important omega-3 fatty acids that are essential and needed to help us function and stay healthy. Make extra to have on hand for when the afternoon munchies arrive!

1 medium banana, peeled, cut into chunks, and frozen

¼ cup old-fashioned oats

1½ tablespoons unsweetened cacao or cocoa powder

1 tablespoon whole or ground flaxseeds

2 tablespoons chia seeds

¼ teaspoon cinnamon

2 medium Medjool dates, pitted

2 cups baby spinach

½ cup fresh or frozen raspberries

Add all ingredients to a blender and blend until smooth, about 1 minute. Refrigerate any leftovers in a sealed container for up to 3 days.

Heart-Healthy Smoothie

SERVES 1

Per Serving:

Calories	298
Fat	9g
Sodium	161mg
Carbohydrates	49g
Fiber	12g
Sugar	18g
Protein	9g

Start out your day with this powerhouse of nutritional goodness packed with fruit, oats, leafy greens, and flaxseeds.

⅓ cup frozen blueberries

⅓ cup frozen strawberries

⅓ cup frozen cranberries

¼ cup old-fashioned oats

1 tablespoon whole or ground flaxseeds

3 large leaves romaine lettuce

¾ cup unsweetened almond milk

¼ cup pomegranate juice

1 Add all ingredients to a blender and blend until smooth. Add water if you'd like it a little thinner.

2 Make smoothies ahead of time and refrigerate 1–3 days in a sealed container. Or, measure out the fruits and freeze in a freezer-safe bag for up to 6 months to make prep quick and easy.

Scrambled Tofu Tacos

This tofu vegetable scramble is an easy and delicious breakfast that's fun to mix up with different vegetables, such as chopped spinach or zucchini. The turmeric provides a beautiful yellow color. Serve with your favorite additions, such as black beans, Avocado Cream Sauce (see recipe in Chapter 9), diced tomatoes, red onion, lettuce, and hot sauce.

1 medium yellow onion, peeled and roughly chopped

1 medium red bell pepper, seeded and roughly chopped

8 ounces button mushrooms, sliced

2 tablespoons water

1 (14-ounce) container firm organic tofu, drained and rinsed

½ teaspoon ground turmeric

½ teaspoon curry powder

¼ teaspoon salt

⅛ teaspoon freshly ground black pepper

8 (6") corn tortillas

1 Heat a large nonstick skillet over medium-high heat. Add onion, bell pepper, mushrooms, and water, and sauté until mostly soft, about 5 minutes.

2 Crumble tofu into skillet and add turmeric, curry powder, salt, and black pepper. Stir to combine. The mixture should turn yellow from the spices and begin to look like eggs.

3 Continue to cook until most of the moisture from the tofu has cooked off and it's heated through, stirring frequently so it doesn't stick, about 4–5 minutes.

4 Wrap tortillas in a damp paper towel and microwave on high until they are softened, about 1 minute, or wrap in foil and heat in a preheated 300°F oven for 10–15 minutes. If you prefer, heat tortillas in a toaster oven until crispy. Divide tofu mixture evenly among tortillas and serve taco-style.

5 Refrigerate any leftovers in a sealed container for up to 3 days.

SERVES 4	
Per Serving:	
Calories	223
Fat	6g
Sodium	176mg
Carbohydrates	30g
Fiber	6g
Sugar	4g
Protein	14g

COOKING WITH TOFU

When cooking with tofu, always drain the water before using it in a recipe. Tofu can be used this way in dips, scrambles, and sauces. You can also press it to remove more of the water (see Chapter 1) and then marinate it to add flavor. It can also be frozen. When thawed, the tofu will have a spongier, chewier, firmer texture and will be filled with holes where the water froze and then defrosted. It can then be marinated.

Tropical Spinach Smoothie

SERVES 2

Per Serving:

Calories	201
Fat	5g
Sodium	144mg
Carbohydrates	6g
Fiber	6g
Sugar	28g
Protein	5g

The combination of tropical fruit and greens makes this smoothie a winner in both the taste and nutrition department. Pineapple not only supplies beneficial digestive enzymes but also makes it easier for your body to absorb nutrients. Prep ingredients ahead of time by freezing smoothie packs that contain fruits and greens already chopped and measured. You can add a variety of additional flavors to this smoothie, such as grated fresh turmeric or ginger, chia seeds, or hemp seeds.

1 cup frozen or fresh chopped pineapple

1 cup frozen or fresh chopped mango

2 medium mandarin oranges or 1 regular medium orange, peeled and seeded

2 cups packed spinach or kale

1 tablespoon ground flaxseeds

1 cup unsweetened almond milk

1 Add all ingredients to a blender and blend until smooth. Serve cold.

2 Refrigerate leftover smoothie in a covered container for no more than 24 hours.

Spinach-Tofu Benedict with Vegan Hollandaise

SERVES 4

Per Serving:

Calories	329
Fat	8g
Sodium	1,714mg
Carbohydrates	40g
Fiber	7g
Sugar	7g
Protein	23g

Substitute tofu for eggs in this savory breakfast Benedict stacked with steamed spinach and a creamy vegan hollandaise sauce. Make extra sauce and serve it over potatoes or in a chickpea flour omelet. If you don't have fresh spinach, you can use frozen; just defrost it in the microwave and squeeze out excess water before sautéing. You can substitute coconut aminos for the soy sauce to lower sodium levels in this recipe.

Tofu Benedict

1 (16-ounce) container firm organic tofu, drained, rinsed, and pressed

1/4 cup plus 2 tablespoons low-sodium soy sauce, divided

1 tablespoon vegan Worcestershire sauce

2 teaspoons maple syrup

1/2 teaspoon liquid smoke

10 ounces fresh spinach leaves, stems removed

Hollandaise Sauce

1 cup unsweetened almond milk, divided

1/8 teaspoon ground turmeric

2 tablespoons unbleached all-purpose flour

4 tablespoons fresh lemon juice

1/2 teaspoon salt

1/4 teaspoon freshly ground black pepper

1/2 tablespoon Dijon mustard

1 tablespoon nutritional yeast

4 whole-grain English muffins, split

2 tablespoons chopped fresh parsley

1 To make the tofu, slice into eight 1/2" slabs. In a small baking dish, combine 1/4 cup soy sauce, Worcestershire sauce, maple syrup, and liquid smoke. Add tofu slices. Marinate in the refrigerator for 20–30 minutes.

Spinach-Tofu Benedict with Vegan Hollandaise—continued

2 Heat a large nonstick skillet over medium heat. Drain marinated tofu slices and add to skillet. Cook until brown on one side, about 5 minutes. Flip and brown on the other side. Remove from heat and set aside.

3 Heat a medium saucepan over medium heat. Add spinach with a little water and sprinkle on remaining 2 tablespoons soy sauce. Cook, stirring frequently, until wilted, about 2 minutes. Remove and set aside and rinse pan.

4 To make the hollandaise sauce, using the same saucepan, add about ¼ cup almond milk and whisk in turmeric and flour. Continuing to whisk, add remaining ¾ cup almond milk.

5 Add lemon juice, salt, and pepper to saucepan. Continue to whisk until sauce thickens. If it's not thick enough, combine a little more flour with almond milk in a separate container and whisk, or shake if you have a cover, and add to the sauce.

6 Remove from heat and add mustard and yeast. Whisk to combine. If sauce is too thick, add a little water or more almond milk.

7 To assemble the Benedict, place 2 English muffin halves on a plate, face up. Top each with about ½ cup spinach. Top spinach with 1 tofu slice, then spoon over hollandaise sauce. Garnish with a sprinkle of parsley.

8 Refrigerate any leftover hollandaise sauce in a sealed container for up to 5 days.

Black Bean Breakfast Tacos

SERVES 4

Per Serving:

Calories	644
Fat	38g
Sodium	863mg
Carbohydrates	69g
Fiber	27g
Sugar	11g
Protein	16g

These quick and easy tacos are great when you have little time but need some morning energy. They're loaded with protein, and you won't feel hungry after eating this flavor-packed dish.

1 (15-ounce) can low-sodium black beans, drained and rinsed

1 cup canned low-sodium fire-roasted diced tomatoes

½ teaspoon ground cumin

1 teaspoon chili powder

¼ teaspoon salt

¼ teaspoon freshly ground black pepper

8 (6") corn tortillas

2 recipes Avocado Cream Sauce (see recipe in Chapter 9)

2 cups diced tomatoes

½ cup diced red onion

4 cups diced romaine lettuce

½ teaspoon hot sauce

1 In a medium saucepan over medium heat, add beans, fire-roasted tomatoes, cumin, and chili powder. Cook for several minutes, until heated through. If you want the mixture a bit thicker, you can mash a few of the beans with the back of your spoon. Stir in salt and pepper.

2 Wrap tortillas in a damp paper towel and microwave on high until softened, about 1 minute, or wrap in foil and heat in a preheated 300°F oven for 10–15 minutes. If you prefer, heat tortillas in a toaster oven until crispy.

3 To prepare tacos, place about ¼ cup black bean mixture onto each tortilla. Top with Avocado Cream Sauce, tomatoes, onion, lettuce, and hot sauce.

4 Refrigerate taco filling and Avocado Cream Sauce separately in covered containers for up to 3 days.

Buttermilk Blueberry Muffins

Be creative and try different fruit, or for an added treat, substitute mini vegan chocolate chips for the blueberries.

Muffins

½ cup soy milk

2 tablespoons fresh lemon juice

1 cup oat flour

1½ cups old-fashioned oats

¼ cup cornmeal

1 tablespoon baking powder

1 teaspoon cinnamon

¼ teaspoon salt

½ cup unsweetened applesauce

¼ cup almond butter

¼ cup maple syrup

½ cup coconut sugar

1 teaspoon vanilla extract

1 cup fresh or frozen blueberries

Topping

1 tablespoon coconut sugar

1 teaspoon cinnamon

MAKES 12 MUFFINS

Per Serving (1 muffin):

Calories	201
Fat	5g
Sodium	161mg
Carbohydrates	33g
Fiber	4g
Sugar	9g
Protein	6g

1 Preheat oven to 375°F. Line a twelve-cup muffin tin with paper liners or spray with nonstick cooking spray.

2 In a measuring cup, combine soy milk and lemon juice; whisk with a fork. Let sit for 10 minutes, until thick and curdled. Set aside.

3 In a large bowl, stir together oat flour, oats, cornmeal, baking powder, cinnamon, and salt.

4 In a medium bowl, whisk together applesauce, almond butter, curdled soy milk, maple syrup, coconut sugar, and vanilla. Add applesauce mixture to oat flour mixture; stir until just combined.

5 Gently fold in blueberries. Spoon batter into prepared muffin cups, filling each ⅔ of the way full.

6 To make the topping, in a small cup, stir together coconut sugar and cinnamon. Sprinkle topping evenly over batter in muffin cups.

7 Bake for 18–20 minutes, until a toothpick inserted in the center of a muffin comes out clean. Let cool slightly, then remove from muffin tin and continue to cool on a wire rack to avoid getting moist.

8 Refrigerate muffins in an airtight container for up to 5 days to keep them from drying out. Or place on a baking sheet lined with parchment paper and freeze for 10 minutes; then transfer to a freezer-safe bag and freeze for up to 2 months.

Anti-Inflammatory Turmeric-Ginger Hot Cocoa

Reap the superfood benefits of this almond milk version of hot chocolate infused with anti-inflammatory powerhouses fresh turmeric and ginger. Serve hot or cold. If you don't have cacao powder, use cocoa.

2 cups water

1 tablespoon grated fresh turmeric

1 tablespoon grated fresh ginger

¼ teaspoon freshly ground black pepper

1 cup unsweetened almond milk

1 tablespoon cacao or cocoa powder

10 drops liquid stevia or 4 tablespoons erythritol sugar substitute

1 In a medium saucepan over medium heat, bring water, turmeric, ginger, and pepper to a boil. Turn off heat and let water infuse for about 5 minutes. Strain with a fine-mesh strainer.

2 Return infused water to saucepan over medium heat and stir in almond milk, cacao, and stevia. Let simmer until warm, about 5–6 minutes.

3 Drink right away or refrigerate in a covered cup and enjoy within 24 hours. Serve cold or reheat in a microwave or saucepan until warm.

Healing Turmeric Smoothie

Creamy, sweet, and loaded with nutrition, this smoothie is a refreshing start to your day. Prep the ingredients ahead of time by freezing several smoothie packs of the fruits so you can grab them and blend in a snap. Add more or less ginger to your taste.

2 cups unsweetened almond milk

2 medium bananas, peeled, cut into chunks, and frozen

1 cup frozen chopped mango

1 teaspoon ground turmeric

1 teaspoon grated fresh ginger

1 tablespoon hemp seeds

1 tablespoon whole or ground flaxseeds

¼ teaspoon vanilla extract

¼ teaspoon cinnamon

⅛ teaspoon freshly ground black pepper

1 Add all ingredients to a high-powered blender.

2 Blend until smooth, scraping the sides as necessary.

3 Refrigerate leftover smoothie in a covered container for no more than 24 hours.

SERVES 2	
Per Serving:	
Calories	256
Fat	8g
Sodium	190mg
Carbohydrates	44g
Fiber	6g
Sugar	26g
Protein	6g

Raspberry Scone Muffins

Scones are a delightful breakfast treat, snack, or even dessert option for a plant-based diet. You can switch out the raspberries for blueberries, raisins, blackberries, or even cranberries, which offer a pop of tartness.

1 tablespoon ground flaxseeds

2 tablespoons water

1¼ cups oat flour

1¼ cups blanched almond flour

1 tablespoon baking powder

2 tablespoons chia seeds

¼ teaspoon salt

¾ cup unsweetened soy milk

2 tablespoons maple syrup

1 tablespoon fresh lemon juice

½ teaspoon vanilla extract

1 cup fresh or frozen raspberries

1 Preheat oven to 300°F. Spray a small amount of nonstick cooking spray into eight muffin cups.

2 In a small cup, mix flaxseeds with water and set aside.

3 In a large bowl, combine oat flour, almond flour, baking powder, chia seeds, and salt. Whisk to mix well.

4 In a separate small bowl, combine flaxseeds mixture with soy milk, maple syrup, lemon juice, and vanilla. Add this mixture to flour mixture and stir until just combined. Very gently fold in raspberries.

5 Evenly divide the batter into eight muffin cups. Bake for 20 minutes until lightly golden brown.

6 These are best eaten fresh. If you have leftovers, refrigerate in an airtight container for up to 7 days or freeze for up to 3 months.

SERVES 8

Per Serving (1 muffin):

Calories	185
Fat	10g
Sodium	221mg
Carbohydrates	19g
Fiber	5g
Sugar	5g
Protein	6g

BENEFITS OF FLAX

Introducing flax to your diet has amazing health benefits, such as lowering cholesterol, leveling hormones, managing diabetes, and reducing your risk of heart disease and cancer. As a plant-based food, flaxseed is also an easy way to boost your health with healthy fats, fiber, antioxidants, and omega-3s.

Carrot Date Nut Bread

This hearty, filling quick bread is a great make-ahead recipe that's tasty for breakfast or for an afternoon snack.

1¼ cups unsweetened soy milk, divided

2 cups pitted medium Medjool dates

¼ cup maple syrup

1 teaspoon apple cider vinegar

1 teaspoon vanilla extract

¼ cup almond butter

½ cup unbleached all-purpose flour

½ cup whole-wheat all-purpose flour

1 cup oat flour

1 teaspoon baking soda

2 teaspoons baking powder

1 teaspoon cinnamon

¼ teaspoon salt

1 cup grated carrots

½ cup chopped walnuts

1 Preheat oven to 350°F. Line a 9" × 5" loaf pan with parchment paper or spray with nonstick cooking spray.

2 In a medium saucepan over medium heat, warm ¼ cup soy milk and dates until dates soften, about 7–8 minutes.

3 Add date-milk mixture to a high-speed blender along with the rest of the soy milk, maple syrup, vinegar, vanilla, and almond butter. Blend until smooth. Some bits of dates can remain.

4 In a large bowl, combine unbleached flour, whole-wheat flour, oat flour, baking soda, baking powder, cinnamon, and salt. Stir in carrots and walnuts.

5 Pour date mixture into flour mixture and stir until just combined. The batter will be thick.

6 Scrape batter into loaf pan and smooth the top. Bake for 45–50 minutes, until a knife inserted in the middle of the loaf comes out clean. Cool bread in the pan on a wire rack for 15 minutes; then remove from pan and set on wire rack to cool completely.

7 Store at room temperature in a sealed plastic bag or bread box for up to 5 days. To freeze, tightly wrap loaf in foil or plastic wrap, place in freezer-safe bag, and store up to 3 months. Thaw overnight in the refrigerator and then let sit at room temperature until ready to serve.

Huevos Rancheros with Tomatillo Sauce

This recipe calls for corn tortillas, but you could also use the recipe for Easy Whole-Wheat Pumpkin Tortillas in Chapter 6. Serve these with hot sauce if you want some extra heat. This is a flavorful breakfast your family will turn to again and again!

½ large yellow onion, peeled and diced

½ large red bell pepper, seeded and diced

¼ cup water

1 (14-ounce) container firm organic tofu, drained and rinsed

½ teaspoon ground turmeric

½ teaspoon salt

¼ teaspoon freshly ground black pepper

1½ cups Instant Pot® Pinto Beans (see recipe in Chapter 8) or 1 (15-ounce) can low-sodium pinto beans, drained and rinsed

8 (6") corn tortillas

1 recipe Tomatillo Sauce (see recipe in Chapter 9)

1 large avocado, peeled, seeded, and sliced

1 Heat a medium nonstick skillet over medium-high heat. Add onion, bell pepper, and water, and sauté until soft, about 5–7 minutes.

2 Crumble tofu into skillet. Add turmeric, salt, and black pepper, and stir to combine. The mixture should turn yellow from the spices and begin to look like eggs. Continue to cook until most of the moisture from the tofu has cooked off and it's heated through, stirring frequently so it doesn't stick, about 4–5 minutes. Remove from heat and set aside.

3 In a small saucepan over medium-high heat, cook beans until heated through, about 5–7 minutes, or microwave on high about 2 minutes.

4 Wrap tortillas in a damp paper towel and microwave on high until softened, about 1 minute, or wrap in foil and heat in a preheated 300°F oven for 10–15 minutes.

5 Put 2 tortillas, slightly overlapping, on each plate and top with black beans, then a large spoonful of Tomatillo Sauce, tofu scramble, and a little more sauce. Top with avocado slices.

6 Refrigerate leftover Tomatillo Sauce and beans separately in covered containers up to 5 days.

SERVES 4

Per Serving:

Calories	334
Fat	14g
Sodium	617mg
Carbohydrates	41g
Fiber	11g
Sugar	8g
Protein	15g

THE BLUE ZONES

Beans are a nutritious food that are a part of every longevity diet on the planet, according to Dan Buettner, author of *The Blue Zones: 9 Lessons for Living Longer from the People Who've Lived the Longest*. The "Blue Zones" are places where people are the longest-lived, such as in Okinawa, Japan; the Italian island of Sardinia; or Loma Linda, California. Beans provide B vitamins, lots of fiber, and protein.

Overnight Chocolate-Chia Oats

SERVES 2

Per Serving:

Calories	313
Fat	16g
Sodium	99mg
Carbohydrates	37g
Fiber	10g
Sugar	9g
Protein	9g

This is a simple breakfast made with creamy oats and chia seeds, almond milk, fresh fruit, and nuts for an energy boost that's ready to go in the morning. Use wide-mouth glass jars that you can eat right out of to make it even simpler.

½ cup old-fashioned oats

1 cup unsweetened almond milk

¼ teaspoon cinnamon

¼ teaspoon vanilla extract

2 tablespoons white chia seeds

½ tablespoon maple syrup

1 teaspoon unsweetened cacao or cocoa powder

½ cup fresh or frozen blueberries

½ cup fresh or frozen strawberries

¼ cup chopped walnuts

1 In a medium bowl, combine oats, almond milk, cinnamon, vanilla, chia seeds, maple syrup, and cacao. Stir to combine. Divide oat mixture evenly between two jars or other airtight containers.

2 Cover jars and refrigerate overnight.

3 In the morning, divide fruit and nuts evenly between the jars and spoon over top.

Pumpkin Pie French Toast

Using a hearty whole-grain bread for this recipe means that you'll stay full until lunch. If you're worried about the bread sticking when you cook it, add a teaspoon of vegan butter to the skillet.

1 cup unsweetened soy milk

¼ cup pumpkin puree

1 teaspoon pumpkin pie spice

¼ teaspoon vanilla extract

2 tablespoons plus ½ cup maple syrup, divided

8 (½") slices whole-grain bread

2 cups fresh or thawed frozen blueberries

SERVES 4

Per Serving:	
Calories	417
Fat	5g
Sodium	341mg
Carbohydrates	82g
Fiber	9g
Sugar	44g
Protein	13g

1 In a shallow dish, whisk together soy milk, pumpkin, pumpkin pie spice, vanilla, and 2 tablespoons maple syrup.

2 Heat a large nonstick skillet or griddle over medium heat.

3 Add 1 slice bread to pumpkin mixture (if the bread is dense, poke a few holes in it with a fork). Let soak for about 20 seconds, flip, and let soak for another 20 seconds.

4 Carefully lift bread into heated skillet. Let it sit without touching for about 4 minutes before turning so that it doesn't stick. It should have some brown marks on it when ready to flip. Flip and heat another 4 minutes. It's better to undercook so French toast doesn't become dry. Repeat with remaining bread slices.

5 For each serving, place 2 slices French toast on a plate. Top with ½ cup blueberries and 2 tablespoons maple syrup.

6 Double or triple the recipe to prep for a future meal. Cool cooked French toast completely (without toppings), then transfer to a freezer-safe bag and freeze until ready to use, up to 3 months. Pop frozen slices in the toaster and heat through before serving with fruit or other toppings.

Steel-Cut Oats with Fruit and Nuts

SERVES 4

Per Serving:

Calories	458
Fat	26g
Sodium	76mg
Carbohydrates	48g
Fiber	11g
Sugar	10g
Protein	14g

Steel-cut oats are one of the healthiest breakfasts you can eat. They take a little longer to cook than old-fashioned oats, but by prepping them ahead of time either in an Instant Pot® or on the stove and storing them in the refrigerator, you'll be ready for breakfast every day of the week. Prep and freeze your favorite combination of fruits ahead of time in plastic freezer bags.

3 cups water

⅛ teaspoon salt

1 cup steel-cut oats

1 teaspoon vanilla extract

½ teaspoon cinnamon

1 cup fresh or thawed frozen blueberries

1 cup chopped fresh or thawed frozen strawberries

1 cup chopped Honeycrisp apple

2 tablespoons ground flaxseeds

2 tablespoons hemp seeds

1 cup chopped walnuts

1 In a large saucepan over medium-high heat, combine water and salt and bring to a boil. Add oats, vanilla, and cinnamon. Reduce heat to medium-low, and cook, stirring often, for 15 minutes. Remove from heat.

2 Divide oats evenly among four bowls, then divide blueberries, strawberries, and apple evenly to top each serving. Sprinkle each bowl with ½ tablespoon flaxseeds, ½ tablespoon hemp seeds, and ¼ cup walnuts.

3 Refrigerate leftovers in an airtight container for up to 3 days.

CHAPTER 3

Appetizers

Basil-Spinach Dip

SERVES 8

Per Serving:

Calories	77
Fat	3g
Sodium	486mg
Carbohydrates	5g
Fiber	2g
Sugar	2g
Protein	8g

HOW TO ADD FLAVOR TO PLANT-BASED DISHES

Use miso paste to give sauces a deep, rich, umami flavor. Nutritional yeast is another addition that enhances "cheesiness" and offers a dose of B_{12}, an essential vitamin that should be monitored when eating a plant-based diet.

Basil and spinach are two flavors that work well together in so many ways. This dip is loaded with these healthy greens and is simple enough to make for a crowd. Serve it with cut-up vegetables or Oil-Free Tortilla Chips (see recipe in this chapter).

1 (14-ounce) container firm organic tofu, drained, rinsed, and pressed for at least 15 minutes (see Chapter 1 for pressing instructions)

¼ cup apple cider vinegar

1 tablespoon spicy mustard

2 tablespoons light miso

½ teaspoon garlic powder

½ teaspoon onion powder

2 tablespoons nutritional yeast

½ teaspoon salt

¼ teaspoon freshly ground black pepper

1 (10-ounce) package frozen spinach, thawed and drained

1 (5-ounce) can water chestnuts, drained

1 cup packed fresh basil

1 In a food processor, blend tofu, vinegar, mustard, miso, garlic powder, onion powder, yeast, salt, and pepper on high until well blended.

2 Add spinach, water chestnuts, and basil to food processor. Pulse a few times to break up water chestnuts, leaving some chunkiness.

3 Transfer to a bowl and chill for 2–3 hours before serving. Refrigerate in a sealed glass container for up to 4 days.

Caramelized Onion Dip

You'll find a surprising depth of sweetness from the caramelized onion in this recipe. Garlic, creamy tofu, and dried onion flakes give this classic favorite that traditional onion dip flavor without using an onion soup mix. Serve it at your next party! Try with oil-free potato chips, Oil-Free Tortilla Chips (see recipe in this chapter), yam chips, crackers, or vegetable sticks. You should be able to find dried onion flakes in the spice aisle.

½ large yellow onion, peeled and thinly sliced

2 medium cloves garlic, peeled and roughly chopped

½ (14-ounce) container firm organic tofu, drained and rinsed

Juice of 1 medium lemon

2 tablespoons light miso

2 tablespoons apple cider vinegar

¼ teaspoon salt

2 tablespoons dried onion flakes

1 Heat a medium nonstick skillet over medium-high heat. Add yellow onion and dry-sauté (using no water), stirring frequently, until lightly browned, about 5–7 minutes. Add garlic as onion browns and sauté for another minute. Remove from heat and set aside to cool.

2 In a food processor, combine tofu, lemon juice, miso, vinegar, salt, and sautéed onion mixture. Process until smooth and transfer to a large bowl.

3 Add dried onion and stir to combine. Cool in refrigerator for about an hour so flavors can blend. Refrigerate leftovers in an airtight container up to 4 days.

SERVES 4

Per Serving:

Calories	114
Fat	5g
Sodium	521mg
Carbohydrates	8g
Fiber	1g
Sugar	3g
Protein	10g

CAN YOU CARAMELIZE ONIONS WITHOUT OIL?

Yes, you can! Heat a nonstick skillet over medium-high heat, then add sliced onions, cover and cook for about 10 minutes, turning 2 or 3 times. Don't touch them until they start to release juices and brown, about 5 minutes. Stir when you see browning and just add a little vegetable broth or water if they start to stick. Uncover for the last 5 minutes and brown until they're the color you like.

Artichoke-Spinach Stuffed Mushrooms

SERVES 6

Per Serving:

Calories	180
Fat	9g
Sodium	212mg
Carbohydrates	19g
Fiber	5g
Sugar	4g
Protein	9g

This dish uses Spinach-Artichoke Dip for the stuffing and tops it with a cheese-like cashew topping. Make a full batch of the dip and keep what you don't use here for dipping vegetables or to top baked potatoes. Mushrooms are high in vitamins and antioxidants and one of the only plant sources of vitamin D.

½ cup unsalted raw cashews

2 tablespoons nutritional yeast

¼ cup bread crumbs

1 pound cremini mushrooms, stems removed

½ recipe Spinach-Artichoke Dip (see recipe in this chapter)

1 Preheat oven to 375°F. Line a baking sheet with parchment paper.
2 Blend cashews in a blender until crumbly. Transfer to a small bowl and combine with nutritional yeast and bread crumbs.
3 Stuff each mushroom cap with 1½ tablespoons Spinach-Artichoke Dip, mounding over the top of the mushroom. Place on baking sheet.
4 Bake, uncovered, for 25 to 30 minutes. About halfway through baking, remove and sprinkle on the cashew mixture. Return to the oven to finish cooking.
5 Let cool for about 5 minutes before serving. Refrigerate leftovers in an airtight glass container for up to 4 days.

Chili "Cheese" Dip

SERVES 6

Per Serving:

Calories	518
Fat	23g
Sodium	824mg
Carbohydrates	66g
Fiber	11g
Sugar	6g
Protein	15g

A LOW-FAT SUBSTITUTE FOR CASHEWS IN DIPS AND SAUCES

Cashews can be used in dips and sauces to add creaminess and subtle nutty flavor. However, if you're avoiding added fats and calories, try substituting the same portion of drained and rinsed cannellini beans. You'll avoid the addition of fats but still enjoy a creamy texture.

This hearty dip is loaded with creaminess and a kick of heat that will satisfy even the strongest of cheese cravings. The complex flavors come from the addition of black beans and fresh salsa. If you don't have store-bought taco seasoning, you can make your own by mixing 1 tablespoon chili powder, ¼ teaspoon garlic powder, ¼ teaspoon onion powder, 1 teaspoon ground cumin, ¼ teaspoon crushed red pepper flakes, ¼ teaspoon dried oregano, ¼ teaspoon smoked paprika, ¼ teaspoon salt, and ¼ teaspoon freshly ground black pepper. It's a well-rounded party staple that will be a hit with your guests. Serve with crackers or Oil-Free Tortilla Chips (see recipe in this chapter).

1 cup unsalted raw cashews, soaked and drained (see Chapter 1 for soaking instructions)

1 cup unsweetened almond milk

2 teaspoons chili powder

¼ cup nutritional yeast

1 medium orange, peeled and roughly chopped, or 1 medium roasted red bell pepper, roughly chopped

Juice of 1 medium lemon

2 teaspoons yellow mustard

½ teaspoon salt

¼ cup minced yellow onion

¼ cup water

1 (15-ounce) can low-sodium black beans, drained and rinsed

1 cup Homemade Cherry Tomato Salsa (see recipe in this chapter)

2 tablespoons taco seasoning

1 (12-ounce) bag tortilla chips or make your own Oil-Free Tortilla Chips (see recipe in this chapter)

1 In a blender, add cashews, almond milk, chili powder, yeast, orange, lemon juice, mustard, and salt. Blend a few minutes until smooth. Set aside.

2 Heat a large nonstick skillet over medium-high heat. Add onion and water and sauté, stirring frequently, until soft, about 5–7 minutes.

3 Add beans, salsa, and taco seasoning, and heat for about 5 minutes to combine flavors.

4 Pour in the "cheese" sauce (cashew mixture) and stir to combine and heat through, about 5 minutes. Refrigerate leftovers in an airtight container for up to 4 days.

High-Protein Trail Mix

If you're like most people, you are always looking for healthy snacks that won't send your healthy diet way off track. If you have a handful of this High-Protein Trail Mix, it'll help you make it to your next meal without derailing your plant-based lifestyle! If you want to lower the sugar and fat content, use cacao nibs instead of the chocolate chips. Likewise, feel free to use freeze-dried blueberries or strawberries as an alternative to the cherries.

½ cup dry-roasted soybeans

¼ cup shelled pistachios

½ cup shelled pumpkin seeds

¼ cup unsalted, dry-roasted almonds

½ cup freeze-dried cherries

¼ cup vegan chocolate chips

½ cup whole oats

1 Line a baking sheet with parchment paper and set aside.

2 In a large bowl, add soybeans, pistachios, pumpkin seeds, almonds, and cherries.

3 In a small microwave-safe bowl, microwave chocolate chips on high for 30 seconds. Stir and heat another 30 seconds or so until melted. Or, if you prefer, melt it on the stove: Place chocolate in a bowl that fits over a saucepan filled with a few inches of water. Heat gently over medium heat for 2 minutes until melted.

4 Stir oats into melted chocolate.

5 Drop ½" spoonfuls of the oats-chocolate mixture onto prepared baking sheet. Place in freezer for 5–7 minutes, until solid.

6 Add chocolate clusters to the bowl with nut mixture and stir to combine.

7 Store trail mix in a sealed container at room temperature for up to 3 months. Extend shelf life by freezing in a freezer-safe bag for up to 6 months.

SERVES 12

Per Serving:

Calories	144
Fat	9g
Sodium	3mg
Carbohydrates	14g
Fiber	4g
Sugar	3g
Protein	6g

THE BEST SNACKING OPTIONS

The best things to satisfy that pesky snack urge are protein and healthy fats. You can find these from nuts, beans, chickpeas, tofu, and other plant-based sources. Trail mix can combine a few of these ingredients, making it a great appetizer for gatherings, keeping you feeling full longer.

Mexican Bruschetta with Guacamole

This unique twist on traditional Italian bruschetta pairs two popular Mexican flavors in a crunchy, creamy bite. It's very quick to pull together if you make the salsa ahead of time.

1 large whole-wheat baguette, cut into ½" slices

2 medium avocados, peeled, seeded, and mashed

1 recipe Homemade Cherry Tomato Salsa (see recipe in this chapter)

1 Preheat oven to 400°F. Place baguette slices on a nonstick baking sheet and bake until lightly browned, about 10 minutes, checking to make sure they're not getting too brown.

2 Top each slice of bread with about 1 tablespoon mashed avocado and top with 2 teaspoons salsa.

3 Refrigerate any leftover salsa in a small airtight container for 5–7 days. Or freeze in a freezer-safe container for up to 6 months.

Homemade Cherry Tomato Salsa

This homemade salsa is a perfect condiment for tacos, burritos, layered bean dip, or burrito bowls.

1 pint cherry tomatoes, cut into ¼" pieces

2 medium cloves garlic, peeled and minced

⅓ heaping cup chopped red onion

⅓ cup lightly packed chopped fresh cilantro

Juice of 1 medium lime

¼ teaspoon salt

⅛ teaspoon freshly ground black pepper

¼ teaspoon hot sauce

1 In a medium bowl, add all ingredients and stir to combine. Taste and adjust seasonings to your liking.

2 Refrigerate in an airtight container for up to 5 days. Note that it's best not to freeze salsa unless you're going to use it in a recipe and not for dipping.

Kale Chips

These superfood-based leafy green chips are delicate and crispy, perfect as a sandwich add-on or salad topper, and just as delicious on their own as a snack. Make plenty, because they'll disappear quickly! If you don't have low-sodium tamari soy sauce, you can use coconut aminos, which are even lower in sodium.

2 tablespoons almond butter

1 teaspoon onion powder

1 teaspoon garlic powder

2 teaspoons nutritional yeast

1 tablespoon low-sodium tamari soy sauce (plus a little water to thin)

4 large leaves kale, stems removed, torn into large pieces, and dried thoroughly

1 Preheat oven to 300°F. Line two baking sheets with parchment paper.
2 In a large bowl, stir together nut butter, onion powder, garlic powder, nutritional yeast, and tamari. Add 1 teaspoon water if it's hard to mix.
3 Using clean hands, add kale to bowl and massage nut butter mixture into kale, then lay kale in a single layer on prepared baking sheets.
4 Bake for 10 minutes, rotate pan, and bake another 10 minutes, checking to see if chips are getting brown. Don't overcook.
5 Let cool a few minutes before eating. They crisp up as they cool and are quite delicate. Keep chips in an airtight container on the counter to enjoy for up to 2 weeks.

SERVES 2

Per Serving:

Calories	123
Fat	9g
Sodium	334mg
Carbohydrates	7g
Fiber	3g
Sugar	2g
Protein	6g

Crispy Baked Mushrooms

SERVES 4

Per Serving:

Calories	209
Fat	2g
Sodium	481mg
Carbohydrates	39g
Fiber	4g
Sugar	5g
Protein	10g

MAKE YOUR OWN SEASONED BREAD CRUMBS

Toast 5 slices whole-grain bread on a baking sheet in a 350°F oven until dry, about 12 minutes. Blend in a food processor until crumbs form. Mix in 2 teaspoons Italian seasonings, ½ teaspoon garlic powder, 2 teaspoons dried parsley, and ¼ teaspoon salt. Refrigerate in an airtight container for 1–2 months, or freeze for up to 3 months.

These mushrooms make for a great appetizer or snack for a crowd. Serve Tartar Sauce (see recipe in Chapter 9) as a dipping sauce.

¾ cups panko bread crumbs

¾ cup Italian seasoned bread crumbs

¼ cup chickpea flour

1 teaspoon ground cumin

1 teaspoon ground turmeric

½ teaspoon smoked paprika

1 teaspoon garlic powder

¼ teaspoon salt

¼ teaspoon freshly ground black pepper

2 tablespoons cornstarch

5 tablespoons aquafaba (liquid from a can of chickpeas)

4 medium portobello mushrooms, sliced ¼" thick

1 Preheat oven to 450°F. Line a baking sheet with parchment paper.

2 In a shallow bowl, mix panko bread crumbs, seasoned bread crumbs, chickpea flour, cumin, turmeric, paprika, garlic powder, salt, and pepper. Set aside. Put cornstarch in a separate shallow bowl.

3 In a third shallow bowl, lightly beat aquafaba with a fork until frothy. Dip each mushroom slice in the cornstarch, then aquafaba, and then into the bread-crumb mixture. Use one hand for the wet aquafaba, and the other for the dry ingredients.

4 Lay mushroom slices on the prepared baking sheet. Bake for 45–50 minutes, until golden brown, then flip mushroom slices and bake for another 7 minutes before serving.

5 Refrigerate any leftovers in a covered container for up to 3 days. To reheat, place on a baking sheet and bake at 400°F for 10 minutes.

Roasted Mexican Cauliflower

Crunchy with a little spice and topped with a creamy easy-to-make avocado sauce, these little bites of heaven will be a big hit at your next party. Try pairing them with a bean dish to continue the Mexican theme. Cauliflower, a cruciferous vegetable, is a nutritional powerhouse that's high in fiber, vitamins B, C, K, and folate. These are wonderful dipped in Avocado Cream Sauce (see recipe in Chapter 9).

½ cup oat flour

¼ cup whole-wheat all-purpose flour

2 teaspoons chili powder

1 teaspoon ground cumin

2 teaspoons garlic powder

2 teaspoons onion powder

½ teaspoon salt

Juice of 1 medium lime

½ cup water

1 medium head cauliflower, cored and broken into bite-sized pieces

1 Preheat oven to 450°F. Line two large rimmed baking sheets with parchment paper.

2 In a shallow bowl, add oat flour, whole-wheat flour, chili powder, cumin, garlic powder, onion powder, salt, lime juice, and water (add enough water to create the consistency of pancake batter). Whisk until well combined.

3 In batches, submerge cauliflower pieces in batter. Remove pieces and place on prepared baking sheets, about 1" apart.

4 Bake for 15 minutes, then flip cauliflower over and bake for 10 more minutes, until golden brown or tender when pierced with a fork.

SERVES 8	
Per Serving:	
Calories	60
Fat	1g
Sodium	189mg
Carbohydrates	12g
Fiber	3g
Sugar	2g
Protein	3g

MAKE YOUR OWN OAT FLOUR

Oat flour can be substituted for all or part of white flour in recipes—and it adds more whole-grain nutrition than white flour. Make your own oat flour by grinding old-fashioned oats in the blender for several seconds. 1 cup whole oats makes about ¾ cup flour.

Black Bean–Mango Salsa

Packed with a sweet and tangy crunch and hearty black beans for protein, this colorful salsa is a flavor explosion perfect for dipping homemade Oil-Free Tortilla Chips (see recipe in this chapter) or serving in tacos or burritos. You can also use it instead of tomato salsa in Layered Bean Dip (see recipe in this chapter).

1 (15-ounce) can low-sodium black beans, drained and rinsed

½ cup diced red onion

½ cup chopped fresh cilantro

1 large avocado, peeled, seeded, and chopped

1 large mango, peeled, seeded, and chopped

½ medium jalapeño pepper, seeded and diced

Juice of 1 medium lime

¼ teaspoon salt

¼ teaspoon freshly ground black pepper

In a large bowl, add all ingredients and stir to combine. If salsa needs more zing, add more lime juice. Refrigerate leftovers in an airtight container for up to 5 days.

SERVES 4

Per Serving:

Calories	243
Fat	8g
Sodium	413mg
Carbohydrates	38g
Fiber	13g
Sugar	13g
Protein	9g

CAN SALSA BE MADE AHEAD OF TIME?

Yes! You can make salsa ahead of time and refrigerate in an airtight container for up to 5 days. It can also be frozen up to 2 months in the freezer, though the texture may not be as crisp. When ready to serve, pull the salsa out of the freezer the day before to thaw in the refrigerator.

Spinach-Artichoke Dip

SERVES 6

Per Serving:

Calories	162
Fat	7g
Sodium	344mg
Carbohydrates	20g
Fiber	7g
Sugar	2g
Protein	8g

HIGH-SPEED BLENDER

Having the proper kitchen equipment is essential for plant-based cooking. A high-speed blender is something you will use almost daily. It's perfect for blending dips and smoothies. You can also use it for blending nuts into a cream sauce, and for making nut milk, gravy, and even soup. If you have a "regular" blender, be sure to soak cashews to soften them before blending or it could overwhelm the motor.

This light and healthy dip uses mashed potato for creaminess but is just as delicious as the unhealthy original. Throw in a little cayenne pepper for a kick, or add diced water chestnuts for a crunchy texture. It's wonderful served with vegetable sticks. If you don't have a high-speed blender, soak the raw cashews in room-temperature water for 2 or more hours or in boiling water for 10 minutes.

½ cup unsalted raw cashews, soaked and drained (see Chapter 1 for soaking instructions)

1¾ cups unsweetened almond milk, divided

¼ cup nutritional yeast

4 medium cloves garlic, peeled and minced

¼ cup fresh lemon juice

2 tablespoons apple cider vinegar

1 cup tightly packed mashed cooked red or Yukon gold potatoes

3 tablespoons flat-leaf parsley

1 (12-ounce) package frozen artichoke hearts, thawed

¼ cup packed fresh basil

1 (10-ounce) package frozen spinach, thawed and squeezed dry

½ teaspoon salt

½ teaspoon freshly ground black pepper

1. Preheat oven to 375°F. Lightly spray a medium baking dish with nonstick cooking spray.
2. In a blender, add cashews, ½ cup almond milk, yeast, garlic, lemon juice, and vinegar. Blend until smooth.
3. Scrape down sides of blender. Add potatoes and ½ cup almond milk. Puree until smooth. Add remaining ¾ cup almond milk and parsley. Puree until very smooth and well combined, scraping down sides of blender when necessary.
4. Add artichokes, basil, spinach, salt, and pepper, and pulse lightly to incorporate the ingredients while retaining a slightly chunky consistency. It will be pretty runny, but will firm up after baking.
5. Pour into prepared baking dish. Bake uncovered for 25–30 minutes, until golden and bubbly.
6. Remove and let cool for about 5 minutes before serving. Refrigerate in a sealed glass container for up to 7 days.

Easy Guacamole

Guacamole is one of those recipes you might not want to make ahead because it so easily turns brown when exposed to air. The addition of lemon juice helps retain the bright green color, but stick with making guacamole on the day you plan to eat it. Serve with Oil-Free Tortilla Chips (see recipe in this chapter), Black Bean Breakfast Tacos (see recipe in Chapter 2), Breakfast Burrito with Tofu Scramble (see recipe in Chapter 2), or sliced vegetables.

SERVES 6	
Per Serving:	
Calories	220
Fat	20g
Sodium	108mg
Carbohydrates	13g
Fiber	9g
Sugar	1g
Protein	3g

4 medium avocados, peeled, seeded, and mashed

¼ cup diced red onion

¼ cup finely chopped fresh cilantro

Juice of 1 medium lemon

½ teaspoon salt

In a medium bowl, add mashed avocados. Add remaining ingredients and mix well.

Beet Hummus

Beet Hummus is a great way to use up roasted beets that you've made during meal prep. It's great for dipping carrot or jicama sticks, cucumber slices, or your favorite crackers. It's also a crowd-pleaser because of its beautiful pink color.

SERVES 4	
Per Serving:	
Calories	168
Fat	6g
Sodium	337mg
Carbohydrates	24g
Fiber	6g
Sugar	8g
Protein	7g

1½ cups chopped Roasted Beets, cooled (see recipe in Chapter 8)

1 (15-ounce) can low-sodium chickpeas, drained (reserve liquid) and rinsed

2 medium cloves garlic, peeled

Juice of 1 medium lemon

2 tablespoons tahini

¼ teaspoon salt

1 Add all ingredients to a food processor and process until smooth, stopping periodically to scrape down the sides. Add about 2 tablespoons liquid from chickpeas to thin, if needed.

2 Refrigerate in a sealed container for up to 5 days.

Tempeh Asian Lettuce Wraps

SERVES 4

Per Serving:

Calories	705
Fat	42g
Sodium	1,528mg
Carbohydrates	54g
Fiber	8g
Sugar	21g
Protein	39g

WHAT'S THE DIFFERENCE BETWEEN SOY SAUCE AND TAMARI?

Both tamari soy sauce and ordinary soy sauce are made from fermented soybeans, but tamari is likely to be a little less salty, has more protein, fewer additives, and is often made without wheat. Be sure to use the low-sodium versions of either one, as they're still high in salt.

These lettuce wraps offer a parade of Asian-inspired flavors in a delicate lettuce cup.

Tempeh Filling

2 (8-ounce) packages original soy tempeh, crumbled

1 large carrot, peeled and grated

1 medium red bell pepper, seeded and cut into thin slices

8 medium green onions, trimmed and sliced

½ cup chopped fresh parsley

¼ (8-ounce) package whole-grain rice noodles, cooked according to package directions

Asian Dipping Sauce

¼ cup all-natural peanut butter

⅓ cup low-sodium tamari soy sauce

2 tablespoons rice vinegar

2 tablespoons chili garlic sauce

1 tablespoon minced fresh ginger

1 tablespoon maple syrup

Lettuce Wraps

8 large leaves butter lettuce, rinsed and dried

¾ cup chopped unsalted dry-roasted peanuts

1 cup mango salsa

1 Heat a large skillet over medium-high heat and dry-sauté tempeh until lightly browned, about 5–7 minutes.

2 Transfer sautéed tempeh to a large bowl and add rest of filling ingredients.

3 In a small bowl, whisk together dipping sauce ingredients.

4 For each wrap, fill 1 lettuce leaf with 2 tablespoons tempeh mixture, 1 teaspoon peanuts, a drizzle of dipping sauce, and 1 tablespoon mango salsa. Fold to eat.

5 Refrigerate filling and dipping sauce separately in airtight containers for up to 5 days. Warm filling by microwaving on high in a microwave-safe dish for a minute when ready to use.

Chickpea "Crab" Cakes

Serve with a traditional Tartar Sauce (see recipe in Chapter 9), flavored with homemade Old Bay seasoning, or with a different pairing, such as tangy mango salsa.

¼ cup water

½ cup diced red onion

½ cup diced celery

¼ cup diced red bell pepper

¼ cup chopped fresh flat-leaf parsley

1 tablespoon drained capers

¼ teaspoon Tabasco sauce

½ teaspoon vegan Worcestershire sauce

½ teaspoon crab boil seasoning (such as Old Bay)

¼ teaspoon salt

¼ teaspoon freshly ground black pepper

1 (15-ounce) can low-sodium chickpeas, drained (reserve liquid) and rinsed

1 teaspoon dulse flakes

⅓ cup bread crumbs

1 tablespoon fresh lemon juice

Zest of ½ medium lemon

2 tablespoons Dijon mustard

WHAT ARE DULSE FLAKES?

Dulse flakes are a type of edible sea vegetable that will impart the flavor of the sea, including some saltiness, to dishes like these Chickpea "Crab" Cakes. Usually eaten dried, it's rich in fiber, vitamin B$_6$, iron, and potassium, and it can be found at most health food stores. Look for flaked dulse, dulse powder, whole-leaf, and seasoning mixes.

1. Preheat oven to 375°F. Line a baking sheet with parchment paper.
2. Heat a large nonstick skillet over medium-high heat. Add water, onion, celery, bell pepper, parsley, capers, Tabasco sauce, Worcestershire sauce, crab boil seasoning, salt, and black pepper. Sauté, stirring frequently, until vegetables are soft, about 15 minutes. Remove from heat and cool to room temperature.
3. In a large bowl, mash chickpeas with a fork and toss with dulse flakes, bread crumbs, lemon juice, lemon zest, and mustard. Add liquid from chickpeas 1 tablespoon at a time until you get a consistency that holds together.
4. Add cooked vegetables and mix well. Refrigerate for 30 minutes.
5. Shape into round cakes about 2" in diameter. Place on prepared baking sheet and bake for 20 minutes, flipping halfway through.
6. If not serving right away, refrigerate in an airtight container for up to 3 days. Reheat in a 350°F oven for about 10 minutes.

Garden Vegetable Dip

SERVES 6

Per Serving:

Calories	78
Fat	5g
Sodium	215mg
Carbohydrates	6g
Fiber	1g
Sugar	2g
Protein	5g

Made with meal prepped Cashew Cream and tofu, this vegetable dip provides a double whammy of nutritional vegetables and a delicious flavor that's addictive to eat. Serve with sliced vegetables such as carrots, peppers, asparagus spears, or crackers. It can also be used over baked potatoes or as a dip for roasted potatoes.

½ (14-ounce) container firm organic tofu, drained, rinsed, and pressed for 20 minutes (see Chapter 1 for pressing instructions)

½ cup Cashew Cream (see recipe in Chapter 9)

½ cup chopped carrot

½ cup chopped red bell pepper

2 tablespoons fresh lemon juice

2 medium cloves garlic, peeled and minced

1 tablespoon dried onion flakes

1 medium green onion, trimmed and chopped

2 tablespoons chopped fresh dill

1 tablespoon chopped fresh chives

1 tablespoon chopped fresh parsley

½ teaspoon salt

¼ teaspoon freshly ground black pepper

1 Crumble tofu into food processor. Add Cashew Cream and remaining ingredients.

2 Process for about 20 seconds, scraping down the sides halfway through, until almost smooth. Don't overprocess because you want to leave some chunky bits.

3 Transfer to an airtight container and refrigerate for 2–4 hours before serving. Refrigerate leftovers for up to 5 days.

Layered Bean Dip

This crowd-pleasing appetizer is easy on the waistline (unlike its traditional counterpart) and easy to pull together if you've meal prepped the Instant Pot® Pinto Beans, Plant-Based Sour Cream, and Homemade Cherry Tomato Salsa. Serve with crunchy homemade Oil-Free Tortilla Chips (see recipe in this chapter).

1½ cups Instant Pot® Pinto Beans, mashed (see recipe in Chapter 8) or 1 (15-ounce) can low-sodium, fat-free refried beans

1 cup Plant-Based Sour Cream (see recipe in Chapter 9)

1 (2.25-ounce) can sliced black olives, drained

½ medium red onion, peeled and diced (about 1 cup)

1 recipe Homemade Cherry Tomato Salsa (see recipe in this chapter)

2 medium avocados, peeled, seeded, and diced

4 medium green onions, trimmed and sliced (including most of the green tops)

½ medium jalapeño pepper, seeded and minced

1 medium lime, halved

1 cup chopped fresh cilantro

SERVES 4	
Per Serving:	
Calories	338
Fat	18g
Sodium	720mg
Carbohydrates	38g
Fiber	15g
Sugar	6g
Protein	12g

1. Layer Instant Pot® Pinto Beans on the bottom of a small 8" × 8" or 7" × 9" baking dish. Top with dollops of Plant-Based Sour Cream and smooth over the beans.
2. Top with a sprinkling of olives, red onion, Homemade Cherry Tomato Salsa, avocados, green onions, and jalapeño. Squeeze lime over everything and sprinkle with cilantro.
3. Refrigerate dip in an airtight container for up to 3 days.

Fresh Spring Rolls with Two Dipping Sauces

Light and refreshing, these spring rolls are great as an appetizer or tasty lunch. You'll quickly get the hang of making these delicious wraps after making a few. You may want to only use half of each of the dipping sauces if you're watching your salt intake.

Nuoc Champ Dipping Sauce

½ teaspoon chili paste

3 medium cloves garlic, peeled and minced

3 tablespoons coconut sugar

⅔ cup warm water

3 tablespoons fresh lime juice

Wraps

10 spring roll rice paper wraps

1 large carrot, peeled and julienned

1 large cucumber, peeled and julienned

2 cups bean sprouts

1 large red bell pepper, seeded and julienned

1 cup roughly chopped fresh cilantro

1 cup whole fresh mint leaves

1 (7-ounce) package Nasoya Teriyaki TofuBaked, sliced

1 recipe Peanut Dipping Sauce (see recipe in Chapter 9)

1 To make the nuoc champ dipping sauce, in a small bowl, whisk together chili paste, garlic, coconut sugar, water, and lime juice. Set aside.

2 Prepare your workspace with a shallow pan of hot water, rice paper wraps, and separate bowls containing tofu, vegetables, cilantro, and mint.

3 Working quickly, carefully place a wrap in the hot water for 10 seconds and then on a cutting board, keeping it smooth.

4 Lay a small amount of each vegetable, a sprinkling of cilantro and mint leaves, and 1 slice tofu across the lower third of the wrap, leaving about 1" on each side.

5 Fold over each side and start rolling from the bottom until you've made a tight roll. Set aside on a plate, keeping spring rolls separated so they don't stick together.

6 Serve at room temperature with nuoc champ dipping sauce and Peanut Dipping Sauce. Refrigerate leftovers in an airtight container for up to 3 days.

Nachos

SERVES 6

Per Serving:

Calories	282
Fat	6g
Sodium	571mg
Carbohydrates	49g
Fiber	6g
Sugar	5g
Protein	11g

WHICH STORE-BOUGHT PLANT-BASED CHEESES ARE BEST?

Use your label-reading skills when deciding which store-bought vegan "cheeses" are best. Most have too many additives and/or the addition of oil. Even coconut oil isn't recommended. Look for those that are made with nuts and little else.

Many of the ingredients in these Nachos are great to keep on hand in your pantry, but if you're making them from scratch, think about how the various parts can be used throughout the week. For example, you could add beans to salads, drizzle cheese sauce over baked potatoes, or use Plant-Based Sour Cream and Homemade Cherry Tomato Salsa in tacos. That's why meal prep comes in handy early in the week.

1½ cups Instant Pot® Pinto Beans (see recipe in Chapter 8) or 1 (15-ounce) can low-sodium pinto beans, drained and rinsed

1 tablespoon taco seasoning

1 (14.5-ounce) can low-sodium fire-roasted corn, drained

1 recipe Oil-Free Tortilla Chips (see recipe in this chapter)

1 (2.25-ounce) can sliced black olives, drained

1 recipe Homemade Cherry Tomato Salsa (see recipe in this chapter)

1 cup Blender "Cheese" Sauce (see recipe in Chapter 9)

½ recipe Plant-Based Sour Cream (see recipe in Chapter 9)

6 medium green onions, trimmed and sliced

½ cup chopped fresh cilantro

1 In a medium microwave-safe bowl, mash Instant Pot® Pinto Beans with taco seasoning. Don't overmash; keep some beans intact for a chunky consistency. Microwave bean mixture on high until heated through, 1–2 minutes. Set aside.

2 In a separate microwave-safe bowl, microwave corn on high for 2–3 minutes, until heated through.

3 On a large platter, arrange Oil-Free Tortilla Chips and top with mashed beans, roasted corn, olives, Homemade Cherry Tomato Salsa, Blender "Cheese" Sauce, and dollops of Plant-Based Sour Cream. Top with green onions and cilantro.

Oil-Free Tortilla Chips

Store-bought tortilla chips are full of salt and oil, but these oil-free chips are a much better nutritional choice. Dress them up with natural seasonings such as chili powder, ground cumin, or smoked paprika, or serve plain to satisfy that craving for crunch. This same cooking technique can also be used for potato chips.

12 (6") corn tortillas
¼ teaspoon salt

1 Stack tortillas four at a time and cut into six wedges.
2 **Oven Method:** Preheat oven to 390°F degrees. Place wedges in a single layer on a baking sheet. Sprinkle or spray a small amount of water over wedges and lightly salt. Bake for 8–10 minutes, then flip wedges over and continue to cook for 5–10 minutes. (Watch them carefully, as they're easy to overcook.)
3 **Microwave Method:** Place wedges in a single layer on a microwave-safe plate. Microwave on high for about 4–5 minutes or until crisp. Some chips will turn a little darker, which is normal, but watch them carefully so they don't burn.
4 Cool chips completely, then store in an airtight container at room temperature for up to 2 weeks.

SERVES 7

Per Serving:

Calories	90
Fat	1g
Sodium	102mg
Carbohydrates	18g
Fiber	3g
Sugar	0g
Protein	2g

Quinoa Oat Crackers

MAKES 20 CRACKERS

Per Serving (1 cracker):

Calories	36
Fat	1g
Sodium	67mg
Carbohydrates	5g
Fiber	1g
Sugar	1g
Protein	1g

MAKE YOUR OWN QUINOA FLOUR

To make your own quinoa flour, simply put quinoa into a blender or grinder and blend until it becomes flour. This usually takes just a few seconds of blending. Half a cup of quinoa will make about ⅔ cup flour. Refrigerate in an airtight container for up to 6 months or in the freezer for up to 1 year.

These crackers pair perfectly with hummus and other dips, plus they're naturally gluten-free.

½ cup quinoa flour

½ cup oat flour

¼ teaspoon baking powder

1 tablespoon ground flaxseeds

1 tablespoon chia seeds

1 tablespoon unsalted shelled sunflower seeds

1 tablespoon sesame seeds

½ teaspoon salt

1 tablespoon cashew butter

1 tablespoon maple syrup

¼ cup water

1 Preheat oven to 325°F.

2 Pulse flours, baking powder, seeds, and salt in a food processor until combined. Add cashew butter and maple syrup and pulse to incorporate. Add water 1 tablespoon at a time and pulse until it starts to come together when pinched with your fingers.

3 Remove from the bowl. If it needs more mixing, knead with your hands until ingredients are well incorporated. Divide into 2 pieces and roll each piece into a large ball.

4 Place one ball on wax paper and flatten with your hand. Top with another piece of wax paper and roll to a little less than ⅛" thick with a rolling pin. The thicker the batter, the more time they'll take to bake. Don't worry about the shape.

5 Cut away rough edges with a knife or pizza cutter and the rest into cracker-sized pieces, about 1½" × 1". Move crackers to baking sheet and bake for 15–20 minutes until they're golden brown. Some crackers will brown faster than others so you can remove these and continue to bake a few more minutes until crisp and golden.

6 Cool completely, then store in an airtight container at room temperature for up to 1 week.

CHAPTER 4

Salads

Asian Noodle Salad

Chock-full of crunchy vegetables, this cold Asian noodle dish can be made in advance for a party or as meal prep for lunches all week. Its savory, spicy sauce is balanced with pasta, tofu, and vegetables.

SERVES 6

Per Serving:

Calories	497
Fat	11g
Sodium	1,373mg
Carbohydrates	79g
Fiber	12g
Sugar	16g
Protein	25g

IS PASTA A HEALTHY CHOICE?

Whole-grain pasta is a great choice. Pasta can also be made with beans, lentils, or chickpeas, all of which are abundant in protein, vitamins, and minerals. Spiralized vegetables such as zucchini or sweet potato are another option. These and whole-grain pasta are minimally processed and full of fiber and nutrients. All this plant-based goodness helps you stay feeling full longer.

Dressing

¼ cup all-natural peanut butter

⅓ cup low-sodium tamari soy sauce

2 tablespoons rice vinegar

2 tablespoons chili garlic sauce

1 tablespoon maple syrup

1 tablespoon minced fresh ginger

Salad

3 cups snow peas, strings removed and cut into thirds

2 medium carrots, peeled and grated

4 medium green onions, trimmed and chopped

1 small red bell pepper, seeded and cut into small strips

1 (15-ounce) can low-sodium kidney beans, drained and rinsed

⅓ cup chopped fresh cilantro

1 (12-ounce) package whole-grain pasta, cooked according to package directions, ¼ cup cooking water reserved

Baked Tofu, cooled (see recipe in Chapter 7)

1 To make the dressing, in a small bowl, whisk together dressing ingredients to combine. Add a little cooking water from the pasta if it's too thick.

2 To make the salad, in a small saucepan over medium-high heat, add snow peas and cook in ¼ cup water for 3–5 minutes until tender. Add them to a large bowl with carrots, green onions, and bell pepper. Add beans and cilantro, and stir to combine.

3 Add cooked pasta and Baked Tofu, and pour dressing over everything. Toss well to coat.

4 Refrigerate in an airtight container for up to 5 days.

Greek Spinach Salad with Falafel

This nutrient-packed lunch is like a falafel sandwich in a bowl. Liberally spread with dressing and add a side of toasted whole-grain pita bread to add some grains. Although this recipe calls for only half of the Falafel Burger recipe, make the full recipe to enjoy as burgers later in the week.

Mixture from ½ recipe Falafel Burger (see recipe in Chapter 7)

1 (5-ounce) bag spinach

1 pound cherry or grape tomatoes, cut in half

1 medium cucumber, cut in half lengthwise and then into slices

2 cups thinly shredded red cabbage

1 cup sliced red onion

⅓ cup Tahini Dressing (see recipe in this chapter)

1 Preheat oven to 400°F. Line a baking sheet with parchment paper.
2 Instead of making a burger, roll falafel mixture into twelve 1" balls. Place on baking sheet and bake for 15–20 minutes, until golden brown.
3 In a large bowl, add spinach, tomatoes, cucumber, cabbage, and onion.
4 Drizzle salad with Tahini Dressing and toss until well coated. Divide among four salad bowls and top with 3 falafel balls each. Refrigerate leftover dressing in an airtight container for up to 7 days and leftover salad for 3–4 days.

SERVES 4

Per Serving:

Calories	149
Fat	2g
Sodium	463mg
Carbohydrates	27g
Fiber	7g
Sugar	8g
Protein	8g

WHY IS SPINACH A SUPERFOOD?

A cup of spinach packs a nutritional punch. It has only 47 calories, yet is a good source of protein, fiber, and micronutrients and is low in carbs and fat. When served with quinoa, tofu, or tempeh, spinach rounds out a meal and provides all of your amino acids.

Chopped Kale-Apple Salad with Lemon Vinaigrette

SERVES 4

Per Serving:

Calories	241
Fat	14g
Sodium	75mg
Carbohydrates	28g
Fiber	9g
Sugar	14g
Protein	6g

This salad is loaded with a rainbow of vegetables, such as carrots, red cabbage, and mint, all tossed in a tangy-sweet lemon dressing. Massaging half of an avocado into the kale makes the leaves more tender. Kale is easy to prep ahead of time. Simply wash, remove the stems, chop, and refrigerate until ready to use. It also does well left-over, unlike most soft greens.

Salad

1 medium bunch kale, stems removed and chopped

1 medium avocado, peeled seeded and chopped, divided

1 large carrot, peeled and grated

1 cup shredded red cabbage

1/3 cup chopped fresh parsley

1/2 cup chopped fresh mint

1/2 cup chopped almonds

1 medium unpeeled Honeycrisp apple, cored and cut into slivers

Lemon Vinaigrette

1/4 cup lemon juice

1 tablespoon nutritional yeast

1 clove garlic, peeled and minced

1 teaspoon mustard

2 tablespoons maple syrup

1 To make the salad, in a large bowl, add kale and 1/2 avocado. Massage avocado into the kale with your hands until leaves soften.

2 To make the vinaigrette, in a small bowl, whisk together all dressing ingredients until smooth.

3 Add remaining 1/2 avocado to kale. Add remaining salad ingredients to kale and top with vinaigrette. Toss to combine.

4 Refrigerate leftover dressing and salad in separate airtight containers for up to 5 days.

Roasted Beet and Arugula Salad

The salad dressing can be made right in your salad bowl, saving you from washing more dishes. This is a great salad for company because it makes a beautiful presentation. You can also use a mixture of arugula and spinach if the taste of arugula is too strong for you.

SERVES 4

Per Serving:

Calories	184
Fat	9g
Sodium	605mg
Carbohydrates	23g
Fiber	5g
Sugar	15g
Protein	6g

Salad

2 medium beets, ends trimmed

3 tablespoons water

½ cup unsalted raw walnuts

1 (5-ounce) package baby arugula

3 medium mandarin oranges, peeled and segments separated

½ (8-ounce) container almond ricotta or ½ cup Almond Ricotta (see recipe in Chapter 9)

Dressing

1 large shallot, sliced

2 teaspoons Dijon mustard

2 teaspoons maple syrup

3 tablespoons rice vinegar

¼ teaspoon salt

GREEN LEAFY LETTUCE CHOICES

Having a variety of different lettuces in your refrigerator will enhance your meal options. Instead of just iceberg, try using romaine, spinach, arugula, or other varieties. This will keep your salads interesting. Each lettuce has its own health benefits and flavor profile.

1 Preheat oven to 400°F.

2 Place beets in a medium baking dish with water. Cover with aluminum foil and roast for 50 minutes, or until tender when poked with a fork. Allow beets to cool slightly. Peel with backside of a paring knife, then cut into ½" cubes.

3 Add walnuts in a single layer to a small baking sheet and toast alongside the beets for about 5 minutes, until golden. Remove and set aside.

4 In a large salad bowl, whisk all dressing ingredients to combine.

5 Add arugula, beets, and oranges to the bowl and toss gently to coat in dressing.

6 Sprinkle each serving with 2 tablespoons toasted walnuts and 2 tablespoons almond ricotta.

7 If you have leftovers, refrigerate salad ingredients and dressing separately in airtight containers up to 5 days until ready to use.

Pasta with Spinach Pesto, Green Beans, and Tomatoes

This cold pasta salad is made with oil-free spinach pesto that is tangy with a touch of sweetness.

Salad

3 cups trimmed and chopped (into thirds) green beans

1 pint cherry tomatoes, halved

1 (16-ounce) package whole-grain penne pasta, cooked according to package directions, ½ cup pasta cooking water reserved

Pesto

¼ cup One-Pot Vegetable Broth (see recipe in Chapter 5)

2 cups packed baby spinach

1 cup packed fresh basil leaves

½ cup chopped fresh mint

2 teaspoons light miso

2 medium cloves garlic, peeled and roughly chopped

1 medium shallot, peeled and roughly chopped

⅓ cup dry-roasted unsalted almonds

Cashew Topping

¾ cup unsalted raw cashews

¼ cup nutritional yeast

¼ teaspoon salt

SERVES 6

Per Serving:	
Calories	495
Fat	15g
Sodium	215mg
Carbohydrates	78g
Fiber	13g
Sugar	7g
Protein	21g

SALAD AND PASTA TOPPING IDEAS

Save time by making simple pasta and salad toppings during your weekly meal prep. Toasted pine nuts, croutons, crispy sliced shallots, or roasted vegetables make great additions to many meals. Store these toppings in an airtight container for up to 1 week, or a few months in the freezer.

1 Boil about 1" water in a medium saucepan with a steamer basket over medium-high heat. Add green beans to steamer basket. Cover and let beans steam until crisp-tender, about 3–5 minutes. Add to a large salad bowl along with tomatoes.

2 In a food processor, add pesto ingredients until combined and mostly smooth, scraping sides as needed.

3 Gently combine pasta, pesto, and green beans in a salad bowl.

4 To make cashew topping, in a small food processor, add cashews, yeast, and salt. Pulse until finely chopped and crumbly.

5 Sprinkle each serving of salad with cashew topping. Store leftover pasta and topping in separate airtight containers and refrigerate until ready to serve, up to 1 week. Refrigerate leftover pesto in a covered container for 3–4 days.

Chia Seed Dressing

Chia seeds are a good source of omega-3 fatty acids and also are a great thickener, as shown in this salad dressing. Using black chia seeds makes this appear similar to poppy seed dressing. It's sweet and tangy and perfect for your next salad.

½ cup unsweetened almond milk

1 tablespoon chia seeds

3 tablespoons maple syrup

⅓ cup rice vinegar

¼ teaspoon salt

1 In a small bowl, combine all ingredients and whisk until smooth.

2 Refrigerate until ready to serve. Stir well before using. This keeps well refrigerated in an airtight container for up to 1 week.

Tahini Dressing

Lemony, garlicky Tahini Dressing goes well with any Greek or Middle Eastern recipes. This recipe uses cannellini beans for creaminess as well as tahini (ground sesame seed paste), which is a good source of vitamin E. They also help keep the recipe's calorie count relatively low, even with the high fat content of the sesame seeds.

Zest and juice of 1 large lemon

½ (15-ounce) can low-sodium cannellini beans, drained and rinsed

2 tablespoons tahini

1 medium clove garlic, peeled

2 tablespoons stone-ground mustard

1½ tablespoons low-sodium tamari soy sauce

1 tablespoon maple syrup

2 tablespoons nutritional yeast

¼ cup water

Place all ingredients in a blender and blend until smooth. Refrigerate in an airtight container for up to 2 weeks.

Green Goddess Dressing

Creamy and delicious and full of plant-based goodness, this recipe combines tahini, avocado, and parsley with green onions for a flavor that brightens any salad. The dressing will thicken up when chilled, making a nice vegetable dip too!

¼ cup tahini

¼ cup chopped avocado

½ cup water

2 tablespoons chopped fresh parsley

2 tablespoons chopped green onions

¼ teaspoon salt

3 medium cloves garlic, peeled and chopped, or 1½ teaspoons garlic powder

1 teaspoon low-sodium tamari soy sauce

2 tablespoons fresh lemon juice

2 tablespoons apple cider vinegar

1 In a blender or food processor, combine all ingredients until smooth.

2 Adjust seasoning to taste and add water, if necessary, until desired texture is achieved. Serve immediately, or store in refrigerator in an airtight container for up to 4 days.

MAKES 1½ CUPS	
Per Serving (2 tablespoons):	
Calories	38
Fat	3g
Sodium	67mg
Carbohydrates	2g
Fiber	1g
Sugar	0g
Protein	1g

Mexican Chopped Salad

SERVES 4

Per Serving:

Calories	322
Fat	9g
Sodium	471mg
Carbohydrates	54g
Fiber	16g
Sugar	6g
Protein	11g

TRY SOMETHING NEW: JICAMA

Jicama (pronounced *HEE-cah-mah*) is a root vegetable that is packed with nutrients. Not only a wonderful source of fiber, it also contains vitamin C, vitamin E, folate, vitamin B_6, pantothenic acid, potassium, magnesium, manganese, copper, iron, and even a small amount of protein! Also, jicama is a great snack for diabetics, as it is low on the glycemic index and regulates blood sugar.

This vibrant and colorful salad has a variety of flavors and textures to keep you feeling full yet light throughout the day. It is protein-rich and has a sweet and tangy vinaigrette that adds a zingy freshness to the salad. Make extra tortilla strips to store in a container on the counter for up to 2 weeks for a quick salad or soup topping.

4 (6") corn tortillas, sliced into 1/3" strips

1/4 teaspoon salt

Salad

2½ cups chopped romaine lettuce

1 (15-ounce) can low-sodium black beans, drained and rinsed

1 cup chopped tomato

1 cup chopped jicama

1 cup canned, unsalted corn kernels

3/4 cup thinly sliced radishes

1 medium red bell pepper, seeded and chopped

1 medium avocado, peeled, seeded, and diced

Dressing

1/3 cup fresh lime juice

2 tablespoons date syrup

2 tablespoons chopped cilantro

1 medium clove garlic, peeled and minced

1 teaspoon chopped and seeded jalapeño pepper

1 Place tortilla strips on a microwave-safe plate. Sprinkle or spray with water or apple cider vinegar and lightly salt. Microwave on high for about 2 minutes. Check for crispness, keeping in mind that the tortilla strips will get crunchier as they cool. Cook in additional 15-second increments if they aren't crispy enough.

2 Toss all salad ingredients except avocado and tortilla strips in a large bowl.

3 In a small bowl, whisk dressing ingredients to combine. Divide salad among four plates. If serving immediately, pour dressing over and top with avocado and crispy tortilla strips.

4 Refrigerate leftover salad, dressing, and tortillas separately in airtight containers for up to 3 days. Toss together when ready to serve.

Middle Eastern Vegetable Salad

This satisfying salad has an intense flavor, heart-healthy vegetables, chickpea protein, plant-based feta, and a brightly flavored dressing. The tofu marinade uses miso, which imparts a smoky, umami flavor.

Salad

10 medium green onions, thinly sliced (green tops included)

2 large tomatoes, cored and chopped

1 medium hothouse cucumber, halved lengthwise and diced into ½" cubes

1 (15-ounce) can low-sodium chickpeas, drained and rinsed

⅓ cup chopped fresh parsley

⅓ cup chopped fresh mint

⅓ cup fresh basil leaves, julienned into thin strips

1 recipe Tofu Feta (see recipe in Chapter 9)

6 pieces whole-grain pita bread, toasted and cut into 6 wedges each

Dressing

4 tablespoons tahini

⅓ cup fresh lemon juice

3 medium cloves garlic, peeled and minced

¼ teaspoon salt

¼ teaspoon freshly ground black pepper

1 In a large salad bowl, add green onions, tomatoes, cucumber, chickpeas, parsley, mint, and basil, and toss to combine.

2 In a small bowl, whisk all dressing ingredients to combine. Pour over salad, tossing gently to coat vegetables. Add feta and toss again gently.

3 Serve salad with wedges of pita bread.

4 Refrigerate prepared salad and dressing in separate covered containers for up to 3 days.

SERVES 6

Per Serving:

Calories	278
Fat	9g
Sodium	1,089mg
Carbohydrates	40g
Fiber	8g
Sugar	7g
Protein	13g

TAHINI, A HEALTHY FAT

Tahini is a paste made from ground sesame seeds and is used here as a source of fat. This fat is infused with a plethora of vitamins and minerals such as calcium, phosphorus, magnesium, potassium, iron, B and E vitamins, and other minerals that aid in liver detoxification. Tahini is a wonderful way to add creaminess and nutrients to any dressing.

Thai Cucumber Salad

This light and refreshing salad can be eaten by itself or added to a lettuce-based salad. It's one of the quickest recipes to make and is always satisfying. There's no need to peel the cucumber, especially if it's organic, and any type works well. Add more red pepper flakes if you want more kick.

Salad

2 hothouse cucumbers, cut in half lengthwise and sliced into ¼" slices

2 medium green onions, trimmed and sliced (including most of the green tops)

¼ cup roughly chopped unsalted dry-roasted peanuts

⅓ cup chopped fresh cilantro

Dressing

2 tablespoons maple syrup

¼ cup lime juice

2 tablespoons rice vinegar

⅛ teaspoon hot pepper flakes

1 In a medium bowl, add cucumbers, green onions, peanuts, and cilantro.

2 In a small bowl, whisk dressing ingredients to combine. Toss with salad to combine.

3 Refrigerate salad and dressing in separate airtight containers for up to 3 days.

Quinoa Salad with Spinach

SERVES 6

Per Serving:

Calories	191
Fat	6g
Sodium	216mg
Carbohydrates	29g
Fiber	6g
Sugar	9g
Protein	7g

ARTICHOKES, THE SUPER VEGETABLE

Did you know that artichokes are one of the most antioxidant-rich vegetables? Their health benefits include aiding heart and liver health, reducing bad cholesterol, acting like a diuretic, and being high in fiber. You can easily use canned, frozen, and fresh artichokes interchangeably. If you find you're sensitive to artichoke, asparagus is the closet substitution with its mild flavor.

Loaded with flavor and vitamins, this recipe will be one you want to share with family and friends.

Salad

8 dry-packaged sun-dried tomatoes

1½ cups One-Pot Vegetable Broth (see recipe in Chapter 5)

1 cup uncooked quinoa

½ medium red onion, peeled and chopped

¼ cup water

1 (10-ounce) bag spinach, stemmed and chopped

1 cup frozen artichoke hearts, thawed and chopped

⅓ cup chopped walnuts

¼ cup raisins

6 medium leaves fresh basil, chopped

Dressing

⅓ cup lemon juice

1 tablespoon white wine vinegar

1 tablespoon maple syrup

¼ teaspoon crushed red pepper flakes

¼ teaspoon salt

¼ teaspoon freshly ground black pepper

1 In a small bowl with hot water to cover, soak sun-dried tomatoes for 10 minutes to soften, then drain and chop. Set aside.

2 In a medium saucepan over medium-high heat, combine broth and quinoa. Bring to a boil, then cover, reduce heat to low, and simmer for 15 minutes, or until liquid is absorbed.

3 Add cooked quinoa to a large bowl and let cool for a few minutes.

4 Heat a large nonstick skillet over medium-high heat. Add onion and water, and sauté until soft, about 5–7 minutes. Add spinach and cook until wilted and tender, about 2 minutes.

5 Add onion mixture, artichokes, walnuts, raisins, tomatoes, and basil to quinoa. Combine well.

6 To make dressing, in a small bowl, whisk dressing ingredients to combine. Pour over salad and mix thoroughly.

7 Refrigerate leftovers in an airtight container for up to 5 days.

Orzo Pasta Salad with Roasted Vegetables

Any kind of roasted vegetables work well in this salad. The Tofu Feta should be made ahead of time to allow the flavors to meld, at least 2 hours ahead or the night before. The recipe will come together quickly if you've already roasted the vegetables.

Dressing

4 tablespoons red wine vinegar

1 tablespoon Dijon mustard

1½ tablespoon maple syrup

2 medium cloves garlic, peeled and minced

½ tablespoon low-sodium soy sauce

¼ teaspoon dried thyme

½ teaspoon salt

½ teaspoon freshly ground black pepper

Salad

1 medium red onion, peeled and sliced into ½" pieces

2 large carrots, peeled and sliced into ½" pieces

2 medium zucchini, trimmed and sliced into ½" pieces

1 large red bell pepper, seeded and sliced into ½" pieces

1 cup whole-wheat orzo, cooked according to package directions

1 recipe Tofu Feta (see recipe in Chapter 9)

1 Preheat oven to 400°F. Line a rimmed baking sheet with parchment paper.
2 In a small bowl, whisk dressing ingredients to combine. Set aside.
3 Spread onion, carrots, zucchini, and bell pepper on prepared baking sheet. Toss with 2 tablespoons dressing. Roast for about 25 minutes, turning halfway through, until the vegetables are crisp-tender. Let cool to room temperature.
4 In a large salad bowl, add cooked orzo and top with roasted vegetables, tofu feta, and remaining dressing. Toss to combine.
5 Refrigerate leftovers in an airtight container for 4–5 days.

SERVES 4

Per Serving:

Calories	252
Fat	5g
Sodium	1,157mg
Carbohydrates	42g
Fiber	7g
Sugar	10g
Protein	13g

SALT SUBSTITUTES

Replace salt with alternatives that will still offer a punch of flavor. Herbs and spices are one of the best ways to flavor food without sodium. Try seasoned blends that have zero added salt, such as Trader Joe's 21 Salute, or simply make your own seasoning that will complement a variety of recipes. For vegetables, salads, and soups, use vinegar and citrus juice to add a vibrant flavor.

Thai Crunch Salad

SERVES 8

Per Serving:

Calories	363
Fat	23g
Sodium	644mg
Carbohydrates	31g
Fiber	11g
Sugar	12g
Protein	16g

OIL-FREE SALAD DRESSINGS

Build a new habit of making your own salad dressings without oil instead of grabbing store-bought options. Use whole-food ingredients like raw cashews or cannellini beans to make your dressing creamy. Sweeteners are always optional. Most dressings will keep refrigerated in an airtight container for up to 7 days.

This salad features a crunchy combo of sweet and tangy flavors made with edamame for a bit of protein. It's a fiber-filled nutritional powerhouse, making it a perfect addition to your weekly meal plan.

3 (6") corn tortillas, sliced into 3" strips

½ medium head Napa cabbage, cored and chopped

1 small head red cabbage, cored and chopped

1 large cucumber, peeled and julienned

2 large carrots, peeled and julienned

12 medium green onions, trimmed and thinly sliced (including most of the green tops)

¾ cup chopped fresh cilantro

2 cups frozen edamame, cooked 5 minutes in boiling water and drained

1 cup unsalted dry-roasted peanuts

2 medium avocados, peeled, seeded, and diced into ½" cubes

Peanut Dressing

¼ cup smooth all-natural peanut butter

⅓ cup low-sodium tamari soy sauce

2 tablespoons rice vinegar

2 tablespoons fresh lime juice

2 tablespoons chili garlic sauce

1 tablespoon maple syrup

1 tablespoon minced fresh ginger

1 Preheat oven to 375°F. Place tortilla strips on a nonstick baking sheet and bake for 10–12 minutes, until crispy.

2 In a large salad bowl, add Napa cabbage, red cabbage, cucumber, carrots, green onions, cilantro, edamame, and peanuts. Toss to mix.

3 Whisk dressing ingredients in a small bowl to combine.

4 Pour peanut dressing on salad and toss. Top with crunchy tortilla strips and avocado.

5 For meal prep, divide undressed vegetable mixture (without avocado topping) into equal portions and refrigerate in airtight containers for up to 5 days. Store tortilla strips at room temperature in an airtight container for up to 7 days, and refrigerate dressing in an airtight container for up to 7 days. When ready to serve, top with tortilla strips and dressing.

Wedge Salad with Homemade Tempeh Bacon

This classic salad has been around for decades, but this plant-based version is easy to throw together if you've prepped your dressing ahead of time. If you're cutting down on fat, use ¾ cup unsweetened almond milk plus 1 tablespoon chia seeds instead of raw cashews in the dressing; the chia seeds will thicken it after several minutes.

4 slices whole-wheat sourdough bread, cut into ½" cubes

1 (6-ounce) package tempeh bacon (8 slices)

1 large head iceberg lettuce, cored and cut into 6 wedges

1 recipe Ranch Dressing (see recipe in this chapter)

1 pint grape tomatoes, halved

1 medium hothouse cucumber, cut in half lengthwise and sliced

3 medium green onions, thinly sliced (including most of the green tops)

1 To make croutons, preheat oven to 375°F. Place bread cubes on ungreased baking sheet and bake for about 5 minutes. Check to see if they're golden brown. If not, bake 5 minutes more. They will crisp up more as they cool. Set aside.

2 While croutons are baking, heat a nonstick skillet over medium-low heat. Add tempeh bacon and cook on each side for 2 minutes, until slightly brown. Remove from heat and set aside.

3 Once croutons and tempeh bacon are ready, assemble salad by placing 1 wedge on each plate. Pour 2 tablespoons dressing over wedge, and then sprinkle one-fourth tomatoes, cucumber, green onions, tempeh bacon, and croutons over lettuce so that some stick to the dressing. Repeat with remaining wedges.

4 Serve remaining dressing on the side. Store dressing and extra croutons in separate airtight containers in refrigerator for up to 5 days.

SERVES 6	
Per Serving:	
Calories	280
Fat	11g
Sodium	357mg
Carbohydrates	35g
Fiber	5g
Sugar	8g
Protein	10g

KEEP LETTUCE FRESH LONGER

To make eating green salads a little easier throughout the week, prep for the whole week's worth on one day. First, wash and dry the greens and vegetables you'll be using. Then store them in the crisper drawer in separate containers or plastic bags with a few paper towels to help absorb any extra moisture. Then when you're ready for a salad, add any toppers (like beans or grains), your salad dressing, and it's ready to go.

Caesar Salad with Homemade Croutons

Crunchy lettuce, pumpkin seeds, and savory croutons make this salad a winner. If you prep the salad greens and dressing early in the week (storing separately), you can quickly throw this together for a healthy lunch. Or whip up a delicious Caesar Salad Wrap with Chickpeas (see recipe in Chapter 6) the next day!

SERVES 6

Per Serving:

Calories	125
Fat	4g
Sodium	400mg
Carbohydrates	18g
Fiber	4g
Sugar	3g
Protein	3g

CHOOSING THE HEALTHIEST BREADS

When it comes to choosing bread, steer clear of white bread, bread that is made with oil and sugar, and bread high in sodium. Instead, choose bread that is 100 percent whole grain. Ezekiel 4:9 and Alvarado St. Bakery brands are good choices, and Trader Joe's has some good options too. If you have trouble finding exactly what you want, don't worry; make the best choice that's available.

Salad

3 slices whole-grain sourdough bread, cut into 3/4" cubes

1/4 teaspoon salt

1 medium head romaine lettuce, torn into pieces

3 tablespoons unsalted shelled pumpkin seeds

Dressing

1/4 cup store-bought hummus or Beet Hummus (see recipe in Chapter 3)

1/4 cup lemon juice

1 1/2 teaspoons vegan Worcestershire sauce

2 large cloves garlic, peeled and minced

2 teaspoons Dijon mustard

2 teaspoons maple syrup

1/4 teaspoon salt

1/8 teaspoon freshly ground black pepper

1 To make the croutons, preheat oven to 375°F. Place bread cubes on an ungreased baking sheet and sprinkle with salt.

2 Bake for about 5 minutes. Check to see if they're golden brown. If not, bake 5 minutes more. They will crisp up more as they cool. Cool completely before using.

3 In a large salad bowl, add lettuce. Sprinkle on the pumpkin seeds and cooled croutons.

4 In a small bowl, whisk dressing ingredients to combine. Pour over salad. Toss to coat.

5 Refrigerate leftover dressing in an airtight container for 3–4 days.

Creamy Strawberry-Cashew Dressing

This sweet and tart dressing is perfect for a fresh green salad, but it also can be used as a dipping sauce for fruit. Or try drizzling it over grilled pineapple or peaches for a sweet treat.

1 cup hulled fresh or frozen strawberries, defrosted

½ cup unsalted raw cashews, soaked and drained (see Chapter 1 for soaking instructions)

2 tablespoons apple cider vinegar

1 medium pitted Medjool date

¼ cup plus 2 tablespoons water

MAKES 1 CUP	
Per Serving (2 tablespoons):	
Calories	61
Fat	4g
Sodium	1mg
Carbohydrates	6g
Fiber	1g
Sugar	4g
Protein	2g

1 In a blender, add all ingredients. Blend until creamy, adding 1–2 tablespoons of water to thin to desired consistency.

2 Refrigerate in an airtight container for up to 3 days.

Ranch Dressing

If you'd rather avoid the extra fat in the cashews, omit them and instead use ¾ cup unsweetened almond milk plus 1 tablespoon chia seeds for the base. These will thicken the dressing after several minutes.

1 cup unsalted raw cashews, soaked (see Chapter 1 for soaking instructions)

3 tablespoons apple cider vinegar

½ cup water

½ teaspoon garlic powder

½ teaspoon onion powder

¼ teaspoon salt

1 tablespoon minced fresh basil

1 tablespoon minced fresh dill

⅛ teaspoon crushed red pepper flakes

MAKES 1 CUP	
Per Serving (2 tablespoons):	
Calories	92
Fat	7g
Sodium	76mg
Carbohydrates	5g
Fiber	1g
Sugar	1g
Protein	3g

1 In a blender, add cashews, vinegar, water, garlic powder, onion powder, and salt. Blend until smooth and creamy.

2 Transfer to an airtight container and add the basil, dill, and red pepper flakes. Refrigerate for up to 5 days.

Panzanella Salad

This is a wonderfully simple salad made with chopped fresh vegetables and a tangy dressing. The homemade oil-free croutons are easy to make in the oven. They are crispy and crunchy and perfect for this salad.

SERVES 4

Per Serving:

Calories	169
Fat	2g
Sodium	359mg
Carbohydrates	32g
Fiber	5g
Sugar	12g
Protein	6g

Salad

4 cups cubed whole-grain bread

2 large tomatoes, cored and diced into 1" cubes (or 1 pint cherry tomatoes)

1 large cucumber, seeded and sliced into ½"-thick coins

1 large red bell pepper, seeded and diced into 1" cubes

1 large yellow bell pepper, seeded and diced into 1" cubes

1 medium red onion, peeled and thinly sliced

20 large fresh basil leaves, coarsely chopped

Vinaigrette

1 medium clove garlic, peeled and finely minced

1 teaspoon Dijon mustard

¼ cup red wine vinegar

2 teaspoons maple syrup

¼ teaspoon salt

⅛ teaspoon freshly ground black pepper

WHY ARE WHOLE GRAINS BEST?

Unlike refined grains, whole grains include all three parts of the kernel, which are the bran, germ, and endosperm. Each part of the grain offers special nutrients and health benefits such as fiber, antioxidants, vitamins, protein, and carbohydrates. The endosperm is what is used in refined products, and it happens to be the least nutritious. So, just by switching to whole grains, you add beneficial nutrients to your diet.

1. Preheat oven to 400°F. Spread bread cubes on an ungreased baking sheet and bake until crispy, about 10 minutes (depending on how hardy your bread is). Keep an eye on them so they don't burn. Remove from oven and allow to cool completely.
2. In a small bowl, whisk vinaigrette ingredients to combine. Set aside.
3. In a large bowl, mix tomatoes, cucumber, red pepper, yellow pepper, onion, and basil.
4. Add bread cubes to vegetable bowl and toss with vinaigrette.
5. If making ahead of time, store croutons, vegetables, and dressing separately. Croutons will keep at room temperature in an airtight container for up to 1 week. Prep vegetables and refrigerate in a sealed container until ready to use, up to 5 days. The vinaigrette will keep refrigerated in a sealed container for up to 2 weeks.

Farro Salad

SERVES 6

Per Serving:

Calories	220
Fat	4g
Sodium	333mg
Carbohydrates	37g
Fiber	8g
Sugar	2g
Protein	10g

FARRO IS A SUPERGRAIN

Farro has a higher nutritional punch than its cousin rice. It's high in complex carbs, which help regulate blood sugar and reduce cholesterol, and it's loaded with protein, vitamins, minerals, and fiber. While it is not the most common grain, you can easily find it at most health food stores.

The addition of beans in this Farro Salad boosts your daily intake of fiber, protein, immune-boosting antioxidants, and minerals. Feel free to mix up the additions, as other chopped vegetables can work quite well too.

Salad

3 leaves Swiss chard, chopped

¼ cup water

1 cup farro, cooked according to package directions

½ cup chopped red onion

1 medium red bell pepper, seeded and chopped

½ medium cucumber, peeled and chopped

½ (14.5-ounce) can low-sodium kidney beans, drained and rinsed

¼ cup chopped or slivered almonds

Dressing

3 tablespoons red wine vinegar

1 tablespoon fresh lemon juice

¼ teaspoon curry powder

½ teaspoon salt

¼ teaspoon freshly ground black pepper

1 Heat a large nonstick skillet over medium-high heat. Add chard and ¼ cup water, and sauté until wilted, about 2–3 minutes.

2 In a large salad bowl, whisk dressing ingredients to combine.

3 Add cooked farro, onion, chard, bell pepper, cucumber, kidney beans, and almonds to the dressing bowl. Mix well and let sit for a few minutes before serving to allow salad to absorb the dressing.

4 Refrigerate leftovers in an airtight container for up to 5 days.

Mason Jar Greek Salad with Roasted Peppers

If you take time to make these Mason jar salads, you'll be set for the workweek. As long as the dressing doesn't touch the lettuce they'll stay as crispy as when you made them. The Tofu Feta and chickpeas add protein that'll keep you full throughout the day.

Dressing

½ cup Tzatziki (see recipe in Chapter 9)

2 tablespoons red wine vinegar

Salad

2 cups halved grape tomatoes

4 mini cucumbers, sliced

½ cup drained bottled roasted red peppers packed in water

1 cup low-sodium Greek olives, rinsed

½ cup sliced red onion

1 cup canned low-sodium chickpeas, drained and rinsed

½ recipe Tofu Feta (see recipe in Chapter 9)

4 cups chopped romaine lettuce

1 In a small bowl, mix Tzatziki and vinegar. Place 2–3 tablespoons dressing each in the bottom of four wide-mouth, quart-sized Mason jars. Layer tomatoes, cucumbers, peppers, olives, onions, chickpeas, and Tofu Feta evenly among the four jars. Put lettuce on top and close jars. Refrigerate for up to 4 days.

2 When ready to serve, pour into a large bowl and toss to incorporate dressing.

SERVES 4	
Per Serving:	
Calories	183
Fat	8g
Sodium	674mg
Carbohydrates	21g
Fiber	4g
Sugar	8g
Protein	8g

Riced Cauliflower Salad

SERVES 6

Per Serving:

Calories	156
Fat	4g
Sodium	132mg
Carbohydrates	25g
Fiber	5g
Sugar	8g
Protein	8g

RICED CAULIFLOWER, A VERSATILE INGREDIENT

Riced cauliflower is low in calories and can be microwaved, roasted, or pan-fried in minutes. It can even be made into a pizza crust. People who eat cauliflower and other cruciferous vegetables have a lower risk of developing cancer, so it's worth it to give cauliflower rice a try.

Riced cauliflower is a great plant-based substitute for grain in a salad. The addition of beans keeps this salad gluten-free and low-carb as well. Use whatever fresh vegetables you have in the refrigerator and vary the fresh herbs as well to make it your own.

Salad

½ medium head cauliflower, cored and roughly broken up

1 (15-ounce) can low-sodium kidney beans, drained and rinsed

1 cup thawed frozen or drained low-sodium canned corn

1 pint grape or cherry tomatoes, halved

1 medium zucchini, trimmed and chopped

¼ cup chopped red onion

4 tablespoons chopped fresh basil

4 tablespoons chopped fresh parsley

¼ cup unsalted shelled sunflower seeds

Lemon Vinaigrette

¼ cup fresh lemon juice

2 medium cloves garlic, peeled and minced

1 teaspoon yellow mustard

2 tablespoons maple syrup

1 In a food processor, add cauliflower and pulse several times until it resembles rice. Alternately, chop it very fine by hand.

2 In a large salad bowl, add riced cauliflower and remaining salad ingredients.

3 In a small bowl, whisk dressing ingredients to combine. Pour over salad and toss to combine flavors.

4 Refrigerate in an airtight container for up to 5 days.

Roasted Mushroom and Cauliflower Salad

Roasting cauliflower and mushrooms brings out their sweetness. This salad is beautiful as a side dish or great tossed with lettuce with a slightly sweet and tangy dressing. Make an extra batch of the dressing and use in the Creamy Mushroom-Cauliflower Soup (see recipe in Chapter 5).

Dressing

½ cup balsamic vinegar

2 teaspoons yellow mustard

1 medium clove garlic, peeled and minced

1 teaspoon maple syrup

¼ teaspoon salt

¼ teaspoon freshly ground black pepper

Salad

1 medium head cauliflower, broken into bite-sized pieces

1 pound cremini mushrooms, halved

6 cups roughly chopped romaine lettuce

1 Preheat oven to 400°F. Line a baking sheet with parchment paper.

2 In a small bowl, whisk dressing ingredients to combine.

3 In a large bowl, add mushrooms, cauliflower, and half of the whisked dressing. Arrange cauliflower and mushrooms on prepared baking sheet and roast until they start to caramelize, about 25 minutes, flipping halfway through baking time.

4 On a large serving platter, arrange lettuce and top with remaining dressing. Serve mushrooms and cauliflower on top.

5 Refrigerate any leftover cauliflower and mushrooms in a covered container for 3–4 days.

SERVES 4	
Per Serving:	
Calories	113
Fat	1g
Sodium	268mg
Carbohydrates	21g
Fiber	5g
Sugar	13g
Protein	8g

Three-Bean Salad

A favorite for picnics and potlucks, this colorful salad has no added oil and very little sugar. It's also delicious served on top of a green salad or as a protein-rich side dish. For less sodium, use no-salt beans.

Salad

1 (15-ounce) can low-sodium kidney beans, drained and rinsed

1 (15-ounce) can low-sodium green beans, drained and rinsed

1 (15-ounce) can low-sodium chickpeas, drained and rinsed

1 (15-ounce) can low-sodium corn, drained

1 medium bell pepper, any color, seeded and chopped

1 cup sliced red onion

2 medium stalks celery, trimmed and finely chopped

1 cup chopped fresh parsley

Dressing

½ cup red wine vinegar

1 tablespoon maple syrup

2 medium cloves garlic, peeled and crushed

¼ teaspoon salt

¼ teaspoon freshly ground black pepper

1 In a large salad bowl, combine all salad ingredients.

2 In a small bowl, whisk dressing ingredients to combine, then pour over salad and toss.

3 Let marinate for a few hours or overnight in the refrigerator before serving.

4 Refrigerate leftovers in an airtight container for 4–5 days.

Toasted Brown Rice Waldorf Salad

SERVES 8

Per Serving:

Calories	212
Fat	4g
Sodium	324mg
Carbohydrates	42g
Fiber	5g
Sugar	18g
Protein	4g

USE FILTERED WATER IF POSSIBLE

Filtered water will remove some of the contaminants or impurities in water, such as chlorine, that may affect the flavor or quality of food. Filtering is especially important if your water has a strong flavor or when water is a part of a recipe.

Eating whole grains has been associated with a reduction of some lifestyle diseases, so ditch the white rice and switch to brown. Making a large pot of brown rice and using it for several recipes is a great way to save time in the kitchen and give a boost to your health.

1 cup uncooked brown rice

3 cups water

½ teaspoon salt

2 cups chopped and stemmed baby kale

1 medium unpeeled Honeycrisp apple, cored and chopped

1 cup chopped celery

½ cup toasted slivered almonds

1 cup chopped medium Medjool dates

½ cup Chia Seed Dressing (see recipe in this chapter)

¼ teaspoon freshly ground black pepper

1 Heat a large skillet over medium-high heat. Rinse rice under running water, then add to the pan. Toast until golden brown, about 5 minutes. Add water and salt to toasted rice and bring to a boil. Lower heat, cover, and simmer for 35 minutes, or until rice is tender. Strain off extra water and set rice aside.

2 Add kale, apple, celery, almonds, and dates to a large bowl. Add cooked rice and top with ½ cup Chia Seed Dressing. Gently toss and add more dressing if desired.

3 For meal prep, divide rice (without kale) among separate airtight containers and refrigerate for up to 3–5 days. When ready to serve, toss rice with kale, other additions, and a drizzle of dressing.

CHAPTER 5
Soups and Stews

Avgolemono Soup

SERVES 4

Per Serving:

Calories	205
Fat	3g
Sodium	528mg
Carbohydrates	36g
Fiber	9g
Sugar	8g
Protein	9g

This soup is a plant-based spin on a traditional Greek recipe that's made with shredded chicken, chicken broth, and eggs as a thickener. It has a burst of citrus flavor in a thick, creamy base. Add chickpeas or Baked Tofu (see recipe in Chapter 7) to boost the amount of protein in it.

2 cups chopped yellow onions

2 medium cloves garlic, peeled and minced

1 cup finely chopped carrot

¼ cup water

4 cups One-Pot Vegetable Broth (see recipe in this chapter)

½ cup fresh lemon juice

2 tablespoons nutritional yeast

½ teaspoon salt

2 cups unsweetened soy milk, divided

3 tablespoons cornstarch

1 cup brown rice, cooked according to package directions

1 (5-ounce) package baby spinach

¼ cup chopped fresh parsley

2 medium sprigs fresh dill, chopped

1 Heat a large soup pot over medium heat. Add onions, garlic, carrot, and water. Sauté until onions are translucent, about 5–7 minutes.

2 Add broth, lemon juice, and yeast, and salt and stir to combine. Continue to cook until carrot is tender, about 3–4 minutes.

3 In the meantime, in a small bowl, combine ½ cup soy milk and cornstarch. Stir with a fork to mix well.

4 Add remaining 1½ cups soy milk to soup pot along with cornstarch mixture; stir to combine. Boil until soup becomes thickened and creamy, about 5 minutes. Add rice and stir for 2 minutes to heat through.

5 Add spinach to pot and stir until wilted, about 2 minutes. Add parsley and dill.

6 Refrigerate leftovers in an airtight container for up to 5 days, or freeze (after cooling) in a freezer-safe container for up to 3 months. Thaw overnight in the refrigerator and reheat on the stovetop or in the microwave.

Cold Cucumber Soup

This easy soup is refreshing on a hot day. It's as good for your skin as it is for your diet: cucumber and avocado are both beautifying foods that hydrate and moisturize your skin and replenish your body with pure mineral hydration.

2 medium English cucumbers, peeled, seeded, and cut into 3" pieces

¼ medium red onion, peeled and roughly chopped

1 medium clove garlic, peeled and minced

8 large mint leaves

1 teaspoon maple syrup

2 tablespoons fresh lemon juice

¾ cup unsweetened plain plant yogurt

½ cup water

¼ teaspoon salt

1 medium avocado, peeled, seeded, and chopped

SERVES 6	
Per Serving:	
Calories	95
Fat	6g
Sodium	106mg
Carbohydrates	11g
Fiber	3g
Sugar	4g
Protein	2g

1 In a food processor, combine all ingredients except avocado. Pulse a few times, until ingredients are coarsely chopped, then process until smooth. Thin with more water if needed.

2 Transfer to a large bowl and refrigerate until chilled, about 2 hours. Ladle soup into soup bowls and top with chopped avocado.

3 For meal prep, divide into equal portions and transfer each portion to an airtight container (without avocado topping). Refrigerate until ready to serve, up to 5 days, or freeze in a freezer-safe container for up to 3 months.

"Cheesy" Broccoli Soup with Kale

DO YOU NEED TO WASH ORGANIC VEGETABLES?

While organic produce is free of unwanted pesticides, it's still a good idea to wash it when you're ready to use it (not before storing). Rinse thoroughly under running water to remove about 98 percent of bacteria. Or use 3 parts water to 1 part vinegar as a wash.

When you're looking for comfort, this quick one-pot broccoli soup really hits the spot.

1 cup chopped yellow onion

2 medium cloves garlic, peeled and minced

1 cup chopped carrots

1 cup chopped celery

¼ cup water

5 cups broccoli florets

1 medium potato, peeled and chopped into ¾" pieces

5 cups chopped, stemmed kale

8 cups One-Pot Vegetable Broth (see recipe in this chapter)

2 cups unsweetened almond milk

⅓ cup nutritional yeast

2 tablespoons fresh lemon juice

½ teaspoon salt

¼ teaspoon freshly ground black pepper

Croutons

4 slices whole-wheat sourdough bread, cut into ½" cubes

1. Heat a large pot over medium-high heat. Add onion, garlic, carrots, celery, and water. Sauté until onion is soft, about 5–7 minutes.
2. Add broccoli, potato, kale, broth, and almond milk. Stir to combine. Add yeast, lemon juice, salt, and pepper. Reduce heat to medium low, cover, and simmer for 10–15 minutes, until vegetables are tender.
3. Preheat oven to 375°F. Place bread cubes on an ungreased baking sheet and bake for about 5 minutes, until golden brown.
4. Cool the soup for about 5 minutes. Add about half to a blender and blend until smooth, about 30 seconds. Top each serving with a few croutons.
5. Refrigerate soup in an airtight container for 3–4 days, or freeze (after cooling) in a freezer-safe container for up to 3 months. Thaw overnight in the refrigerator and reheat on the stovetop or in the microwave.

Asian Vegetable-Noodle Soup

This easy, low-calorie Asian Vegetable-Noodle Soup is perfect for a quick meal. It's full of healthy vegetables, protein-packed tofu, and noodles, all in a savory broth with a hint of spice. If you have trouble finding soba noodles, you can substitute rice noodles.

¼ cup water

1 cup thinly sliced carrots

2 large cloves garlic, peeled and minced

1 teaspoon minced fresh ginger

8 cups One-Pot Vegetable Broth (see recipe in this chapter)

2 cups thinly sliced button mushrooms

4 cups broccoli florets

1 cup snow peas, cut into thirds

3 small heads baby bok choy, cored and sliced

1 (8-ounce) package soba noodles, cooked according to package directions and rinsed

2 tablespoons low-sodium soy sauce

1½ teaspoons chili garlic paste

3 tablespoons rice vinegar

6 medium green onions, sliced (including most of the green tops)

4 tablespoons chopped fresh cilantro, divided

½ teaspoon salt

¼ teaspoon freshly ground black pepper

SERVES 4	
Per Serving:	
Calories	341
Fat	1g
Sodium	1,242mg
Carbohydrates	65g
Fiber	10g
Sugar	7g
Protein	26g

1 Heat a large soup pot over medium heat. Add water and carrots, and stir-fry until carrots are crisp-tender, about 5–7 minutes.

2 Add garlic, ginger, and broth, and bring soup to a boil.

3 Stir mushrooms, broccoli, snow peas, and bok choy into the soup. Cook for another 3–4 minutes, until vegetables are tender.

4 Once vegetables are cooked, add noodles, soy sauce, chili garlic paste, vinegar, green onions, 1 tablespoon cilantro, salt, and pepper. Stir to combine.

5 Serve topped with a sprinkling of chopped cilantro.

6 Refrigerate in an airtight container for 3–4 days, or freeze (after cooling) in a freezer-safe container for up to 3 months. Thaw overnight in the refrigerator and reheat on the stovetop or in the microwave.

Butternut Squash and Apple Soup

This hearty soup is a great choice for holiday menus because it features classic autumn and winter flavors. If you'd like to use store-prepared cubed squash, buy 24 ounces. Bake on a rimmed baking sheet lined with parchment for 20–25 minutes, until tender.

1½ pounds butternut squash, seeded (reserve seeds) and cut in half lengthwise

1 medium yellow onion, peeled and chopped

½ cup chopped celery

¼ cup water

2 medium Honeycrisp apples, peeled, cored, and chopped

8 cups One-Pot Vegetable Broth (see recipe in this chapter)

1½ teaspoons ground cumin

½ teaspoon chopped fresh thyme

½ teaspoon ground ginger

½ teaspoon coriander

¼ teaspoon cinnamon

¼ teaspoon cayenne pepper

½ teaspoon salt

¼ teaspoon freshly ground black pepper

1 Preheat oven to 400°F. Line a large rimmed baking sheet with parchment paper.

2 Lay squash halves cut side down on one end of prepared rimmed baking sheet. Spread seeds on the other end of the baking sheet.

3 Bake squash seeds about 15 minutes. Remove and cool.

4 Continue to bake squash for 30 more minutes, until tender. Cool and scoop out flesh; discard skins. Chop squash into 2" pieces.

5 When squash is nearly done, heat a large soup pot over medium heat. Add onion, celery, and water, and sauté until soft, about 5–7 minutes. Add apples, squash, broth, and remaining ingredients.

6 Turn the heat to low and simmer for about 30 minutes, until apples are soft. Add more water if soup is too thick.

7 Cool slightly before using an immersion blender to blend soup to a creamy smoothness. Or, working in batches, put soup in a blender and carefully blend on slow speed. Then blend at high speed until smooth. Serve in bowls topped with additional thyme or roasted squash seeds.

8 Refrigerate leftover soup in an airtight container for up to 7 days, or freeze in a freezer-safe container for up to 3 months.

SERVES 6

Per Serving:

Calories	123
Fat	1g
Sodium	481mg
Carbohydrates	25g
Fiber	6g
Sugar	10g
Protein	7g

HEALTH BENEFITS OF BUTTERNUT SQUASH

Butternut squash is loaded with vitamins A, C, E, and B$_6$, not to mention zinc, protein, folate, and many other essential nutrients. A cup of cubed squash offers more potassium than a banana! Save the fiber-rich seeds and toast in the oven for a lovely nutty flavor, perfect atop a creamy soup.

Creamy Curried Cauliflower Soup

SERVES 5

Per Serving:

Calories	245
Fat	5g
Sodium	596mg
Carbohydrates	42g
Fiber	11g
Sugar	10g
Protein	12g

COCONUT MILK AND ITS ALTERNATIVE

Canned coconut milk is a tasty, creamy addition to soups and Indian and Thai dishes; however, it is high in fat and unfortunately has some saturated fat. If you'd prefer, substitute 1 teaspoon coconut extract with 1 cup of unsweetened plant milk for coconut milk in most recipes.

A bowl of this warm and comforting soup is great on a cool winter day and provides a burst of plant-based nutrition from cauliflower, yams, red peppers, and chickpeas. It can easily be made in a slow cooker as well as on the stove—just add all ingredients at once to the cooker and set it on high for 4 hours or on low for 8 hours.

½ pound russet potatoes, peeled and cut into 1½" pieces

½ pound yams, peeled and cut into 1½" pieces

1 large head cauliflower, cored and cut into 1½" pieces

1½ cups sliced carrots

¾ cup coarsely chopped red bell pepper

½ cup chopped yellow onion

1 (15-ounce) can low-sodium chickpeas, drained and rinsed

3 teaspoons curry powder

2 teaspoons grated fresh ginger

⅛ teaspoon crushed red pepper flakes

½ teaspoon salt

4 cups One-Pot Vegetable Broth (see recipe in this chapter)

1 (14-ounce) can light coconut milk

1 In a large pot over medium heat, combine potatoes, yams, cauliflower, carrots, bell pepper, onion, and chickpeas.

2 Sprinkle curry powder, ginger, red pepper flakes, and salt into pot. Add broth and stir to combine.

3 Bring soup to a boil, cover, and reduce heat to low. Simmer for about 45 minutes, until vegetables are tender.

4 Stir in coconut milk and cook until heated through, about 5 minutes.

5 Cool completely and refrigerate in a covered container for up to 3–4 days, or freeze in a freezer-safe container for up to 3 months. Thaw overnight in the refrigerator and reheat on the stovetop or in the microwave.

Gazpacho

Gazpacho is easy to make in the blender. It's refreshingly sweet and tart on a hot day, and it's full of nutrition! You can add protein with black beans, chickpeas, or even chia seeds, which will also act as a thickener.

3 cups low-sodium tomato juice

1 medium cucumber, peeled and roughly chopped

½ medium red onion, peeled and roughly chopped

1 green or red bell pepper, seeded and roughly chopped

¼ teaspoon Tabasco or other hot sauce

¼ teaspoon salt

¼ teaspoon freshly ground black pepper

1 In a blender, combine all ingredients. Start blending on low speed and quickly turn up to high. Blend for 30–45 seconds, leaving some of the soup a little chunky. Refrigerate to chill before serving.

2 Refrigerate in an airtight container until ready to serve, up to 3 days. Freeze in a freezer-safe container for up to 6 months.

SERVES 4	
Per Serving:	
Calories	64
Fat	0g
Sodium	256mg
Carbohydrates	13g
Fiber	3g
Sugar	8g
Protein	2g

Curried Red Lentil Soup

SERVES 6

Per Serving:

Calories	213
Fat	5g
Sodium	457mg
Carbohydrates	31g
Fiber	7g
Sugar	6g
Protein	15g

COCONUT MILK VERSUS COCONUT WATER

Coconut milk in a can contains coconut cream, and that's what's used in most soup recipes. You can find regular or low-calorie versions. If it's in a carton, it is used as dairy milk, such as in cereal or coffee. There's also coconut water, which comes straight from the middle of a coconut and is much thinner than coconut milk. It's a good source of nutrients without being high in calories and is used for hydration.

This easy-to-make one-pot lentil soup variation is delightfully yummy as a weeknight meal. The addition of Swiss chard and mushrooms increases the nutritional value, and the lentils provide some protein to keep you full.

¼ cup water

½ large yellow onion, peeled and chopped

1 large carrot, peeled and diced

1 large stalk celery, trimmed and diced

2 medium cloves garlic, peeled and minced

2 teaspoons curry powder

1 teaspoon garam masala

1 (1") piece fresh ginger, peeled and grated

1 cup dry red lentils, rinsed and debris removed

4 cups One-Pot Vegetable Broth (see recipe in this chapter)

1 (14.5-ounce) can low-sodium diced tomatoes

1 (12-ounce) bunch Swiss chard, stems removed and thinly sliced

8 ounces cremini mushrooms, sliced

1 (13.5-ounce) can light coconut milk

½ teaspoon salt

¼ teaspoon freshly ground black pepper

½ cup chopped fresh cilantro

1 medium lime, cut into wedges

1 Heat a large soup pot over medium heat. Add water, onion, carrot, and celery, and sauté until onion is soft, about 5–7 minutes.

2 Add garlic, curry powder, garam masala, and ginger. Sauté for another minute, until garlic becomes fragrant.

3 Stir in lentils, broth, tomatoes, Swiss chard, and mushrooms.

4 Bring soup to a boil, then reduce heat to low. Continue simmering, uncovered, until lentils are soft, about 25–30 minutes.

5 Add coconut milk, salt, and pepper. Stir to combine and heat through, about 5–7 minutes.

6 Serve with a sprinkling of cilantro and a wedge of lime.

7 Refrigerate in an airtight container for 3–4 days. To freeze, cool completely and store in freezer-safe containers for up to 3 months. Thaw in refrigerator before reheating.

Roasted Tomato Bisque

This soup freezes well, so make a double batch! Just pour it into individual freezer-safe containers. Pull a container from the freezer the night before and your soup will be ready for a quick, no-thought packable work lunch on the go.

5 large tomatoes, cored and quartered

2 large yellow onions, peeled and quartered

1 medium red bell pepper, seeded and quartered

¼ teaspoon salt

¼ teaspoon freshly ground black pepper

½ teaspoon sweet paprika

4 medium cloves garlic, peeled

2½ cups One-Pot Vegetable Broth (see recipe in this chapter)

½ cup unsweetened almond milk

1 Preheat oven to 400°F. Line a large rimmed baking sheet with parchment paper.
2 Spread tomatoes, onions, and bell pepper on prepared baking sheet. Sprinkle with salt, black pepper, and paprika.
3 Bake for about 5 minutes, and then add garlic to baking sheet. Continue to roast vegetables until they soften and start to caramelize, about 15 minutes, stirring about halfway through baking time.
4 In a large soup pot over medium heat, add roasted vegetables and broth. Use an immersion blender to process until smooth and then heat through, about 10 minutes. If you'd like to use a regular blender, add roasted vegetables to it after they've cooled slightly; add enough broth to blend. Then transfer to pot with remaining broth and heat through.
5 Add almond milk and stir to combine. Taste and add up to ½ cup more milk, if needed. Season with more salt and pepper if needed.
6 Refrigerate soup in a covered container for up to 5 days, or freeze (after cooling) in a freezer-safe container for up to 3 months.

SERVES 4

Per Serving:

Calories	107
Fat	1g
Sodium	362mg
Carbohydrates	20g
Fiber	5g
Sugar	11g
Protein	6g

STORING AND REHEATING LEFTOVERS

Remember to put cooked food directly from your pan into airtight containers and store in the refrigerator. If you want to freeze them, cool in the refrigerator before transferring to freezer-safe containers in the freezer. When reheating food, the temperature should reach 165 degrees, and soups, sauces, and gravies should be brought back up to a boil before eating.

Slow Cooker Italian Soup with Spinach

This soup is an easy way to get more vegetables into your day. It's very easy to throw together, and you can start it in the morning so it's ready for dinnertime. Plus, you can add in crumbled seitan sausage links for a nice protein boost. Top with a dollop of homemade soy yogurt for creaminess and tang. Enjoy with crusty whole-grain bread.

SERVES 6

Per Serving:

Calories	231
Fat	2g
Sodium	532mg
Carbohydrates	44g
Fiber	6g
Sugar	7g
Protein	12g

HOMEMADE SOY YOGURT

To make your own soy yogurt, heat 2 cups soy milk over medium-low heat. Once it steams, whisk in ½ cup cold soy milk mixed with 3 tablespoons cornstarch until it reaches 148°F and starts to thicken. Remove from heat, whisk in another 1½ cups soy milk, and cool to 110°F. Then, whisk in 1 package yogurt starter (a blend of bacteria to start fermentation) and pour into containers to ferment in either a warm spot in the kitchen or in a yogurt maker for about 11 hours.

1 small yellow onion, peeled and diced

2 medium cloves garlic, peeled and minced

3 cups One-Pot Vegetable Broth (see recipe in this chapter)

1 (14.5-ounce) can low-sodium Italian-style diced tomatoes, undrained

1 (14.5-ounce) can low-sodium fire-roasted diced tomatoes, undrained

1 (15-ounce) can low-sodium pinto beans, drained and rinsed

2 large carrots, peeled and sliced

2 medium stalks celery, trimmed and sliced

2 small red potatoes, peeled and diced into ½" cubes

1 large green bell pepper, seeded and chopped

1 teaspoon Italian seasoning

2 teaspoons dried oregano

½ tablespoon dried basil

¾ cup uncooked whole-wheat orzo pasta

3 cups packed fresh spinach

½ teaspoon salt

¼ teaspoon freshly ground black pepper

1 In a large slow cooker, add onion, garlic, broth, both cans tomatoes, beans, carrots, celery, potatoes, and bell pepper.

2 Add Italian seasoning, oregano, and basil. Stir to combine. Set slow cooker on low heat for 8 hours or on high for 4 hours.

3 Add orzo pasta and spinach in the last 30 minutes of cooking, and continue cooking until orzo is tender. Add salt and black pepper. Taste and adjust seasonings to your preference.

4 Refrigerate in a covered container for up to 5 days, or freeze (after cooling) in a freezer-safe container up to 3 months. Thaw overnight in the refrigerator and reheat on the stovetop or in the microwave.

Spring Asparagus, Pea, and Zucchini Soup

This beautiful soup fuses the fresh flavors of springtime vegetables with tasty herbs and is then blended into a smooth, light, and delicious soup. It's great served cold or warm and is easy enough to make on a weeknight, but also impressive enough to serve to company. Top the soup with a dollop of delicious Oil-Free Basil Pesto.

1 medium yellow onion, peeled and chopped

2 medium cloves garlic, peeled and chopped

¼ cup water

3 cups (1" pieces) chopped asparagus

3 (6") zucchini, trimmed and sliced

1 cup frozen peas

5 cups One-Pot Vegetable Broth (see recipe in this chapter)

1 (13.5-ounce) can light coconut milk

2 tablespoons fresh lemon juice

1 teaspoon salt

¼ teaspoon freshly ground black pepper

½ recipe Oil-Free Basil Pesto (see recipe in Chapter 9)

1 Heat a large soup pot over medium heat. Add onion, garlic, and water, and sauté until fragrant, about 1 minute.

2 Add asparagus to pot along with zucchini, peas, broth, and coconut milk. Cover and reduce heat to low. Simmer for about 25 minutes, or until asparagus is tender.

3 Add lemon juice, salt, and pepper. Cool slightly, then, working in batches, blend in a high-speed blender until smooth and creamy.

4 Transfer back to soup pot until ready to serve. Ladle soup into bowls and garnish with a dollop of Oil-Free Basil Pesto.

5 Pesto can be refrigerated covered in a glass jar up to 1 week.

6 Refrigerate soup in a covered container for up to 5 days, or freeze (after cooling) in a freezer-safe container for up to 3 months. Thaw overnight in the refrigerator and reheat on the stovetop or in the microwave.

SERVES 6

Per Serving:

Calories	139
Fat	6g
Sodium	653mg
Carbohydrates	16g
Fiber	6g
Sugar	7g
Protein	10g

TO LIGHTEN THE DISH

Skip the coconut milk if you don't like the added fat and instead add 1 teaspoon coconut extract plus 1 cup plant milk. You'll be able to enjoy the lovely coconut flavor without the fat, and still get some plant-based goodness from the almond milk.

Hearty Lentil-Kale Soup

SERVES 6

Per Serving:

Calories	177
Fat	1g
Sodium	504mg
Carbohydrates	34g
Fiber	9g
Sugar	7g
Protein	11g

LENTILS ARE A YEAR-ROUND PANTRY STAPLE

Lentils offer a healthy nutritional punch. One cup has 18 grams of protein, 15 grams of fiber, less than 1 gram of fat, plus a high dose of folate, potassium, iron, and B vitamins. Buy them precooked to save time and have dinner ready to serve that much quicker!

If you like to get dinner on the table in a flash, this lentil soup is the perfect option, especially if you use prepared lentils. (You can find them canned or in pouches at most stores.) This soup freezes well too.

1 cup chopped yellow onion

3 medium carrots, peeled and chopped

2 medium stalks celery, trimmed and chopped

3 medium cloves garlic, peeled and minced

2¼ cups water, divided

4 cups One-Pot Vegetable Broth (see recipe in this chapter), divided

½ (6-ounce) can no-salt-added tomato paste

½ teaspoon coriander

½ teaspoon ground cumin

½ teaspoon salt

¼ teaspoon freshly ground black pepper

1 large Yukon gold potato, peeled and chopped

2 cups cooked brown lentils

3 large leaves kale, stemmed and roughly chopped

1 Heat a large pot over medium heat. Add onion, carrot, celery, garlic, and ¼ cup water, sauté until vegetables are soft, about 5–7 minutes.

2 Add ½ cup broth and tomato paste, and stir into the pot.

3 Add remaining 3½ cups broth and remaining 2 cups water. Add coriander, cumin, salt, pepper, potato, and lentils. Stir to combine. Cook on medium heat for 20 minutes.

4 Stir in kale and continue to cook for 15 minutes, until kale and lentils are soft.

5 Refrigerate leftovers in a covered container for 3–4 days. Or divide equal portions into airtight containers and freeze for up to 4 months. Thaw in the refrigerator the night before for a quick and easy lunch.

Beefless Beef Stew

SERVES 6

Per Serving:

Calories	219
Fat	1g
Sodium	354mg
Carbohydrates	46g
Fiber	8g
Sugar	10g
Protein	10g

This hearty stew's rich broth is so satisfying, you'll want to savor every bite. Serve with crusty bread and a salad for a complete meal.

1 large yellow onion, peeled and sliced

3 large stalks celery, trimmed and cut into ¾" chunks

3 large carrots, peeled and cut into ¾" chunks

¾ cup water or more as needed, divided

6 medium cloves garlic, peeled and minced

1 pound cremini mushrooms, left whole or if large cut into ¾" chunks

2 cups One-Pot Vegetable Broth (see recipe in this chapter)

2 pounds russet potatoes, cut into 1" chunks (peel if you prefer)

½ (6-ounce) can no-salt-added tomato paste, mixed with ¼ cup water to thin

1 tablespoon Italian seasoning

1 tablespoon chopped fresh rosemary

½ teaspoon smoked paprika

½ teaspoon salt

½ teaspoon freshly ground black pepper

2 cups thawed frozen peas

1 Heat a large soup pot over medium-high heat. Add onion, celery, carrots, and ¼ cup water. Sauté until onion is soft, about 5–7 minutes. Add garlic and mushrooms, and sauté for 2 minutes more.

2 Add broth, potatoes, thinned tomato paste, Italian seasoning, rosemary, paprika, salt, and pepper. Reduce heat to medium low and cook, covered, until potatoes and carrots are tender, about 20 minutes. Add remaining ½ cup water (or more as needed) if the stew is too thick.

3 In a blender, add about 1½ cups of the broth with a few of the vegetables. Blend until smooth. Return the blended soup to the pot and stir to combine. Add peas and heat through for about 5 minutes.

4 Refrigerate leftovers in an airtight container for 3–4 days, or freeze (after cooling) for up to 3 months. Thaw overnight in the refrigerator and reheat on the stovetop or microwave.

Creamy Garlic Soup with Kale

When you're feeling sick with a cold or the seasonal flu, this creamy garlic soup is sure to give your immune system a boost. Don't worry about it being too strong; garlic mellows when it's cooked.

1 medium yellow onion, peeled and chopped

¼ cup water

1 head garlic, cloves separated, peeled, and chopped

4 cups One-Pot Vegetable Broth (see recipe in this chapter)

1 (10-ounce) bag spinach

4 tablespoons cornstarch

4 cups unsweetened almond milk, divided

½ cup nutritional yeast

Juice of 2 medium lemons

½ teaspoon salt

¼ teaspoon freshly ground black pepper

1 Heat a soup pot over medium heat. Add onion and water, and sauté for about 5–7 minutes. Add garlic, broth, and spinach. Cook until spinach is soft, about 5 minutes.

2 In a cup, mix cornstarch with about ½ cup almond milk; stir with a fork to combine. Add cornstarch mixture to the pot along with remaining 3½ cups almond milk. Stir to combine well. Continue to stir until soup starts to thicken slightly, about 3–5 minutes.

3 Add yeast, lemon juice, salt, and pepper.

4 Refrigerate in an airtight container for up to 5 days, or freeze (after cooling) in a freezer-safe container for up to 3 months. Thaw overnight in the refrigerator and reheat on the stovetop or in the microwave.

SERVES 6

Per Serving:

Calories	115
Fat	3g
Sodium	504mg
Carbohydrates	16g
Fiber	3g
Sugar	2g
Protein	9g

THE BENEFITS OF THE COMPOUND ALLICIN IN GARLIC

Garlic contains the immune-stimulating compound allicin, which promotes the activity of white blood cells, so it's a perfect boost when you have a cold or other upper respiratory illness. When chopped, it takes a few minutes for allicin to be released, so it's best to let the garlic sit for 10–15 minutes before cooking.

Creamy Mushroom-Cauliflower Soup

SERVES 4

Per Serving:

Calories	200
Fat	7g
Sodium	550mg
Carbohydrates	27g
Fiber	6g
Sugar	8g
Protein	10g

Roast double the cauliflower and mushrooms, and use them in the Roasted Mushroom and Cauliflower Salad (see recipe in Chapter 4).

Soup

8 ounces cremini mushrooms

½ medium head cauliflower, cored and broken into florets

⅓ cup brown rice, cooked according to package directions

4 cups One-Pot Vegetable Broth (see recipe in this chapter), divided

1 (13.5-ounce) can light coconut milk

½ teaspoon salt

¼ teaspoon freshly ground black pepper

½ cup chopped fresh parsley

Marinade

¼ cup balsamic vinegar

1 teaspoon yellow mustard

1 medium clove garlic, peeled and minced

1 teaspoon maple syrup

1 Preheat oven to 400°F. Line a baking sheet with parchment paper.

2 In a large bowl, combine mushrooms and cauliflower.

3 In a small bowl, whisk marinade ingredients to combine. Pour over mushrooms and cauliflower, and stir to combine.

4 Spread mushrooms and cauliflower on prepared baking sheet. Roast for about 20 minutes, until they start to caramelize, turning halfway through baking time.

5 Allow mushrooms and cauliflower to cool. Working in batches if necessary, add them to a blender along with cooked brown rice and about 1 cup broth.

6 Blend until everything is smooth, adding more broth to thin if needed. When all vegetables are blended, add to a large soup pot over medium heat.

7 Add remaining 3 cups broth and coconut milk to soup pot. Add salt and pepper and heat through, about 10 minutes.

8 Garnish each serving with parsley.

9 Refrigerate soup in a covered container for up to 5 days, or freeze (after cooling) in a freezer-safe container for up to 3 months. Thaw in refrigerator overnight and reheat on the stovetop or in the microwave.

Creamy Vegetable Noodle Soup

This soup is comforting and creamy with a burst of vegetables. For extra protein, add a can of cannellini beans or No Evil Foods Comrade Cluck, a meatless chicken product made with vital wheat gluten and no added oil.

½ cup unsalted raw cashews, soaked and drained (see Chapter 1 for soaking instructions)

½ cup unsweetened almond milk

8 ounces uncooked fettuccini noodles

¼ cup water

2 medium leeks (white part only), chopped

3 medium cloves garlic, peeled and minced

2 medium carrots, peeled and chopped

2 medium stalks celery, trimmed and chopped

½ medium head broccoli, trimmed and chopped

2 medium Yukon Gold potatoes, peeled and chopped

6 cups One-Pot Vegetable Broth (see recipe in this chapter)

½ teaspoon salt

¼ teaspoon freshly ground black pepper

1½ teaspoon poultry seasoning

¼ cup nutritional yeast

1 cup canned low-sodium chickpeas, drained and rinsed

1 In a blender, combine cashews and ½ cup almond milk. Blend until smooth, adding more milk as needed to make it creamy. Set aside.

2 Cook fettuccini noodles according to package directions. Set aside.

3 Heat a large soup pot on medium-high heat. Add ¼ cup water, leeks, garlic, carrots, and celery, and sauté until they begin to soften, about 10 minutes. Add broccoli, potatoes, broth, salt, pepper, poultry seasoning, and yeast. Cook until vegetables soften, about 10 minutes.

4 Add cashew cream, chickpeas, and noodles and stir to combine and heat through, 2–3 minutes.

5 Refrigerate soup in a covered container for up to 5 days, or freeze (after cooling) in a freezer-safe container for up to 3 months. Thaw in refrigerator overnight and reheat on the stovetop or in the microwave.

SERVES 6

Per Serving:

Calories	282
Fat	7g
Sodium	572mg
Carbohydrates	44g
Fiber	8g
Sugar	6g
Protein	15g

MAKE AND STORE MIREPOIX

For speedier cooking, make and freeze your very own mirepoix—the combination of onion, carrots, and celery that's often used in stock, soups, and stews. It's traditionally sautéed in butter or oil, but for a plant-based version, slowly sauté in vegetable broth and lightly season with salt and pepper. Cool before freezing in an airtight freezer-safe container for 2-3 months.

Instant Pot® Black Bean and Rice Soup

Per Serving:

Calories	312
Fat	2g
Sodium	425mg
Carbohydrates	59g
Fiber	11g
Sugar	2g
Protein	16g

LOWER THE RISK OF ARSENIC IN RICE

Unfortunately, all rice, including organic and brown rice (even more so than white), contains tiny amounts of arsenic. To lower the risk that you'll consume all the arsenic present in the uncooked rice, first rinse rice in a strainer under running water for several seconds. Then add 1½ times the amount of water called for. When the rice is done cooking, strain off the excess water and you're ready to go.

Finding ways to add beans to your diet is easy with so many wonderful recipes. Your gut bacteria love them, and they help you stay healthy, so don't miss an opportunity to eat beans every day. If desired, top each bowl with chopped avocados, chopped red bell pepper, minced fresh cilantro, and unsweetened plain plant yogurt.

3¼ cups water, divided

½ medium yellow onion, peeled and chopped

4 medium cloves garlic, peeled and minced

2 teaspoons ground cumin

2 teaspoons chili powder

1 teaspoon dried oregano

½ teaspoon smoked paprika

¾ teaspoon salt

¼ teaspoon freshly ground black pepper

3 cups One-Pot Vegetable Broth (see recipe in this chapter)

1½ cups dry black beans, rinsed and debris removed

1 cup uncooked brown rice

Juice of 1 medium lime

1 Set Instant Pot® to sauté and add ¼ cup water and onion. Stir occasionally until onion starts to wilt, about 7–8 minutes.

2 Add garlic, cumin, chili powder, oregano, paprika, salt, and pepper. Cook for 15 seconds more. Turn off Instant Pot®.

3 Add broth, remaining 3 cups water, black beans, and rice. Stir to combine. Put lid on Instant Pot® and close steam vent. Set to high pressure using manual mode. Cook for 22 minutes.

4 Pressure release naturally for about 10 minutes, then release pressure all the way. Squeeze lime juice into pot and stir to combine.

5 Serve each bowl with toppings, if desired.

6 Refrigerate leftovers (without toppings) in an airtight container up to 5 days, or freeze (after cooling) in a freezer-safe container for up to 3 months. Reheat on stovetop over medium heat until heated through.

Instant Pot® Pea Soup with Spinach

If you don't have an Instant Pot®, you can also make this soup right on the stove or in a slow cooker. Its warm, cozy goodness is perfect on a chilly night. The addition of spinach adds both nutrition and a deep green color. Serve with crusty bread and a salad for a complete meal.

SERVES 6	
Per Serving:	
Calories	320
Fat	3g
Sodium	514mg
Carbohydrates	52g
Fiber	20g
Sugar	9g
Protein	23g

¼ cup water

1 large yellow onion, peeled and diced

3 medium cloves garlic, peeled and diced

2 medium carrots, peeled and diced

2 medium stalks celery, trimmed and diced

2 cups dry split peas, rinsed and debris removed

8 cups One-Pot Vegetable Broth (see recipe in this chapter)

1 (10-ounce) bag spinach

½ teaspoon salt

¼ teaspoon freshly ground black pepper

1 tablespoon chopped fresh thyme

6 tablespoons Cashew Cream (see recipe in Chapter 9)

½ teaspoon crushed red pepper flakes

3 tablespoons chopped fresh parsley

1 Turn Instant Pot® to sauté. Add water, onion, garlic, carrots, and celery, and sauté for 7–8 minutes. Turn off sauté.

2 Add peas, broth, spinach, salt, pepper, and thyme. Set pressure vent to "sealing" and push "pressure cooking on high" for 15 minutes. Natural release for 10 minutes.

3 Serve chunky or blend with an immersion blender.

4 Top each serving with 1 tablespoon Cashew Cream, a dash of red pepper flakes, and ½ tablespoon parsley.

Curried Chickpea-Vegetable Stew

Top this with mango chutney or chopped unsalted peanuts.

SERVES 6

1 large yellow onion, peeled and diced

4 medium cloves garlic, peeled and minced

2 cups water, divided

1 teaspoon ground cumin

1 teaspoon coriander

1 teaspoon ground ginger

½ teaspoon crushed red pepper flakes

½ teaspoon salt

¼ teaspoon freshly ground black pepper

3 tablespoons no-salt-added tomato paste

1 (28-ounce) can low-sodium crushed tomatoes

2 cups One-Pot Vegetable Broth (see recipe in this chapter)

1 large sweet potato, peeled and cut into ¾" dice

3 medium red potatoes, unpeeled, cut into ¾" dice

½ large head cauliflower, broken into bite-sized pieces

1 medium head broccoli, trimmed and cut into bite-sized pieces

1 (15-ounce) can low-sodium chickpeas, drained and rinsed

1 (10-ounce) bag spinach

2 tablespoons fresh lemon juice

1½ cups uncooked whole-wheat couscous

Per Serving:

Calories	458
Fat	2g
Sodium	479mg
Carbohydrates	91g
Fiber	15g
Sugar	15g
Protein	21g

HOW TO MAKE SOUPS AND STEWS THICK AND CREAMY

An easy way to make a stew or a soup thick and creamy is to take a portion of the broth along with a few vegetables in the dish and blend until you have a sauce. Add this back into the pot and voilà, you have creaminess without added oil or dairy.

1 Heat a large saucepan over medium-high heat. Add onion, garlic, and ¼ cup water and sauté about 8–10 minutes. Stir in cumin, coriander, ginger, red pepper flakes, salt, and black pepper. Add tomato paste. Cook 1 minute, stirring constantly.

2 Stir in crushed tomatoes, broth, and sweet and red potatoes; bring to a boil. Reduce heat to medium low and simmer, covered, about 10 minutes. Add cauliflower, broccoli, chickpeas, and spinach. Simmer until vegetables are tender, about another 10 minutes.

3 Bring remaining water and lemon juice to a boil. Remove from heat. Stir in couscous. Cover and let sit about 5 minutes. Fluff with a fork.

4 Serve stew over couscous, adding toppings as desired.

5 Refrigerator leftovers in an airtight container for up to 5 days, or freeze (after cooling) in a freezer-safe container for up to 3 months. Thaw overnight in the refrigerator and reheat on the stovetop or in the microwave.

Lasagna Soup

SERVES 6

Per Serving:

Calories	477
Fat	19g
Sodium	669mg
Carbohydrates	55g
Fiber	11g
Sugar	11g
Protein	22g

This plant-based version of lasagna is a healthy alternative to meat and dairy lasagna. It will help beat cravings and keep you on track. The Almond Ricotta is easy to make in the blender, or use the Kite Hill brand, which is made without added oil.

¼ cup water

½ large yellow onion, peeled and chopped

3 medium cloves garlic, peeled and minced

1½ teaspoon dried oregano, divided

½ teaspoon salt

¼ teaspoon freshly ground black pepper

⅛ teaspoon crushed red pepper flakes

3 tablespoons no-salt-added tomato paste

3 cups Basil Marinara (see recipe in Chapter 9) or 1 (25.5-ounce) jar prepared marinara sauce

½ cup red wine

6 cups One-Pot Vegetable Broth (see recipe in this chapter)

½ medium head broccoli, trimmed and cut into ¾" pieces

8 ounces uncooked lasagna noodles, broken into bite-sized pieces

1 recipe Almond Ricotta (see recipe in Chapter 9)

½ cup chopped fresh basil, divided

¼ teaspoon garlic powder

1 Heat a large pot over medium-high heat. Add water, onion, garlic, 1 teaspoon oregano, salt, black pepper, and red pepper flakes. Sauté until onion is soft, about 5–7 minutes.

2 Stir in tomato paste and cook for 2 minutes more before adding the Basil Marinara sauce, red wine, and broth. Stir to combine. Bring just to a boil, then reduce heat to low and simmer for 12 minutes. Add broccoli and simmer for 3 more minutes.

3 Meanwhile, in a separate large pot, cook lasagna noodles according to package directions and drain.

4 In a medium bowl, combine Almond Ricotta, 1 tablespoon basil, remaining ½ teaspoon oregano, and garlic powder. Set aside.

5 To serve, ladle soup over cooked pasta. For each serving, add 1 tablespoon ricotta mixture and ½ tablespoon basil.

Farro-Sausage Stew

Many store-bought vegan sausages contain added oil. If you choose to use those, do so only infrequently. If possible, choose No Evil Foods sausages, which are made without oil. Serve alongside crusty bread for dipping the delicious broth!

1 large yellow onion, peeled and diced

3 large cloves garlic, peeled and minced

¼ cup water

2 medium stalks celery, trimmed and chopped

2 medium sweet potatoes, peeled and chopped

8 ounces cremini mushrooms, sliced

3 tablespoons no-salt-added tomato paste

1 cup uncooked farro

½ teaspoon dried thyme

1 teaspoon dried rosemary

½ teaspoon salt

½ teaspoon freshly ground black pepper

4 cups One-Pot Vegetable Broth (see recipe in this chapter)

3 vegan sausage links, cut into coins

1 cup thawed frozen peas

6 cups thinly sliced Swiss chard

½ cup chopped fresh parsley

SERVES 6	
Per Serving:	
Calories	200
Fat	7g
Sodium	714mg
Carbohydrates	22g
Fiber	6g
Sugar	6g
Protein	15g

1 Heat a large soup pot over medium-high heat. Add onion, garlic, and ¼ cup water, and sauté until soft, about 5–7 minutes. Add celery, sweet potatoes, and mushrooms, and continue to sauté until mushrooms are wilted, about 7–8 minutes.

2 Add tomato paste and stir to incorporate.

3 Add farro, thyme, rosemary, salt, pepper, and broth. Cook until farro is soft, about 20 minutes, adding more water if it becomes too dry.

4 Add sausage, peas, and Swiss chard and stir to combine and heat through until chard is wilted, about 10 minutes.

5 Garnish with chopped fresh parsley.

6 Refrigerate leftovers in a covered container for 4–5 days, or freeze (after cooling) in a freezer-safe container filled halfway for up to 3 months.

One-Pot Vegetable Broth

MAKES 10 CUPS

Per Serving (1 cup):

Calories	19
Fat	0g
Sodium	140mg
Carbohydrates	2g
Fiber	4g
Sugar	2g
Protein	1g

Vegetable broth is an important part of a plant-based diet, but no-salt varieties are almost impossible to find in the store. Your best option is to make homemade broth and store it in the freezer. It's especially handy for using leftover vegetable scraps. After chopping vegetables, keep any scraps in a freezer bag until you're ready to make broth.

1 large yellow onion, skin on, roughly chopped

10¼ cups water, divided

4 medium cloves garlic, skin on

½ teaspoon salt

5 medium stalks celery, cut into large chunks

3 large carrots, cut into large chunks

⅓ medium head broccoli, trimmed and cut into chunks

3 cups roughly chopped kale

2 medium tomatoes, chopped into large chunks

1 cup roughly chopped parsley

2 cups button mushrooms, cut in half

2 medium bay leaves

1 teaspoon whole black peppercorns

1 Heat a large pot over medium-high heat. Add onions and ¼ cup water, and sauté until fragrant, about 2 minutes. Add garlic and salt, and cook another 30 seconds.

2 Add the rest of the ingredients to the pot and bring to a boil. Gently stir to combine.

3 Simmer, covered, on low heat for about 1 hour. The longer you simmer it, the more concentrated the broth will be.

4 Strain broth through a large colander to remove larger pieces and then through a fine-mesh strainer to remove the rest.

5 Refrigerate in an airtight container for up to 3–4 days, or freeze (after cooling) in a freezer-safe container for up to 3 months. Thaw overnight in the refrigerator and reheat over medium heat on the stovetop or in the microwave. For smaller quantities, freeze in ice cube trays. Pop out cubes when frozen and store in a freezer bag for those times when you'd like to sauté in vegetable broth instead of water, make a sauce, or reheat leftovers.

Roasted Corn and Red Pepper Soup

The roasted flavors of corn and red peppers blend with the fiery tomatoes and chipotle for a bowl of nutritious goodness.

2 (16-ounce) packages frozen corn kernels

8 medium cloves garlic, peeled and chopped

½ teaspoon salt

¼ teaspoon freshly ground black pepper

1 medium sweet onion, peeled and diced

¼ cup water

1 (8-ounce) jar roasted red bell peppers, drained and roughly chopped

1 (15-ounce) can low-sodium fire-roasted tomatoes, undrained

8 cups One-Pot Vegetable Broth (see recipe in this chapter)

½ teaspoon chipotle chili powder (use less if you want less heat)

1 large medium avocado, peeled, seeded, and diced

2 tablespoons chopped fresh cilantro

SERVES 6

Per Serving:

Calories	259
Fat	6g
Sodium	565mg
Carbohydrates	44g
Fiber	8g
Sugar	8g
Protein	12g

HOW TO RIPEN AVOCADOS

Ripen avocados in a paper bag for 2–3 days with another fruit that's already ripe, such as a banana or apple. Do not place in direct sunlight. Check daily. They're ripe when the flesh gives. If you need to slow down or halt ripening, put them in the refrigerator. They easily turn brown once cut, so use up quickly.

1 Preheat oven to 400°F. Line one (or more, as needed) baking sheets with parchment paper.

2 Spread corn and garlic on prepared baking sheet. Sprinkle with salt and black pepper. Bake for 20 minutes.

3 Meanwhile, heat a large soup pot over medium-high heat. Add onion and water, and sauté until soft, about 5–7 minutes.

4 Add roasted peppers, tomatoes, broth, and chipotle chili powder. Add corn and garlic to the pot once they are done roasting.

5 Bring soup to a simmer, cover, and cook for 20 minutes.

6 Let soup cool a little before blending in a blender or with an immersion blender until smooth. If corn kernels are a little tough, use the standing blender.

7 Ladle soup into bowls and garnish with a few kernels of corn, diced avocado, and cilantro.

8 Refrigerate leftovers in a covered container for up to 5 days, or freeze (after cooling) in freezer-safe containers for up to 3 months. Thaw overnight in the refrigerator and reheat on the stovetop or in the microwave for a quick lunch.

Corn Chowder

Serve this creamy Corn Chowder any time of year. It's dairy-free, rich, delicious, and all made in one pot for a simple and satisfying dish.

SERVES 8

Per Serving:

Calories	80
Fat	1g
Sodium	235mg
Carbohydrates	16g
Fiber	3g
Sugar	3g
Protein	4g

CORN OFF THE COB

Have an abundance of fresh corn? When in season, it's the perfect time to stock your freezer. Shave the kernels off cooked cob into a bowl. Portion into airtight freezer bags to store up to 2–3 months. For longer freeze time, blanch corn for about 3–4 minutes before storing.

1 medium yellow onion, peeled and finely chopped

2 medium cloves garlic, peeled and minced

1 cup diced red bell pepper, divided

2 medium stalks celery, trimmed and chopped

¼ cup water

1 medium Yukon Gold potato, peeled and diced

2 cups One-Pot Vegetable Broth (see recipe in this chapter)

1 cup unsweetened almond milk

½ teaspoon crushed red pepper flakes

1 tablespoon Capitol Hill Seasoning Blend

½ teaspoon salt

¼ teaspoon freshly ground black pepper

2 tablespoons nutritional yeast

Juice of ½ medium lemon

2 cups fresh or frozen corn kernels

½ cup chopped fresh cilantro

½ cup chopped green onions

1 Heat a large pot over medium heat. Add onion, garlic, ¾ cup red bell pepper, celery, and water, and sauté until soft, about 10 minutes.

2 Add potato, broth, and almond milk, and stir well.

3 Add red pepper flakes, seasoning blend, salt, black pepper, yeast, and lemon juice, and stir to combine. Bring to a boil, then reduce heat to low, cover pot, and simmer gently for 15–20 minutes, or until potatoes are tender.

4 Add corn and stir to combine. Let cook for another 5–10 minutes, or until corn is tender.

5 Transfer about one-third of soup to a blender, and blend until smooth.

6 Pour blended portion back into pot and stir well.

7 Top each serving with cilantro, green onions, and remaining red pepper.

8 Refrigerate leftovers in an airtight container for 3–4 days, or freeze (after cooling) in freezer-safe plastic or glass containers for up to 3 months. Thaw overnight in the refrigerator and reheat on the stovetop or in the microwave.

CHAPTER 6

Lunch

Easy Whole-Wheat Pumpkin Tortillas

Per Serving:

Calories	80
Fat	1g
Sodium	52mg
Carbohydrates	17g
Fiber	3g
Sugar	1g
Protein	3g

THE POWERFUL BENEFITS OF PUMPKIN

Pumpkin is chock-full of nutrient-rich benefits. Don't let the fact that it's associated with autumn stop you from using it in recipes year-round. Pumpkin is high in fiber but low in calories. Like carrots, it has antioxidants as well as beta-carotene to improve eyesight. Don't forget to roast the seeds, which have just as many health benefits!

These tortillas, a great oil-free substitute for regular flour tortillas, boost the nutritional value with the addition of pumpkin puree. They are perfect for meal prep because they work well in a number of dishes, including Hummus-Vegetable Wrap or Pinto Bean Quesadillas (see recipes in this chapter), or Black Bean Breakfast Tacos (see recipe in Chapter 2).

1½ cups whole-wheat all-purpose flour
½ cup corn flour
¼ teaspoon salt
1½ cups pumpkin puree

1 In a large bowl, combine whole-wheat flour, corn flour, salt, and pumpkin puree. Use your hands to fully incorporate puree with flours. The dough will be sticky.

2 Divide dough in half and then into six equal parts. Flour hands and roll each piece of dough into a ball.

3 Place one ball of dough on a lightly floured surface and either use a rolling pin to roll into a very thin tortilla, about 8" in diameter, or use your hands to flatten. (They're still delicious if they look rustic!) Repeat with remaining dough.

4 Heat a large nonstick skillet over medium-high heat. Place 1 tortilla in the skillet and cook for about 1½ minutes, or until one side starts to brown. Flip and cook on the other side for another minute or so. Make sure you don't overcook tortilla, or it will become crispy.

5 Cool tortillas completely. Refrigerate leftovers in an airtight container for up to 1 week. Or place between sheets of wax paper in a large freezer bag and freeze for up to 6 months.

Caesar Salad Wrap with Chickpeas

This delicious wrap comes together quickly at lunchtime when you have leftover ingredients from a Caesar salad. The chickpeas add protein, helping you to stay full longer.

1 recipe Caesar Salad with Homemade Croutons (including dressing; see recipe in Chapter 4)

1 (15-ounce) can low-sodium chickpeas, drained and rinsed

4 Easy Whole-Wheat Pumpkin Tortillas (see recipe in this chapter)

1 In a large bowl, top Caesar Salad with chickpeas and dressing. Toss to combine flavors.

2 Top half of each tortilla with one-fourth of the salad and chickpeas. Fold in half.

SERVES 4	
Per Serving:	
Calories	358
Fat	8g
Sodium	792mg
Carbohydrates	60g
Fiber	13g
Sugar	9g
Protein	12g

Black Bean Barbecued Meatloaf Sandwich

These Black Bean Barbecued Meatloaf Sandwiches are a great use for your meatloaf leftovers. Mix up the condiments and toppings to suit your taste buds.

4 slices "meatloaf" from Black Bean Meatloaf (see recipe in Chapter 7)

4 tablespoons Basic Barbecue Sauce (see recipe in Chapter 9)

8 slices hearty whole-grain bread

4 (⅛") slices red onion

4 bread-and-butter pickle chips or slices dill pickle

4 leaves green leaf lettuce

1 Heat a large nonstick skillet over medium heat. Add "meatloaf" slices and heat for 3–4 minutes. Flip slices over and heat on other side for another minute.

2 For each sandwich, spread 1 tablespoon Basic Barbecue Sauce on 1 slice of bread. Top with onion slice, pickle slice, lettuce leaf, and meatloaf slice. Top with second slice of bread and cut in half.

SERVES 4	
Per Serving:	
Calories	405
Fat	8g
Sodium	896mg
Carbohydrates	66g
Fiber	13g
Sugar	17g
Protein	19g

Curried Tempeh Lettuce Wraps

These wraps are a quick low-fat, low-carb idea for a light lunch. Made with Indian-inspired flavors and wrapped in delicate, crispy lettuce, their flavor is kicked up with the addition of mango chutney. Add more or less cayenne pepper to your desired level of spice. You can also top with sprouts if you like. Make a double batch of the tempeh for lunch all week. You can add tempeh to soups, stews, salad, or crumbed in tacos.

1 (8-ounce) package original soy tempeh, crumbled

1 medium unpeeled Honeycrisp apple, cored and diced

⅓ cup raisins

¼ cup unsalted shelled walnuts

1 medium stalk celery, trimmed and diced

½ medium unpeeled cucumber, diced

½ teaspoon curry powder

¼ cup mango chutney

⅛ teaspoon cayenne pepper

¼ cup diced red onion

2 tablespoons Cashew-Tofu Mayonnaise (see recipe in Chapter 9)

2 tablespoons fresh lemon juice

¼ teaspoon salt

⅛ teaspoon freshly ground black pepper

4 large green leaf lettuce leaves

1. In a medium bowl, mash tempeh with the back of a fork. Add remaining ingredients except lettuce, and stir to combine.
2. For each wrap, spoon one-fourth tempeh filling onto 1 lettuce leaf and roll up.
3. If you make extra curried tempeh filling, refrigerate in an airtight container for up to 5 days.

Hummus-Vegetable Wrap

This wrap goes well alongside a soup, such as cold Gazpacho or warm Butternut Squash and Apple Soup (see recipes in Chapter 5). You can mix up the vegetables for variety or even try adding an apple and a few shakes of hot sauce if you like spice. Top with your favorite dressing. You might want to cut up extra vegetables and refrigerate in airtight containers for up to 3 days. Use them in a lettuce salad.

½ cup Beet Hummus (see recipe in Chapter 3)

4 Easy Whole-Wheat Pumpkin Tortillas (see recipe in this chapter)

4 large green leaf lettuce leaves

1 cup slivered carrots

1 cup slivered bell pepper

1 cup slivered cucumber

½ cup broccoli sprouts

1 For each wrap, spread 2 tablespoons Beet Hummus on 1 tortilla, leaving about ½" around edges. Top with a lettuce leaf.

2 In a row across one end lay ¼ cup each carrot, pepper, and cucumber. Top with 2 tablespoons sprouts.

3 Carefully start rolling the tortilla from the vegetable end, holding on to vegetables to make it tight. Slice in half.

SERVES 4

Per Serving:

Calories	149
Fat	2g
Sodium	143mg
Carbohydrates	29g
Fiber	7g
Sugar	6g
Protein	6g

HUMMUS AS A SALAD DRESSING

Hummus is a great staple to have on hand. Use it as a dip, as a spread on sandwiches, or make it into a dressing by thinning it with a little vinegar or lemon juice. Enjoy using hummus in recipes that are full of crunchy vegetables and healthy greens.

Tempeh BLT

SERVES 2

Per Serving:

Calories	285
Fat	7g
Sodium	438mg
Carbohydrates	39g
Fiber	10g
Sugar	7g
Protein	17g

Finding good alternatives to our non-plant-based favorites can sometimes be a struggle. Luckily, this pan-fried tempeh "bacon" is smoky and sweet, and when layered with crisp, fresh vegetables and toasty bread, it satisfies a bacon craving.

8 slices store-bought tempeh bacon

1 tablespoon Cashew-Tofu Mayonnaise (see recipe in Chapter 9)

4 pieces whole-grain bread, toasted

2 medium leaves iceberg lettuce

4 (¼") slices tomato

4 (¼") slices avocado

1 Heat a medium nonstick skillet over medium-high heat. Add slices of tempeh bacon and cook until lightly browned on each side, about 2–3 minutes per side.

2 For each sandwich, divide ½ tablespoon Cashew-Tofu Mayonnaise between 2 slices toasted bread and spread on each. Top 1 slice bread with 2 slices bacon, 1 lettuce leaf, 2 slices tomato, and another 2 slices bacon. Top with second slice of bread and slice sandwich in half. Repeat with remaining bread and fillings.

3 If not eating both sandwiches at once, refrigerate tempeh bacon, lettuce, and tomato in separate sealed containers for up to 3 days. (Slice fresh avocado as needed at serving time.)

Tofu Eggless Salad Sandwich

You won't believe how much this tofu salad tastes like the original egg version! Just like its cousin, this recipe is simple, flavorful, and easy on the budget. You could add some currants or raisins and walnuts for sweetness (and omega-3s!) and use broccoli sprouts as an alternative to lettuce. This could be your child's new favorite school lunch sandwich!

1 (14-ounce) container firm organic tofu, drained, rinsed, and pressed for at least 15 minutes (see Chapter 1 for pressing instructions)

⅓ cup chopped celery

¼ cup chopped red onion

2 medium sweet pickles, chopped

¼ cup chopped fresh parsley

2 tablespoons Cashew-Tofu Mayonnaise (see recipe in Chapter 9)

2 tablespoons yellow mustard

½ teaspoon ground turmeric

⅛ teaspoon salt

⅛ teaspoon freshly ground black pepper

8 pieces whole-grain bread

1 medium tomato, cored and sliced

4 medium leaves green leaf lettuce

1 medium avocado, peeled, seeded, and sliced

1 In a large bowl, break tofu up into small pieces with a fork.

2 Add celery, onion, pickles, parsley, Cashew-Tofu Mayonnaise, mustard, turmeric, salt, and pepper. Stir to combine.

3 For each sandwich, spoon one-fourth eggless salad on 1 slice bread. Top with one-fourth sliced tomato, 1 lettuce leaf, and one-fourth sliced avocado. Top with second slice bread.

4 Refrigerate eggless salad in an airtight container for up to 5 days.

Vegetable Sandwich

This sandwich is simple, but you'll love the flavor and texture of hummus, roasted red pepper, crisp lettuce and onion, and cooked zucchini on toasty bread. Make extra hummus to snack on throughout the week.

1 medium zucchini, trimmed and cut lengthwise into ¼" slices

¼ cup water

2 teaspoons low-sodium tamari soy sauce

4 slices whole-grain bread, lightly toasted

2 teaspoons yellow mustard

2 slices bottled roasted red pepper packed in water, drained

2 (⅛") slices red onion

2 medium leaves green leaf lettuce

4 tablespoons Beet Hummus (see recipe in Chapter 3) or store-bought hummus

SERVES 2	
Per Serving:	
Calories	213
Fat	4g
Sodium	560mg
Carbohydrates	35g
Fiber	7g
Sugar	9g
Protein	11g

1 Heat a medium nonstick skillet over medium-high heat. Add zucchini, water, and tamari. Cover and heat until zucchini is wilted, about 5–7 minutes.

2 For each sandwich, spread 1 slice toasted bread with 1 teaspoon mustard.

3 Layer half the zucchini, red pepper, and onion onto bread. Top with 1 leaf lettuce.

4 Spread 1 tablespoon Beet Hummus on a second slice of bread and place on top of first slice. Cut sandwich in half.

5 Refrigerate any extra Beet Hummus in an airtight container for up to 7 days.

Creamy Polenta with Sautéed Mushrooms

Polenta is a versatile cornmeal dish that can also be used for breakfast much like oatmeal, topped with fruit and nuts. If you prefer not to use wine to sauté the mushrooms, you can use vegetable broth instead. Cremini mushrooms are sometimes called baby portobellos in the grocery store. Feel free to add a cashew "parmesan" topping as well by blending ½ cup unsalted raw cashews, 3 tablespoons nutritional yeast, ½ teaspoon garlic powder, and ¼ teaspoon salt in a blender until the cashews have almost turned into fine crumbs.

Polenta

3 cups One-Pot Vegetable Broth (see recipe in Chapter 5)

1 cup unsweetened almond milk

1 cup polenta

¼ cup nutritional yeast

½ teaspoon salt

¼ teaspoon freshly ground black pepper

Mushrooms

1½ pounds cremini mushrooms, cut into 1" pieces

¼ cup water

4 medium cloves garlic, peeled and minced

¼ cup red wine

1 teaspoon chopped fresh rosemary

1½ tablespoons chopped fresh thyme, divided

½ cup One-Pot Vegetable Broth (see recipe in Chapter 5)

1 tablespoon cornstarch

2 tablespoons balsamic vinegar

1 To make polenta, in a large saucepan over medium heat, combine broth and almond milk. Bring to a simmer.

continued

THE BEST STORE-BOUGHT PLANT MILKS

Unless you make your own, the best plant milks for a plant-based diet are unsweetened and made with the fewest ingredients. Unfortunately, most have additives or preservatives. The brands with the fewest ingredients are WestSoy brand Unsweetened Soymilk, Trader Joe's Unsweetened Soy Beverage, Elmhurst unsweetened brands (various plant milks), and MALK Unsweetened Almond.

Creamy Polenta with Sautéed Mushrooms—continued

2 Slowly add the polenta in a stream, whisking the whole time. This helps prevent lumps. Cook, stirring occasionally with a heavy spoon to avoid burning, until it starts to thicken but is still loose and creamy, at least 20–30 minutes.

3 Add yeast, salt, and pepper.

4 To prepare mushrooms, heat a large skillet over medium heat. Add mushrooms and water, and cook, stirring occasionally, until water evaporates and mushrooms turn golden brown, about 10 minutes. Stir in garlic, wine, rosemary, and 1 tablespoon thyme.

5 In a measuring cup, combine broth and cornstarch and stir with fork. Add cornstarch mixture to mushrooms and continue to simmer until sauce is thickened, about 2 minutes. Drizzle with vinegar and stir to combine. Taste and adjust seasonings if needed.

6 To serve, divide polenta evenly among four bowls. Top with sautéed mushrooms and remaining ½ tablespoon thyme.

7 Store leftover mushrooms and polenta separately in airtight containers for 4–5 days. Polenta will firm up in the refrigerator and can then be sliced easily and reheated in a dry nonstick skillet on medium heat for 3 minutes per side. It can also be thinned again by stirring in a couple of tablespoons of water at a time until it reaches the desired consistency.

8 To freeze polenta, wait until it's completely cool and slice into individual servings. Wrap in parchment and then plastic and store in freezer bags for up to 3 months.

Crustless Tofu Quiche

You won't miss eggs in this dish because it has a similar consistency and is stuffed with vegetables. If you don't have aquafaba, you can leave it out, but it acts very similarly to egg whites.

1 (14-ounce) container firm organic tofu, drained, rinsed, and pressed for 10 minutes (see Chapter 1 for pressing instructions)

¼ cup unsweetened almond milk

⅓ cup aquafaba (liquid from a can of chickpeas)

1 teaspoon Dijon mustard

2 tablespoons nutritional yeast

2 tablespoons chickpea flour

¼ teaspoon onion powder

¼ teaspoon ground turmeric

¼ teaspoon nutmeg

½ teaspoon salt

¼ teaspoon freshly ground black pepper

2 medium leeks, trimmed and chopped (white part only)

3 medium cloves garlic, peeled and minced

¼ cup water

1 cup diced red bell pepper

2 cups chopped asparagus

SERVES 6

Per Serving:

Calories	101
Fat	3g
Sodium	225mg
Carbohydrates	10g
Fiber	3g
Sugar	3g
Protein	8g

SAVE THE CHICKPEA JUICE!

The juice from a can of chickpeas is called aquafaba. Instead of dumping it down the drain, save it to use in later recipes. It will last refrigerated in a sealed container for 3–4 days. Or put it into ice cube trays and freeze. Then pop out the cubes and store in freezer bags for up to 2 months.

1. Preheat oven to 375°F. Spray a 9" pie plate with nonstick cooking spray.
2. In a food processor, combine tofu, almond milk, aquafaba, mustard, yeast, chickpea flour, onion powder, turmeric, nutmeg, salt, and black pepper. Process until smooth. Transfer to a large bowl and set aside.
3. Heat a medium nonstick skillet over medium-high heat. Add leeks, garlic, and water, and sauté for 5 minutes. Add red bell pepper and asparagus, and continue to cook until vegetables are crisp-tender, about 5 more minutes.
4. Add vegetables to tofu mixture and carefully stir.
5. Pour into pie plate and bake for 35–40 minutes, or until quiche is set. Allow to cool for 5 minutes before cutting.
6. Leftovers will keep refrigerated in an airtight container for up to 3 days. To reheat, cover with aluminum foil and warm in a preheated 325°F oven for about 25 minutes.

Easy Italian Pita Pizzas

SERVES 4

Per Serving:

Calories	355
Fat	16g
Sodium	483mg
Carbohydrates	45g
Fiber	9g
Sugar	6g
Protein	15g

These quick little individual pizzas use Oil-Free Basil Pesto and Almond Ricotta for a tasty lunch or snack. Experiment with toppings and find your favorite combo, or try flavors from different cuisines, like Asian or Greek. For an even quicker lunch, bake these individually in a toaster oven instead of heating up your large oven.

4 (5¼") whole-grain pita breads

½ recipe Oil-Free Basil Pesto (see recipe in Chapter 9)

½ medium red onion, peeled and sliced

1 medium bell pepper, seeded and sliced

4 ounces button mushrooms, sliced

2 cups packed chopped baby spinach

1 cup Almond Ricotta (see recipe in Chapter 9)

½ cup sliced fresh basil

1 Preheat oven to 350°F.

2 Place pita breads on a large baking sheet and spread each with 2 tablespoons Oil-Free Basil Pesto. Evenly distribute vegetables over each pita.

3 Bake 6 minutes, then remove and add ¼-cup dollops Almond Ricotta on each pita. Return to oven and bake until pita breads become crisp and vegetables start to wilt, about another 6 minutes. Sprinkle with basil and cut pitas into quarters. Serve warm.

4 Refrigerate leftovers in an airtight container for 2–3 days.

Falafel-Tahini Buddha Bowl

The variations for making a Buddha bowl are endless. You can mix it up by using any grains, greens, vegetables, or beans that you like. They're perfect for meal prep or lunches.

½ recipe Falafel Burger mixture (see recipe in Chapter 7)

1½ cups cubed sweet potatoes

1½ cups farro, cooked according to package directions

4 cups arugula

1½ cups halved cherry tomatoes

½ cup Tahini Dressing (see recipe in Chapter 4)

1 cup broccoli sprouts

4 (5¼") whole-grain pita breads, sliced into 6 wedges each and toasted

SERVES 4	
Per Serving:	
Calories	564
Fat	5g
Sodium	801mg
Carbohydrates	111g
Fiber	18g
Sugar	9g
Protein	22g

1 Preheat oven to 400°F. Line a baking sheet with parchment paper.

2 Form falafel mixture into 12 small patties with your hands using 1 rounded tablespoon for each. Place on prepared baking sheet. On the other half of the baking sheet, spread cubed sweet potatoes. Bake falafels for 15–20 minutes, flipping halfway through, until they are golden. Check potatoes and if they're not soft enough, bake them for another 10 minutes or so. Set aside.

3 Divide farro, arugula, tomatoes, and sweet potatoes evenly among 4 bowls. Top each with 3 falafel balls and drizzle with 2 tablespoons Tahini Dressing. To each bowl, add ¼ cup broccoli sprouts and 6 pita wedges.

4 Premade bowls can be refrigerated in airtight containers for 3–4 days without the pita, sprouts, or dressing, which can be added when ready to eat.

Pinto Bean Quesadillas

SERVES 4

Per Serving:

Calories	328
Fat	8g
Sodium	665mg
Carbohydrates	53g
Fiber	5g
Sugar	6g
Protein	11g

Quesadillas are an easy-to-make lunch or dinner, especially if you have already made a pot of homemade pinto beans for another recipe. You can also use black beans or different vegetables, depending on your preference and what's in your refrigerator. Broccoli sprouts are baby shoots of broccoli from broccoli seeds and can be found in the produce section of your grocery store.

4 (10") whole-grain tortillas

1⅓ cups Instant Pot® Pinto Beans (see recipe in Chapter 8)

¼ teaspoon hot sauce

½ cup chopped red onion

½ cup chopped red bell pepper

1½ cups chopped green or red cabbage

1 cup broccoli sprouts

¼ cup unsweetened plain plant yogurt

1 Heat a large nonstick skillet over medium heat. Place 1 tortilla in skillet and let sit until it turns golden and slightly crispy, about 5–7 minutes, being careful not to overcook.

2 Transfer to a cutting board and add another tortilla to the skillet. Add ⅓ cup pinto beans on one side of the tortilla on the board. Smash them slightly with the back of your spoon and top with a little hot sauce. Add a sprinkling of onion, pepper, cabbage, and sprouts on the same side of the tortilla.

3 Smear 1 tablespoon yogurt on the other side of the tortilla.

4 Carefully crease the middle of the tortilla with the edge of a knife and fold over. Cut in half and serve.

5 These are best made right before you plan to eat them, but they can also be made ahead of time and frozen without the cabbage and sprouts. To freeze, once the quesadillas are folded, place individually on a parchment-topped baking sheet and place in the freezer until they're frozen. Then, wrap individually and store in a freezer bag. To reheat them once they're defrosted, place in the oven at 325°F or in a dry nonstick skillet over medium heat until crispy, about 5–7 minutes. Lift one side of the quesadilla and add fresh cabbage, sprouts, and yogurt at serving time.

Chili-Stuffed Potatoes

SERVES 4	
Per Serving:	
Calories	586
Fat	3g
Sodium	711mg
Carbohydrates	119g
Fiber	21g
Sugar	15g
Protein	25g

These loaded Chili-Stuffed Potatoes are a great way to use leftover chili. Add hot sauce or salsa for a touch of heat.

4 large russet potatoes

1 recipe Quick Chili (see recipe in this chapter)

½ cup Plant-Based Sour Cream (see recipe in Chapter 9)

4 tablespoons sliced green onions

1 Preheat oven to 425°F. Pierce potatoes a few times with a knife to allow steam to escape.
2 Place potatoes directly on the rack in the oven and bake for about 50 minutes, flipping halfway through baking time, until tender when pierced with a knife.
3 Make a split down the center of each potato and fluff with a fork. Top with ¼ cup chili, 2 tablespoons Plant-Based Sour Cream, and 1 tablespoon green onions.

Mushroom Pita Pockets

SERVES 4	
Per Serving:	
Calories	232
Fat	3g
Sodium	515mg
Carbohydrates	42g
Fiber	6g
Sugar	7g
Protein	11g

This earthy lunch comes together in a flash when you've already prepped the mushrooms and made the Tzatziki sauce.

2 (5¼") whole-wheat pita pockets

1 cup chopped romaine lettuce

½ recipe Sautéed Mushrooms (from the Creamy Polenta with Sautéed Mushrooms recipe in this chapter)

8 (¼") slices tomato

12 slices dill pickles

1 cup thinly sliced red cabbage

½ cup Tzatziki (see recipe in Chapter 9)

1 Preheat oven to 350°F. Lay pita pockets on a baking sheet and warm for about 3 minutes, until heated through but not crispy. Remove and cut in half. Or, warm in the microwave on high for 10–15 seconds.
2 For each pita pocket, stuff with ¼ cup chopped lettuce, ⅓ cup mushrooms, 2 slices tomato, 3 pickles, ¼ cup cabbage, and 2 tablespoons Tzatziki.
3 Refrigerate leftovers in an airtight container for 3–5 days.

Quick Chili

Beans are an important part of a plant-based diet, providing protein, fiber, and B vitamins. You can use homemade beans for this recipe or used canned in a pinch. Top with vegan sour cream, green onions, and a sprinkling of chopped fresh cilantro for a quick and easy lunch.

1 small yellow onion, peeled and diced

¼ cup water

1 (15-ounce) can low-sodium diced tomatoes with green chilies, undrained

1 (8-ounce) can low-sodium tomato sauce

1 (15-ounce) can low-sodium pinto beans, drained and rinsed

1 (15-ounce) can low-sodium black beans, drained and rinsed

1½ tablespoons chili powder

1 teaspoon garlic powder

1 teaspoon ground cumin

½ teaspoon smoked paprika

¼ teaspoon salt

SERVES 4

Per Serving:

Calories	288
Fat	2g
Sodium	685mg
Carbohydrates	53g
Fiber	13g
Sugar	12g
Protein	17g

1 Heat a large saucepan over medium-high heat. Add onion and water, and sauté until soft, about 5–7 minutes.

2 Add remaining ingredients to saucepan and stir to combine. Bring to a boil, then reduce heat to medium low, cover, and simmer for 10 minutes, adding more water if it's too thick.

3 Refrigerate leftovers in an airtight container for 3–4 days, or freeze (after cooling) in a freezer-safe container for up to 3 months.

Roasted Vegetable–Quinoa Bowl

SERVES 4

Per Serving:

Calories	308
Fat	12g
Sodium	463mg
Carbohydrates	39g
Fiber	8g
Sugar	7g
Protein	13g

PARCHMENT PAPER VS. SILICONE MATS: WHICH IS BETTER?

Both parchment paper and silicone baking mats make baking cleanup fast and easy. Parchment paper is flexible and can be cut to fit any size pan, and it keeps the bottom of your food crispier. Silicone baking mats have the benefit of being reusable, fitting easily into standard baking sheets, and staying flat.

This vegetable bowl is a treat for the eyes and the stomach. You can change up the vegetables to use what you have on hand or what you have left over from other meal prepping. The Almond Ricotta adds a delicious creaminess, but leave it out if you prefer.

1 large sweet potato, peeled and chopped

½ medium red onion, peeled and sliced

2 cups ½" slices zucchini

4 cups halved, or quartered if large, cremini mushrooms

1 large red bell pepper, seeded and sliced

½ teaspoon salt

¼ teaspoon freshly ground black pepper

1 cup uncooked quinoa

4 cups chopped fresh spinach

½ cup Almond Ricotta (see recipe in Chapter 9)

½ cup Green Goddess Dressing (see recipe in Chapter 4)

1 Preheat oven to 400°F. Line two baking sheets with parchment paper.

2 Spread sweet potatoes and onions on one prepared baking sheet, making sure they are spread out a little. To the second baking sheet, add zucchini, mushrooms, and bell pepper. Season both trays with salt and black pepper.

3 Place potatoes and onions in the oven and roast for 15 minutes. Toss and return to the oven, and add the other baking sheet. Remove both from the oven after another 15 minutes or until vegetables are tender but slightly crisp.

4 While roasting vegetables, prepare quinoa according to package directions.

5 To assemble, divide cooked quinoa, an assortment of roasted vegetables, and chopped spinach evenly among 4 bowls. Dollop 2 tablespoons Almond Ricotta on top and drizzle with 2 tablespoons Green Goddess Dressing.

6 Refrigerate leftover roasted vegetables, quinoa, and dressing in separate airtight containers for 3–4 days.

CHAPTER 7

Main Dishes

Black Bean Meatloaf

SERVES 6

Per Serving:

Calories	229
Fat	6g
Sodium	596mg
Carbohydrates	35g
Fiber	8g
Sugar	8g
Protein	11g

WHAT IS TEMPEH?

If you're new to tempeh, you'll find that it is a great substitute for protein in any dish. It's made with fermented soybeans and has a bit of a nutty flavor. Using a steamer basket over a saucepan of boiling water, steam it for a few minutes to soften and to help pull in the recipe's flavor better. Tempeh is easy to crumble and makes a great addition to salads.

You'll be delighted with the flavor, texture, and appearance of this meatless loaf, as it is so much like the original.

⅓ cup dry-packaged sun-dried tomatoes

⅓ medium yellow onion, peeled and chopped

2 medium carrots, peeled and chopped

3 medium cloves garlic, peeled and chopped

¼ cup water

½ (8-ounce) package original soy tempeh, sliced

1 (15-ounce) can low-sodium black beans, drained and rinsed, divided

½ cup cornmeal

3 tablespoons ground flaxseeds

⅓ cup pitted and halved Kalamata olives

¾ cup Basic Barbecue Sauce (see recipe in Chapter 9), divided

2 tablespoons red wine

½ teaspoon salt

¼ teaspoon freshly ground black pepper

1 Spray a 9" × 5" loaf pan with nonstick cooking spray.

2 In a small bowl with hot water to cover, soak sun-dried tomatoes for 10 minutes to soften, then drain and set aside.

3 Heat a medium skillet over medium-high heat. Add onion, carrots, garlic, and water. Sauté about 5–7 minutes.

4 Transfer onion mixture to a food processor. Add tempeh and half the black beans. Pulse a couple of times.

5 Add cornmeal, flaxseeds, sun-dried tomatoes, olives, ½ cup Basic Barbecue Sauce, red wine, salt, and pepper. Pulse processor, scraping sides to make sure all is mixed. Don't overprocess.

6 Mash remaining black beans slightly with a fork and add them to the food processor bowl. Pulse to just combine.

7 Scrape mixture into prepared loaf pan and spread to all corners with a spatula, flattening the top. Spread remaining ¼ cup Basic Barbecue Sauce on top. Let sit for about 20 minutes.

8 Meanwhile, preheat oven to 350°F. Bake for 60 minutes or until firm. (Cover with foil if top is getting too brown.)

9 Refrigerate leftovers in an airtight container for up to 5 days, or freeze (after cooling) in a freezer-safe container for up to 3 months.

Tempeh Burrito Bowl

A delicious marinade turns tempeh into a "meaty" satisfying protein. The Avocado Cream Sauce whips up in seconds, and leftovers are great for dipping vegetables.

SERVES 4

Per Serving:

Calories	481
Fat	24g
Sodium	746mg
Carbohydrates	51g
Fiber	9g
Sugar	4g
Protein	24g

Marinade

3 tablespoons water

1 tablespoon no-salt-added tomato paste

1 tablespoon chili powder

1 teaspoon ground cumin

$1/8$ teaspoon cayenne pepper

$1/2$ teaspoon garlic powder

2 tablespoons fresh lime juice

$1/4$ teaspoon salt

$1/4$ teaspoon freshly ground black pepper

Bowls

1 (8-ounce) package original soy tempeh, cut into $1/2$" cubes

$1^1/3$ cups brown rice, cooked according to package directions

1 (15-ounce) can low-sodium pinto beans, drained and rinsed or $1^1/2$ cups Instant Pot® Pinto Beans (see recipe in Chapter 8)

1 medium avocado, peeled, seeded, and diced

1 cup frozen grilled corn kernels, thawed and warmed in the microwave

1 cup slivered green cabbage

$1/2$ cup salsa

$1/2$ recipe Avocado Cream Sauce (see recipe in Chapter 9)

2 tablespoons chopped fresh cilantro

1 In a shallow dish, whisk together water, tomato paste, chili powder, cumin, cayenne pepper, garlic powder, lime juice, salt, and black pepper. Add the tempeh pieces and toss to coat. Marinate in the refrigerator for at least 20 minutes, flipping the pieces once.

2 Heat a medium nonstick skillet over medium heat. Add marinated tempeh and cook until bottom side is golden, 3–4 minutes. Flip and cook the other side until nice and crispy, about 3–4 minutes. Remove from heat and set aside.

3 Divide rice and beans evenly among four bowls. Top with evenly divided tempeh, avocado, corn, cabbage, and salsa. Finish with about $1/4$ cup Avocado Cream Sauce and $1/2$ tablespoon cilantro per bowl.

4 Refrigerate leftover ingredients separately in airtight containers for up to 3 days.

Cauliflower Pasta Alfredo

SERVES 8

Per Serving:

Calories	342
Fat	7g
Sodium	276mg
Carbohydrates	62g
Fiber	9g
Sugar	3g
Protein	15g

A SAUCE FOR ANYTHING

Plant-based sauces are extremely versatile and can really make a dish burst with flavor. Use leftover sauces from dinner to top your vegetables, as a quick pizza sauce, as a base for soup, or for topping Buddha bowls. Most sauces will keep refrigerated for up to 3 days or frozen for 6 months.

This cauliflower Alfredo sauce is a great alternative to the traditional recipe. It eliminates the fattening and unhealthy dairy and cheese ingredients while still retaining a beautiful flavor and texture. If you'd like to add some vegetables, stir in green peas or fresh spinach after you add the sauce and heat through before serving.

1 (16-ounce) package whole-wheat fettuccine

3½ cups One-Pot Vegetable Broth (see recipe in Chapter 5)

4 cups cauliflower florets (mixed medium and small pieces)

2 medium russet potatoes, peeled and cut into 1" chunks

½ cup unsalted raw cashews

3 medium cloves garlic, peeled and minced

1 teaspoon mustard powder

2 tablespoons fresh lemon juice

2 teaspoons vegan Worcestershire sauce

½ teaspoon salt

¼ teaspoon freshly ground black pepper

¼ cup chopped fresh basil

1 Cook pasta according to package directions. Drain and set aside.

2 While pasta is cooking, in a large pot over medium-high heat, bring broth to a boil. Add cauliflower, potatoes, cashews, garlic, and mustard powder. Reduce heat to low, cover, and simmer until cauliflower and potatoes are fork-tender, about 15–20 minutes. Do not drain.

3 Once cauliflower mixture has cooled slightly, transfer ingredients to blender. Add lemon juice, Worcestershire sauce, salt, and pepper.

4 Blend until sauce becomes very smooth, about 1 minute.

5 Pour over noodles and stir to distribute Alfredo sauce. Top each serving with chopped basil.

6 Refrigerate leftovers in an airtight container for 3–4 days.

Falafel Burger

Falafel Burgers are a delicious variation on Middle Eastern vegetarian falafel balls, served on a whole-grain bun with your preferred toppings and a creamy Tahini Dressing. They are low in fat, high in fiber, and protein rich, which makes for a well-rounded meal.

1 (15-ounce) can low-sodium chickpeas, drained and rinsed

2 medium cloves garlic, peeled and smashed

1 small yellow onion, peeled and chopped

¼ cup chopped fresh parsley

¼ cup chopped fresh mint

½ teaspoon ground cumin

½ teaspoon coriander

½ teaspoon baking powder

¾ teaspoon salt

Juice of 1 medium lemon

¼ teaspoon Tabasco sauce

2 tablespoons chickpea flour

4 whole-wheat burger buns

1 recipe Tahini Dressing (see recipe in Chapter 4)

1 Preheat oven to 400°F. Line a baking sheet with parchment paper.

2 In a food processor, add half the chickpeas and pulse a few times until chopped but not smooth. Transfer to a large bowl.

3 Place remaining chickpeas in food processor with garlic, onion, parsley, mint, cumin, coriander, baking powder, salt, lemon juice, and Tabasco. Pulse until mixture resembles a thick paste. Transfer to bowl with chopped chickpeas.

4 Add chickpea flour and stir to combine until mixture comes together in a ball. Add more flour if needed. Shape into four patties and place on prepared baking sheet.

5 Bake 15 to 20 minutes, flipping burgers halfway through, until golden and firm.

6 Serve burger patties on buns with preferred toppings and a dollop of Tahini Dressing.

7 Refrigerate leftovers in an airtight container for up to 3–4 days, or freeze uncooked patties between parchment paper in an airtight container for up to 6 months. To use, thaw overnight in the refrigerator, then heat on a baking sheet in a 400°F oven for 15 minutes.

SERVES 4

Per Serving:

Calories	374
Fat	9g
Sodium	1,312mg
Carbohydrates	58g
Fiber	11g
Sugar	11g
Protein	18g

GET CREATIVE WITH BURGER TOPPINGS

Kick your burger up several notches by adding fresh pico de gallo, sliced avocado, or some grilled peppers for a Southwestern-style burger. You could even liven it up with mango salsa and use leafy lettuce instead of a bun.

Vegetable Divan

SERVES 6

Per Serving:

Calories	164
Fat	4g
Sodium	399mg
Carbohydrates	26g
Fiber	9g
Sugar	6g
Protein	10g

This version of the traditional comfort-food dish is a delicious, hearty meal. It uses the same fresh vegetables as the original but leaves out the heavy dairy and oils. Round this meal out by serving it over a bowl of quinoa.

Vegetables

1 medium head broccoli, trimmed and cut into bite-sized florets

½ medium head cauliflower, cut into bite-sized florets

4 medium carrots, peeled and sliced into ¾" coins

1 large yellow onion, peeled and chopped

Divan "Cheese" Sauce

1 (15-ounce) can low-sodium cannellini beans, drained and rinsed

½ cup drained bottled roasted red peppers packed in water

⅓ cup nutritional yeast

4 tablespoons fresh lemon juice

2 tablespoons tahini

1 teaspoon yellow mustard

½ teaspoon salt

½ teaspoon garlic powder

½ teaspoon onion powder

1½ cups One-Pot Vegetable Broth (see recipe in Chapter 5), divided

1 Preheat oven to 350°F. Spray bottom of a 9" × 12" baking pan with nonstick cooking spray.

2 Add a steamer basket to a large pot over medium-high heat and fill with about 1" water, making sure the water isn't touching the bottom of the basket. Add broccoli, cauliflower, carrots, and onions. Cover and let vegetables steam until crisp-tender, about 7–10 minutes. Remove from heat and transfer to prepared baking pan.

Vegetable Divan—continued

3 To make "cheese" sauce, in a blender, combine beans, red peppers, yeast, lemon juice, tahini, mustard, salt, garlic powder, onion powder, and ½ cup broth.

4 Blend until very smooth, adding a few tablespoons more broth to thin as needed.

5 Scrape cheese sauce from blender into a large saucepan over medium heat. Add remaining broth.

6 Mix carefully with a whisk until sauce is smooth and liquid is incorporated together with cheese sauce. Heat through, about 5–7 minutes.

7 Pour sauce over vegetables and move them around a little to coat. Cover baking pan with foil and bake for 30 minutes, or until heated through.

8 Refrigerate leftovers in an airtight container for up to 5 days, or freeze (after cooling) in a freezer-safe container for up to 3 months. Thaw in the refrigerator for 24 hours before reheating in a 350°F oven for 30 minutes.

Fiesta Mac and "Cheese"

This classic is a favorite of both kids and adults alike. Leave out the jalapeño if you want less spice. The cheese sauce comes together quickly right in the blender and actually heats in the blender for easy cleanup.

½ medium red onion, peeled and thinly sliced

2 cups fresh or frozen corn kernels

½ jalapeño pepper, seeded and minced

2 (4-ounce) cans diced green chilies, undrained

¼ cup water

½ (16-ounce) package whole-wheat elbow macaroni, cooked according to package directions

½ teaspoon salt

¼ teaspoon freshly ground black pepper

2 cups Blender "Cheese" Sauce (see recipe in Chapter 9)

¼ cup chopped fresh cilantro

SERVES 4	
Per Serving:	
Calories	420
Fat	8g
Sodium	745mg
Carbohydrates	78g
Fiber	11g
Sugar	5g
Protein	17g

1 Preheat broiler to high. Spray an 8" × 8" baking dish with non-stick cooking spray.

2 Heat a large, ovenproof skillet over medium-high heat. Add onion, corn, jalapeño, green chilies, and water. Season with salt and pepper. Sauté until onions start to turn golden brown, about 5–7 minutes. To char corn mixture, place skillet under the broiler for 30–60 seconds, being careful to watch it so it doesn't burn. (If you do not have an ovenproof pan, add the corn to a small baking sheet and broil for 30–60 seconds.) Remove from oven and turn off broiler. Preheat oven to 375°F.

3 In a large bowl, combine cooked macaroni with Blender "Cheese" Sauce and corn mixture. Stir to coat. If mixture seems too thick, add more cheese sauce.

4 Pour into an 8" × 8" baking dish and bake for 20–25 minutes, until bubbly and hot.

5 Sprinkle with chopped cilantro and serve.

6 Refrigerate leftovers in an airtight container for up to 3 days. (Note that this recipe does not freeze well.)

Lightly Curried Vegetable Wraps

SERVES 8

Per Serving:

Calories	305
Fat	8g
Sodium	775mg
Carbohydrates	48g
Fiber	6g
Sugar	7g
Protein	10g

OIL-FREE WATER SAUTÉING

A plant-based diet uses little processed oil, therefore when sautéing ingredients such as onions, vegetables, and tofu, use the water sauté or vegetable broth method. This is done by adding a small amount of water or broth to a nonstick pan to keep ingredients loose.

This vegetable wrap is like a burrito and is perfect for lunches on the go or just a simple, guilt-free meal when you want something flavorful. Choose any vegetables you have on hand—potatoes, green beans, squash...it all works.

½ large green bell pepper, seeded and diced

½ large red bell pepper, seeded and diced

1 medium red onion, peeled and diced

4 medium cloves garlic, peeled and minced

1 teaspoon curry powder

2 tablespoons water

1 cup chopped broccoli

1 cup chopped zucchini

1 cup chopped sweet potatoes

1 cup chopped cauliflower

4 cups shredded butter lettuce

8 (10") whole-grain tortillas or homemade Easy Whole-Wheat Pumpkin Tortillas (see recipe in Chapter 6)

½ cup store-bought hummus or Beet Hummus (see recipe in Chapter 3)

½ recipe Tofu Feta (see recipe in Chapter 9)

1 Heat a large pot over medium-high heat. Add green and red peppers, onion, garlic, curry powder, and water. Sauté for about 5 minutes.

2 Add broccoli, zucchini, sweet potatoes, cauliflower, and lettuce. Cover, reduce heat to low, and steam for about 10 minutes.

3 Meanwhile, heat a large nonstick skillet over medium heat. Add tortillas and warm until pliable, about 5 minutes. Or wrap tortillas in a damp paper towel and microwave on high until softened, about 1 minute.

4 For each wrap, spread about 2 tablespoons hummus on 1 tortilla. Top with ½ cup cooked vegetables and a sprinkling of Tofu Feta down the middle.

5 Fold over both sides of tortilla and then roll up tightly.

6 Refrigerate in an airtight container for up to 3–4 days, or freeze whole prepared wraps wrapped in waxed paper and foil for up to 2 months. Thaw overnight in the refrigerator and reheat over medium heat on the stovetop or in the microwave.

Penne Pasta with Roasted Vegetables

This simple and elegant dinner is quick to get to the table, especially if you've already meal prepped vegetables or marinara sauce for another dish this week. (If you haven't made sauce, just grab a store-bought version that quickly heats on the stove.) Serve with a large green salad. If you make extra Parmesan "cheese," store in an airtight container to enjoy over salads and other pasta dishes for the next 5 days.

Pasta

1 (16-ounce) package whole-grain penne, cooked according to package directions

3 cups Basil Marinara (see recipe in Chapter 9)

1 recipe Balsamic-Roasted Vegetables (see recipe in Chapter 8)

2 Black Bean Mushroom Burgers, crumbled (see recipe in this chapter; do not include buns)

1 cup chopped fresh basil, divided

Cashew Parmesan Cheese

½ cup unsalted raw cashews

2 tablespoons nutritional yeast

½ teaspoon salt

1. In a large skillet over medium heat, add Basil Marinara along with Balsamic-Roasted Vegetables, Black Bean Mushroom Burger crumbles, and ½ cup basil. Heat through, about 10 minutes.
2. To make Parmesan "cheese," in a blender, combine cashews with yeast and salt. Blend until it resembles Parmesan cheese. Set aside.
3. To serve, add ¼ cup cooked pasta to each plate and top with one-fourth of the sauce. Top with 2 tablespoons cashew Parmesan and 2 tablespoons fresh basil.
4. Refrigerate leftovers in an airtight container for 3–5 days, or freeze (after cooling) in a freezer-safe container for up to 3 months.

SERVES 4

Per Serving:

Calories	838
Fat	14g
Sodium	1,896mg
Carbohydrates	149g
Fiber	27g
Sugar	23g
Protein	38g

CHOOSE YOUR PASTA FOR HEALTH

Quinoa pasta, a wonderful gluten-free noodle that holds its integrity, offers a healthy dose of dietary fiber and tastes very similar to the traditional wheat noodle. It's a healthier alternative to white flour pasta, which converts to sugar in your body.

Pineapple Fried Rice with Baked Tofu

Per Serving:

Calories	386
Fat	10g
Sodium	1,399mg
Carbohydrates	59g
Fiber	6g
Sugar	22g
Protein	17g

IS SOY OK TO EAT?

Although some people are concerned about eating soy because of conflicting news reports, rest assured that soy is indeed a healthy food to consume. (See Chapter 1 for more about this topic.) Tofu is a great source of protein and is full of vitamins, minerals, and omega-3 and omega-6 fatty acids. When marinated, it takes on the flavor of any dish, making it a great addition to plant-based recipes.

The balance of textures and flavors with the sweet pineapple, crunchy vegetables, and creamy tofu is what makes this rice that much better. This is also a great way to use leftover rice as you create your meal plan for the week. For a lower-sodium version, substitute the tamari soy sauce for coconut aminos.

Fried Rice

3 tablespoons One-Pot Vegetable Broth (see recipe in Chapter 5)

½ medium yellow onion, peeled and chopped

3 medium cloves garlic, peeled and chopped

1 medium red bell pepper, seeded and chopped

2 medium carrots, peeled and diced

¼ cup water

½ cup unsalted roasted cashews

3 cups brown rice, cooked according to package directions

1½ recipes (21 ounces) Baked Tofu (see recipe in this chapter)

1 cup chopped pineapple

¼ cup frozen peas

¼ cup raisins

2 medium green onions, trimmed and sliced

¼ cup chopped fresh cilantro

Asian Sauce

⅓ cup low-sodium tamari soy sauce

2 tablespoons rice vinegar

2 tablespoons chili garlic sauce

1 tablespoon maple syrup

1 tablespoon minced fresh ginger

1 Heat a large nonstick skillet over medium-high heat. Add yellow onion, garlic, pepper, carrots, and water, and sauté until crisp-tender, about 5–7 minutes.

2 Add cashews and cooked rice, breaking up any clumps, and stir-fry for another 7–8 minutes.

3 Add Baked Tofu, pineapple, peas, and raisins, and stir to heat through, another 5 minutes.

4 In a small bowl, whisk Asian sauce ingredients to combine. Pour over rice mixture and stir to mix well.

5 Serve garnished with green onions and cilantro.

6 Refrigerate leftovers in an airtight container for 3–5 days, or freeze (after cooling) in a freezer-safe container for up to 3 months.

Roasted Beet and Mushroom Tacos

This recipe pairs two very nutritious ingredients that can easily be used in other dishes such as hummus or beet salad. To keep your hands from turning red while preparing the beets, use dishwashing gloves.

8 ounces button mushrooms, sliced

¼ cup water

¼ teaspoon salt

⅛ teaspoon freshly ground black pepper

8 (6") corn tortillas

1 recipe Tofu Feta (see recipe in Chapter 9)

½ recipe Roasted Beets (see recipe in Chapter 8)

½ medium head green cabbage, cored and sliced

1 cup roughly chopped fresh cilantro

¼ teaspoon hot sauce

SERVES 4	
Per Serving:	
Calories	250
Fat	5g
Sodium	895mg
Carbohydrates	42g
Fiber	8g
Sugar	12g
Protein	12g

1. Heat a medium skillet over medium-high heat. Add mushrooms and water, and sauté until cooked through, about 7–8 minutes. Sprinkle with salt and pepper. Remove from heat and set aside.
2. Heat a small nonstick skillet over medium heat. Add a tortilla and warm it for 3–4 minutes, until it is still pliable but starting to crisp. Repeat with remaining tortillas.
3. For each taco, crumble 1 or 2 tablespoons Tofu Feta on a tortilla. Add 2–3 tablespoons Roasted Beets and 2–3 tablespoons mushrooms, and sprinkle with cabbage and cilantro. Serve with hot sauce.
4. Refrigerate extra filling and tofu in separate airtight containers and extra tortillas in a large sealable plastic bag for up to 5 days.

Roasted Vegetable Tacos

These Roasted Vegetable Tacos taste amazing thanks to the smoky chipotle sauce. Top the roasted vegetables with creamy avocado, chopped tomato, and a few alfalfa sprouts or lettuce for extra crunch. If you want to turn up the heat, add more chipotle chili powder, but be careful to add in small increments—it's very hot.

1 large red onion, peeled and cut into ½" cubes

1 large yellow or red bell pepper, seeded and cut into ½" cubes

2 medium zucchini, cut into ½" cubes

½ teaspoon salt

¼ teaspoon freshly ground black pepper

6 (8") corn tortillas

1 medium avocado, peeled, seeded, and chopped

1 recipe Chipotle Dipping Sauce (see recipe in Chapter 9)

2–3 large leaves romaine lettuce, chopped

1 Preheat oven to 400°F. Line a large rimmed baking sheet with parchment paper.

2 Combine chopped vegetables on baking sheet and add salt and pepper.

3 Roast until they begin to brown and are softened, about 20 minutes. Watch carefully so they don't burn.

4 Wrap tortillas in a damp paper towel and microwave on high until softened, about 1 minute, or wrap in foil and heat in a preheated 300°F oven for 10–15 minutes.

5 To assemble tacos, place roasted vegetables into warmed tortillas, then top evenly with avocado slices, chipotle sauce, and lettuce.

6 Roasted vegetables can be refrigerated in an airtight container for up to 5 days or frozen for up to 3 months. To reheat from the refrigerator, microwave for 30-second intervals until heated through and add to warmed tortillas.

African Vegetable Stew

If you prefer, switch out the beans for cubed tofu or tempeh for a heartier dish. The jalapeño adds a pleasant heat; removing the seeds makes it more mellow and is always optional.

1 cup uncooked whole-wheat couscous

1 medium yellow onion, peeled and chopped

2 medium cloves garlic, peeled and minced

¾ cup water, divided

1 medium jalapeño pepper, seeded and finely chopped

1 tablespoon finely grated fresh ginger

2 teaspoons coriander

½ teaspoon cardamom

2 medium Yukon Gold potatoes, peeled and chopped

1 (14.5-ounce) can low-sodium diced fire-roasted tomatoes

1 (15-ounce) can low-sodium kidney beans, drained and rinsed

1 cup canned light coconut milk

⅓ cup all-natural peanut butter

4 cups broccoli florets (with some stems)

2 tablespoons fresh lemon juice

1 cup chopped fresh cilantro

½ teaspoon salt

¼ teaspoon freshly ground black pepper

SERVES 4	
Per Serving:	
Calories	548
Fat	14g
Sodium	467mg
Carbohydrates	86g
Fiber	14g
Sugar	10g
Protein	23g

WHAT ABOUT TVP FOR PROTEIN?

Texturized vegetable protein (TVP) is made from soy and is used as a meat substitute. It's made from defatted soy flour and, unfortunately, is not a good choice for vegans. In addition to being highly processed, it may be derived from genetically modified organisms (GMOs). A better option is a product called Soy Curls from Butler Foods, which is made from dehydrated non-GMO soybeans.

1 Prepare couscous according to package directions.

2 Heat a large nonstick skillet over medium heat. Add onion, garlic, and ¼ cup water, and sauté until soft, about 5–7 minutes. Add jalapeño, ginger, coriander, and cardamom, and continue to sauté for another minute.

3 Stir in potatoes, tomatoes, kidney beans, coconut milk, remaining ½ cup water, and peanut butter. Cook for 10 minutes. Add broccoli and cook until potatoes are tender, about another 10 minutes. Add more water if mixture becomes too thick.

4 Remove from heat and stir in lemon juice and cilantro. Season with salt and black pepper.

5 Serve over couscous.

6 Refrigerate in an airtight container for up to 3–4 days, or freeze (after cooling) in a freezer-safe container for up to 3 months. Thaw overnight in the refrigerator and reheat over medium heat on the stovetop or in the microwave.

Easy Spaghetti and Black Bean Meatballs

SERVES 4

Per Serving:

Calories	403
Fat	7g
Sodium	1,349mg
Carbohydrates	73g
Fiber	13g
Sugar	14g
Protein	16g

Meatballs made with leftover Black Bean Mushroom Burger ingredients makes this dish come together in a flash. It's just like the classic comfort food dish, but with the healthy addition of plant-based goodness!

1 recipe Black Bean Mushroom Burger, mixed but not baked (see recipe in this chapter)

½ (16-ounce) package whole-wheat spaghetti

1 (32-ounce) jar marinara sauce or 1 recipe Basil Marinara (see recipe in Chapter 9)

1 cup chopped fresh basil

1 Preheat oven to 350°F. Line a rimmed baking sheet with parchment paper.

2 Using Black Bean Mushroom Burger mixture, roll into 16–20 1" meatballs and place on prepared baking sheet.

3 Bake for 30–35 minutes, turning once halfway through baking time, until they start to turn golden. In the meantime, cook spaghetti according to package directions.

4 In a large saucepan over medium-high heat, heat marinara sauce. Add baked meatballs and spaghetti to the sauce, and stir to coat and heat through.

5 Serve each plate of spaghetti and meatballs with a sprinkle of fresh basil.

6 Refrigerate leftovers in an airtight container for 3–4 days.

Sheet Pan Ratatouille with Creamy Polenta

SERVES 4

Per Serving:

Calories	314
Fat	3g
Sodium	673mg
Carbohydrates	61g
Fiber	11g
Sugar	16g
Protein	15g

FINDING DELICIOUS TOMATOES

Choosing the best tomatoes at the store can be a challenge, especially in the winter. Some of the most consistently best-tasting tomatoes are the heirloom, smaller cherry or grape tomatoes, so look for those varieties when you shop. Store them on the counter and not the refrigerator for best flavor.

This easy recipe uses an entire garden full of fresh herbs and flavors. This dish is as easy as it is clean and healthy, and it works for lunch, dinner, potlucks, and holiday meals.

Ratatouille

1 large eggplant, peeled and chopped into 1" cubes

2 medium zucchini, chopped into 1" cubes

1 large yellow onion, peeled and chopped into 1" wedges

1 large green bell pepper, seeded and chopped into 1" wedges

8 ounces button mushrooms, cut in half

¼ teaspoon salt

¼ teaspoon freshly ground black pepper

4 large Roma tomatoes, cored and chopped into 1" cubes

4 medium cloves garlic, peeled and cut in half

2 tablespoons chopped fresh marjoram

½ cup chopped fresh basil

1 tablespoon chopped fresh parsley

Polenta

3 cups One-Pot Vegetable Broth (see recipe in Chapter 5)

1 cup polenta

½ cup unsweetened almond milk (or more as needed)

¼ cup nutritional yeast

¼ teaspoon salt

¼ teaspoon freshly ground black pepper

1 Preheat oven to 400°F. Line a rimmed baking sheet with parchment paper or spray with nonstick cooking spray.

2 Spread eggplant, zucchini, onion, bell pepper, and mushrooms on prepared baking pan. Season with salt and black pepper. Roast for 20 minutes.

Sheet Pan Ratatouille with Creamy Polenta—continued

3 Remove baking sheet and add tomatoes and garlic. Sprinkle marjoram, basil, and parsley over roasted vegetables and toss to coat.

4 Roast for another 20 minutes. Vegetables should be wilted and a bit soft.

5 To make polenta, in a large saucepan over medium heat, add broth and heat to a slow simmer.

6 Slowly add polenta in a stream, whisking constantly. Reduce heat to low and cook, stirring frequently, until thick and creamy, about 15 minutes. Scrape bottom to avoid burning cornmeal mixture.

7 Stir in almond milk, yeast, salt, and black pepper before removing pan from heat.

8 Serve creamy polenta topped with roasted vegetables.

9 Roasted vegetables and polenta can be refrigerated separately in airtight containers for up to 5 days.

Baked Tofu

SERVES 4

Per Serving:

Calories	133
Fat	4g
Sodium	765mg
Carbohydrates	14g
Fiber	1g
Sugar	9g
Protein	10g

CAN TOFU BE FROZEN?

Yes, it can be frozen, but it does change the consistency of the tofu. When the water inside of tofu freezes, it leaves holes throughout the tofu so that when it's defrosted, it becomes chewier. It's a popular way to use tofu for a meaty texture.

These yummy tofu bites are a great palette for other flavors. Tofu is high in protein, low in fat, and is extremely versatile.

¼ cup low-sodium tamari soy sauce

2 tablespoons maple syrup

2 tablespoons ketchup

1 tablespoon rice vinegar

1 dash hot sauce

¼ teaspoon garlic powder

¼ teaspoon freshly ground black pepper

1 (14-ounce) container firm organic tofu, drained, rinsed, and pressed for 20 minutes, then diced into 1" cubes

1 Preheat oven to 375°F. Line a baking sheet with parchment paper.
2 In a small bowl, stir together tamari, maple syrup, ketchup, vinegar, hot sauce, garlic powder, and pepper.
3 Gently stir tofu cubes into sauce. Cover and marinate at room temperature for at least 10 minutes.
4 Place tofu on prepared baking sheet in a single layer. Bake for 15 minutes. Turn tofu, then bake until it turns golden brown, about 15 minutes more.
5 Refrigerate tofu in an airtight container for 3–5 days.

Grilled Portobello Mushroom Burgers

These delicious portobello burgers are easy to make and really address a burger craving! They have a savory flavor that even a meat lover can't resist. Serve them with Thick-Cut Seasoned Fries with Chipotle Sauce (see recipe in Chapter 8) for a full pub meal experience.

SERVES 4	
Per Serving:	
Calories	297
Fat	11g
Sodium	521mg
Carbohydrates	41g
Fiber	9g
Sugar	12g
Protein	12g

Marinade

4 tablespoons low-sodium soy sauce

4 tablespoons balsamic vinegar

½ teaspoon garlic powder

½ teaspoon smoked paprika

½ teaspoon freshly ground black pepper

Burgers

4 large portobello mushrooms (about ½ pound), stems removed

4 whole-wheat buns, split

4 tablespoons Cashew-Tofu Mayonnaise (see recipe in Chapter 9)

4 tablespoons ketchup

4 medium leaves romaine lettuce, stem removed and cut in half

½ medium red onion, peeled and sliced into rings

2 medium tomatoes, cored and sliced

1 medium avocado, peeled, seeded, and sliced

1 In a small bowl, stir together soy sauce, vinegar, garlic powder, paprika, and pepper.

2 Place the portobello mushroom caps in a shallow dish, gill sides up. Pour some of the marinade into the caps, then flip and pour the rest over the top. Marinate at room temperature for 30 minutes, flipping occasionally.

3 Heat a grill or grill pan to medium-high heat. Spray with non-stick cooking spray. Grill mushrooms for about 7 minutes on each side, or until they are soft and have released most of their liquid.

4 During the last few minutes of cooking, toast the buns in a toaster.

5 For each burger, spread ½ tablespoon each of vegan mayonnaise and ketchup on both halves of bun. On bottom half, place 1 leaf lettuce, onion, tomato, avocado, a grilled mushroom cap, and the top bun.

6 Grilled portobello mushrooms can be refrigerated in an airtight container in the refrigerator for 3–5 days.

Black Bean Mushroom Burgers

SERVES 4

Per Serving:

Calories	367
Fat	4g
Sodium	1,625mg
Carbohydrates	60g
Fiber	14g
Sugar	9g
Protein	20g

THE AMAZING MUSHROOM

Mushrooms are a wonderful addition to a plant-based diet. They're considered a superfood—they're loaded with amazing health benefits and are even recognized for their medicinal qualities. Mushrooms are an excellent source of B and D vitamins and are high in fiber and protein. Plus, they're naturally cholesterol-free, fat-free, low-sodium, and low-calorie.

The umami flavors of tomatoes, mushrooms, red wine, and tamari really make this burger "beefy" tasting. It's hearty and filling and sticks together well when cooked because of the addition of moist ingredients. Top with your favorite condiments, such as lettuce, pickles, and tomatoes.

¼ cup dry-packaged sun-dried tomatoes

¼ cup water

1 cup chopped yellow onion

8 ounces button mushrooms, roughly chopped

1 medium clove garlic, peeled and minced

½ teaspoon ground cumin

½ cup red wine

⅓ cup low-sodium tamari soy sauce

3 slices whole-grain bread, lightly toasted

1 (15-ounce) can low-sodium black beans, drained and rinsed

½ teaspoon salt

¼ teaspoon freshly ground black pepper

4 whole-grain buns

1 Preheat oven to 375°F. Line a baking sheet with parchment paper.

2 In a small bowl with hot water to cover, soak sun-dried tomatoes for 10 minutes to soften, then drain. Set aside.

3 In the meantime, heat a large skillet over medium-high heat. Add onion and ¼ cup water, and sauté until soft, about 5–7 minutes. Stir in mushrooms, garlic, and cumin, and cook until mushrooms are just tender, about 4–6 minutes. Add red wine and tamari, and cook until liquid is reduced by half, about 5 minutes. Remove from heat and set aside to cool slightly.

Black Bean Mushroom Burgers—continued

4 Tear toasted bread into pieces and place in food processor. Process until broken down into crumbs. Pour crumbs into a medium bowl. Add mushroom mixture and beans to food processor along with sun-dried tomatoes; pulse until combined, leaving some chunky bits. Scoop mixture into bowl with bread crumbs; season with salt and pepper.

5 Mix ingredients together well. With dampened hands, divide mixture into four portions. Shape each portion into a thick patty. Place burgers on prepared baking sheet. Bake burgers for about 10 minutes, until brown on one side. Flip to brown on other side for another 10 minutes, watching to make sure they don't overcook.

6 Toast buns. Top with burgers and any desired condiments.

7 Refrigerate burger patties in a covered container for up to 3 days. Or wrap patties tightly in foil, place in a freezer bag, and freeze for up to 1 month. Thaw in the refrigerator and reheat in a 350°F oven for 10–15 minutes until heated thoroughly to an internal temperature of 165°F.

Pulled "Pork" Burgers

If you'd like leftovers, prepare two packages of the pulled "pork" and make extra cabbage. If you've made the Cabbage Carrot Slaw (see recipe in Chapter 8), you can use that in place of the cabbage in this recipe. Serve with a side of baked fries or barbecued beans.

1 (10-ounce) package No Evil Foods Pit Boss Pulled "Pork" BBQ

6 tablespoons Basic Barbecue Sauce (see recipe in Chapter 9), divided

2 tablespoons water

4 whole-grain buns, split

2 cups shredded cabbage

SERVES 4	
Per Serving:	
Calories	270
Fat	3g
Sodium	379mg
Carbohydrates	42g
Fiber	6g
Sugar	15g
Protein	20g

1 In a saucepan over medium heat, combine pulled "pork," 2 tablespoons Basic Barbecue Sauce, and water to thin it a little. Stir to heat through, about 5 minutes.

2 Toast buns. For each burger, top one half of a bun with 1 tablespoon Basic Barbecue Sauce and one-fourth of the pulled "pork." Add ¼ cup cabbage and the other side of the bun.

3 Refrigerate leftover "pork" and cabbage in separate airtight containers for up to 5 days. Reheat "pork" in the microwave for 2 minutes or on the stovetop in a saucepan over medium heat for 5–7 minutes.

Jackfruit Enchiladas with Green Sauce

WHAT IS GREEN JACKFRUIT?

Jackfruit, a fruit native to southeast Asia and India, is often used in vegetarian or vegan recipes as a meat replacement because it shreds much like cooked meat does. Green, or unripe, jackfruit is best used in savory dishes as the riper versions are sweeter. The fruit itself is huge, and can get as big as 40 pounds. It's most often found canned and has become easier to find in most markets because of its recent popularity.

Enchiladas can seem like a lot of work, but if you meal prep the Tomatillo Sauce, roasted butternut squash, spice mix, and Cashew Cream ahead of time, it comes together much faster. Serve with a side of black or pinto beans.

Spice Mix

½ teaspoon chili powder

1 tablespoon ground cumin

½ teaspoon onion powder

½ teaspoon garlic powder

½ teaspoon smoked paprika

1 teaspoon coconut sugar

½ teaspoon salt

Enchiladas

1 (12-ounce) package chopped butternut squash

1 medium yellow onion, peeled and chopped

3 medium cloves garlic, peeled and minced

¼ cup water

1 (20-ounce) can green jackfruit, drained and large seeds removed

Double recipe Tomatillo Sauce (see recipe in Chapter 9), divided

12 (6") corn tortillas

8 tablespoons Cashew Cream (see recipe in Chapter 9)

2 medium avocados, peeled, seeded, and chopped

⅓ cup chopped fresh cilantro

1 Preheat oven to 400°F. Line a baking sheet with parchment paper. Spray a 9" × 13" baking dish with nonstick cooking spray.

2 In a small bowl, combine spice mix ingredients. Set aside.

3 Spread squash on the baking sheet and roast until tender, about 25 minutes. Remove from oven and turn down heat to 350°F.

Jackfruit Enchiladas with Green Sauce—continued

4 To prepare the filling, heat a large nonstick skillet over medium-high heat. Add onion, garlic, and water, and sauté until soft, about 5–7 minutes. Add jackfruit and mash it with the back of a spoon to break it up into shredded pieces. Add roasted squash and sprinkle mixture with the spice mix. Add 1 cup Tomatillo Sauce. Stir to combine flavors and continue to cook, adding a little more water or sauce if mixture gets too dry.

5 Spoon remaining 1 cup Tomatillo Sauce into the bottom of prepared baking dish.

6 Wrap tortillas in a damp paper towel and microwave on high until softened, about 1 minute, or wrap in foil and heat in a preheated 300°F oven for 10–15 minutes.

7 Spoon about 2–3 tablespoons of the jackfruit-squash filling into the center of a tortilla, top with 1 tablespoon Cashew Cream, and roll it up. Place the tortilla seam-side down in the baking dish. Repeat with remaining tortillas.

8 Pour most of the enchilada sauce evenly over the tortillas so they are completely covered. Bake for 25–30 minutes, until bubbly. Remove from oven and allow to sit for 5 minutes.

9 Top each serving with avocado, cilantro, more Cashew Cream, and any leftover Tomatillo Sauce.

10 Refrigerate leftover enchiladas in an airtight container for 3–4 days.

Creamy Zucchini and Tomato Lasagna

SERVES 4

Per Serving:

Calories	318
Fat	14g
Sodium	609mg
Carbohydrates	30g
Fiber	13g
Sugar	9g
Protein	21g

TOFU RICOTTA

The tofu "ricotta" adds a substantial creaminess to this dish. Sometimes tofu can be bland, so be sure to taste the ricotta filling as you're making it to see if it needs more salt, pepper, or fresh basil. If you want to add a kick to the ricotta, try adding some lemon zest for tang or crushed red pepper flakes for spice.

Loaded with flavor, this dish has it all except traditional noodles, which are swapped out for zucchini. The tomatoes pair perfectly with zucchini, creamy pesto, and rich tofu ricotta. Use leftovers for tasty lunches throughout the week.

Lasagna

3 medium zucchini, sliced lengthwise into long 1/4" pieces

1 teaspoon salt

1 (14-ounce) package frozen artichoke hearts, thawed and coarsely chopped

4 tablespoons Oil-Free Basil Pesto (see recipe in Chapter 9) or store-bought pesto

3 large tomatoes, cored and sliced into 1/4" slices

Tofu "Ricotta"

1 (14-ounce) package firm organic tofu, drained, rinsed, and pressed for 15 minutes (see Chapter 1 for pressing instructions)

3 tablespoons nutritional yeast

1 tablespoon fresh lemon juice

2 teaspoons chopped garlic

1/2 teaspoon cayenne pepper

1/2 teaspoon salt

1/4 teaspoon freshly ground black pepper

1/2 cup chopped fresh basil

1/2 cup chopped fresh parsley

Cashew Topping

1/2 cup unsalted raw cashews

3 tablespoons nutritional yeast

1/2 teaspoon garlic powder

1/4 teaspoon salt

Creamy Zucchini and Tomato Lasagna—continued

1 Preheat oven to 400°F. Spray a baking sheet with nonstick cooking spray. Spray the bottom and sides of a 9" × 9" baking dish with nonstick cooking spray.

2 Place zucchini in a colander in the sink and salt generously. Let sit and drain for about 20 minutes.

3 Rinse zucchini to remove salt and place in a single layer on prepared baking sheet. Roast for about 10 minutes, until softened and pliable. Set aside and turn the oven down to 350°F.

4 When cooled, in a large bowl, gently toss zucchini with artichokes and Oil-Free Basil Pesto to coat.

5 To prepare the tofu ricotta, in a food processor, combine tofu, yeast, lemon juice, garlic, cayenne pepper, salt, and black pepper. Process until the mixture is creamy but still has a little texture.

6 Add basil and parsley, and pulse a few times to incorporate, but don't totally blend. The mixture should show flecks of green. Set aside.

7 To make the cashew topping, in a food processor, combine cashews, yeast, garlic powder, and salt. Process until you have fine crumbs.

8 To assemble lasagna, place about half zucchini mixture in a single layer in prepared baking dish and top with a layer of artichokes. Spoon half tofu ricotta filling evenly over zucchini and flatten with the back of spoon. Top with tomato slices. Repeat layers one more time.

9 Cover with foil and bake lasagna for about 30 minutes, until bubbly and hot. Remove from oven, remove foil, and top with cashew topping. Return to oven uncovered for another 4–5 minutes, until top is very lightly browned.

10 Refrigerate leftovers in a covered container for up to 3 days.

Lentil and Vegetable Cobbler

SERVES 6

Per Serving:

Calories	363
Fat	6g
Sodium	789mg
Carbohydrates	63g
Fiber	10g
Sugar	9g
Protein	14g

If you prefer, leave out the wine and use vegetable broth instead. Meal prep extra lentils ahead of time and use leftovers in salad or soup for your weekly meal plan.

1 medium yellow onion, peeled and chopped

2 medium cloves garlic, peeled and minced

¼ cup water

2 cups halved fresh green beans

8 ounces cremini mushrooms, sliced

3 medium sweet potatoes, peeled and chopped

3 tablespoons no-salt-added tomato paste

3 sprigs fresh thyme

½ cup red wine

½ teaspoon salt

¼ teaspoon freshly ground black pepper

¾ cup One-Pot Vegetable Broth, divided (see recipe in Chapter 5)

½ tablespoon cornstarch

1 cup frozen peas

1 cup cooked lentils

Biscuits

¾ cup unsweetened almond milk

1 tablespoon apple cider vinegar

½ cup unsalted raw cashews, soaked and drained (see Chapter 1 for soaking instructions)

1¼ cups unbleached all-purpose flour

½ cup whole-wheat pastry flour

1 tablespoon baking powder

1 teaspoon baking soda

¼ teaspoon salt

⅓ cup chopped mixed fresh herbs (chives or dill)

Lentil and Vegetable Cobbler—continued

1. Heat a large soup pot over medium-high heat. Add onion, garlic, and water, and sauté until soft, about 5–7 minutes.
2. Add green beans, mushrooms, sweet potatoes, tomato paste, thyme, wine, salt, and pepper. Stir in ½ cup broth and combine.
3. In a measuring cup, mix remaining ¼ cup of broth with cornstarch with a fork; add to the pot. Stir and cook until vegetables are just tender and sauce is thickened, 8–10 minutes. Add more broth if it becomes too thick.
4. Add peas and lentils during the last 5 minutes of cooking.
5. Transfer to a 2-quart baking dish and set aside.
6. Preheat oven to 400°F.
7. While the oven is preheating, make the biscuits. In a blender, combine almond milk, vinegar, and cashews. Blend on high until you have a thick cashew cream.
8. In a large bowl, combine all-purpose flour, pastry flour, baking powder, salt, and herbs.
9. Add cashew cream to flour mixture and stir until just mixed. The batter will be thick.
10. Drop ¼ cup of the batter for each biscuit onto the top of the lentil mixture, spacing them evenly. You should have about 10 biscuits. Bake for 20–25 minutes, until the biscuits are done and the vegetables are hot. Alternatively, place biscuits on a nonstick baking sheet and bake alongside the casserole. Allow to rest about 10 minutes before serving.
11. Refrigerate leftovers in an airtight container for 3–4 days.

Vegetable Fajitas with Mexican Tofu

SOY AS A PROTEIN SOURCE

Soy is a great source of plant-based protein. It balances hormones, contains all eight essential amino acids, offers nutrients vital to maintaining skin health, and lowers cholesterol. Because tofu is also low in fat, it makes a great low-fat protein source. Allergic to soy? Some recipes can use soaked cashews blended with water instead, which also are rich in protein.

Make-ahead tofu bites are great to have on hand for an addition to your weekday lunch or dinner.

Tofu

1 (14-ounce) container firm organic tofu, drained, rinsed, and pressed for 15 minutes, then cut into 2" × ½" strips (see Chapter 1 for pressing instructions)

Marinade

3 tablespoons fresh lime juice

1 teaspoon chili powder

½ teaspoon ground cumin

½ teaspoon onion powder

¼ teaspoon garlic powder

½ teaspoon salt

Vegetables

¼ cup water

1 red bell pepper, seeded and cut into thin strips

1 green bell pepper, seeded and cut into thin strips

1 medium yellow onion, peeled and thinly sliced

4 (10") whole-grain flour tortillas

Toppings

¼ cup chopped fresh cilantro

½ medium avocado, peeled, seeded, and chopped

¼ cup salsa

¼ cup Plant-Based Sour Cream (see recipe in Chapter 9)

1 medium lime, sliced into wedges

Vegetable Fajitas with Mexican Tofu—continued

1 Place tofu in a shallow dish.

2 In a small bowl, mix lime juice, chili powder, cumin, onion powder, garlic powder, and salt. Pour half of marinade over tofu.
Toss gently to coat tofu, cover, and refrigerate for 15 minutes or
overnight.

3 Heat a large nonstick skillet over medium-high heat. Drain tofu
and add to skillet. Cook, stirring occasionally, until browned,
about 10 minutes. Remove from skillet and set aside.

4 Return skillet to medium-high heat. Add ¼ cup water and stir
to loosen any bits stuck to the bottom of the skillet. Then add
red bell pepper, green bell pepper, and onion, and stir-fry until
crisp-tender, about 7–10 minutes. Return tofu to skillet and heat
through, about 5 minutes. Stir carefully so tofu doesn't break
apart.

5 Wrap tortillas in a damp paper towel and microwave on high until
softened, about 1 minute, or wrap in foil and heat in a preheated
300°F oven for 10–15 minutes.

6 Divide tofu mixture evenly among tortillas. Serve mixture in
tortillas topped with cilantro, avocado, salsa, Plant-Based Sour
Cream, and lime wedges.

7 Refrigerate tofu strips in an airtight container until ready to use,
up to 1 week.

Hawaiian Stuffed Peppers

SERVES 4

Per Serving:

Calories	492
Fat	10g
Sodium	2,354mg
Carbohydrates	89g
Fiber	10g
Sugar	32g
Protein	16g

Make a double batch of Pineapple Fried Rice without the Baked Tofu (see recipe in this chapter) and use the leftovers for these delicious stuffed peppers with teriyaki sauce. It's a unique spin on a traditional stuffed pepper recipe, but still packs in all the great nutrition. Keep in mind that the nutritional stats include the entire amount of sauce—you might find that less sauce still works great for you, especially if you're trying to watch your salt intake.

Peppers

4 medium bell peppers, stemmed, and then cut in half top to bottom

1 recipe Pineapple Fried Rice, prepared without tofu or sauce (see recipe in this chapter)

½ cup chopped fresh cilantro

2 teaspoons sesame seeds

Teriyaki Sauce

1 cup low-sodium soy sauce

¼ cup maple syrup

2 tablespoons rice vinegar

2 tablespoons grated fresh ginger

2 medium cloves garlic, peeled and crushed

¼ cup water

1 tablespoon cornstarch

1. Preheat oven to 400°F. Spray a 9" × 13" baking dish with nonstick cooking spray.
2. In a large pot over medium-high heat, add enough water to cover peppers. Heat water to boiling, add peppers, and cook about 2 minutes; drain.
3. Place pepper halves in prepared baking dish and scoop about ½ cup Pineapple Fried Rice into each half.
4. To make the teriyaki sauce, in a small saucepan over medium-high heat, combine soy sauce, maple syrup, vinegar, ginger, and garlic; whisk well. In a small bowl, mix water and cornstarch, then slowly add to saucepan. Whisk until sauce has thickened, about 30 seconds. Remove from heat and drizzle stuffed peppers with half of the teriyaki sauce.
5. Cover peppers with foil and bake 30 minutes.
6. Remove foil and serve 2 pepper halves per person. Top with the cilantro and sesame seeds, and serve the remaining sauce on the side.

CHAPTER 8

Side Dishes

Pan-Seared Artichoke Hearts with Spinach and Sun-Dried Tomatoes

SERVES 3

Per Serving:	
Calories	309
Fat	3g
Sodium	224mg
Carbohydrates	61g
Fiber	16g
Sugar	10g
Protein	12g

This side dish is versatile and can be served alongside sautéed tempeh, roasted potatoes, or as a topping for crackers as an appetizer. Add your favorite plant protein to make it even more filling!

½ cup One-Pot Vegetable Broth (see recipe in Chapter 5), divided

1 (12-ounce) bag frozen artichoke hearts, thawed, or 1 (12-ounce) can artichoke hearts packed in water, drained

2 large shallots, peeled and sliced

1 cup chopped dry-packaged sun-dried tomatoes, softened in water to cover for about 10 minutes

4 cups baby spinach

½ cup low-sodium canned or homemade chickpeas

2 cups brown rice, cooked according to package directions

1 Heat a medium nonstick skillet over medium-high heat. Add ¼ cup broth and artichokes. Let them cook for a minute until the broth evaporates.

2 Add shallots and stir until artichokes start to sear and lightly brown, about 5 minutes.

3 Add remaining ¼ cup broth, sun-dried tomatoes, spinach, and chickpeas. Turn frequently until spinach has wilted, about 2 minutes, adding more broth if it comes too dry.

4 Serve over brown rice.

5 For meal prep, refrigerate each portion in separate airtight containers for up to 5 days.

Barbecue Baked Beans

MAKES 7½ CUPS

Per Serving (¾ cup):

Calories	262
Fat	1g
Sodium	743mg
Carbohydrates	52g
Fiber	11g
Sugar	17g
Protein	13g

These Barbecue Baked Beans are sweetened with crushed pineapple, a healthier alternative to added sugar.

1 large red onion, peeled and diced

¾ cup water, divided

2 (15-ounce) cans low-sodium kidney beans, drained and rinsed

2 (15-ounce) cans vegetarian barbecue beans, undrained

1 (15-ounce) package frozen low-sodium lima beans

1 (6-ounce) can no-salt-added tomato paste

1 cup canned unsweetened crushed pineapple in its own juice

½ cup apple cider vinegar

¼ cup low-sodium tamari soy sauce

3 medium Medjool dates, pitted and cut into quarters

½ teaspoon liquid smoke

1 Preheat oven to 350°F. Spray a 9" × 13" baking pan with nonstick cooking spray.

2 Heat a medium nonstick skillet over medium heat. Add onion and ¼ cup water, and sauté until soft, about 5–7 minutes.

3 Pour all beans into a large bowl.

4 In a small saucepan over medium heat, whisk remaining ingredients. Simmer for about 5–7 minutes to soften dates. Remove from heat and cool a few minutes.

5 Transfer tomato paste mixture to a blender and blend until smooth (be careful if it's too hot, as it can splatter). Add a little water if it's too thick.

6 Add onion to the bowl with beans along with blended barbecue sauce, and stir to combine well.

7 Pour into prepared baking pan and cover with foil. Bake for 45–50 minutes, stirring every 20 minutes or so. Remove foil for the last 20 minutes. The beans are done when they are bubbly and heated through.

8 Refrigerate leftovers in an airtight container for up to 3–5 days or freeze (after cooling) in a freezer-safe container for up to 3 months. Thaw overnight in the refrigerator and reheat over medium heat on the stovetop or in the microwave.

Squash, Brussels Sprouts, and Apple Stuffing

This beautiful dish is especially easy to make if you use 12 ounces of prechopped butternut squash from your grocery store.

1 pound butternut squash, peeled, seeded, and cubed

1 pound Brussels sprouts, trimmed and halved

1 medium Honeycrisp apple, cored and cut into ½" dice

½ teaspoon salt, divided

¼ teaspoon freshly ground black pepper, divided

2¼ cups One-Pot Vegetable Broth (see recipe in Chapter 5), divided

1 cup sliced yellow onion

1 cup diced celery

10 slices whole-grain bread, cubed

⅓ cup dried cranberries

⅓ cup shelled raw walnuts

2 teaspoons chopped fresh rosemary

1 teaspoon chopped fresh thyme

1 teaspoon chopped fresh sage

SERVES 6

Per Serving:

Calories	288
Fat	7g
Sodium	448mg
Carbohydrates	51g
Fiber	12g
Sugar	18g
Protein	11g

1. Preheat oven to 400°F. Line a 9" × 13" baking sheet with parchment paper.
2. Place squash, Brussels sprouts, and apple on prepared baking sheet and toss with ¼ teaspoon salt and ⅛ teaspoon pepper. Roast vegetables about 25–30 minutes, until tender. Remove from oven and set aside. Reduce oven heat to 350°F.
3. In a large nonstick skillet over medium-high heat, add onion, celery, and ¼ cup broth. Sauté until liquid has evaporated, about 5–8 minutes. Add bread cubes and cook until golden brown, about 10 minutes. Add remaining salt and pepper.
4. In a large bowl, add celery and bread mixture along with roasted vegetables, remaining broth, and rest of ingredients. Stir until toasted bread has absorbed broth.
5. Transfer to a baking dish, cover with foil, and bake for 30 minutes. Uncover and bake another 10–15 minutes until top is golden.
6. Refrigerate leftovers in an airtight container for up to 5 days. Reheat in a 350°F oven in a glass baking dish until the center reaches 165°F.
7. Freeze (after cooling) in a freezer-safe container for up to 3 months. Thaw overnight in the refrigerator and reheat over medium heat on the stovetop or in the microwave.

STORING AND CUTTING SQUASH

Whole squash lasts up to 4 weeks or more in a cool, dry location. Some squashes, especially butternut squash, are difficult to cut. To make this easier, pierce squash with a sharp knife in a few places, then microwave on high for 3–5 minutes to soften the skin and make it easier to cut.

Cauliflower–Sweet Potato Mash

SERVES 8

Per Serving:

Calories	49
Fat	0g
Sodium	197mg
Carbohydrates	10g
Fiber	2g
Sugar	3g
Protein	2g

MORE ABOUT SWEET POTATOES

Did you know that most yams we find in the market are actually a variety of sweet potatoes? True yams, unrelated to sweet potatoes, are native to Africa and Asia and are drier and starchier. You'll find yellow, orange (called yams in the United States), and even purple sweet potatoes, and any of these works well in this recipe. They're an excellent source of vitamin A, fiber, vitamin C, manganese, copper, pantothenic acid, and vitamin B$_6$.

Simple yet elegant, this delightful combination of cauliflower and sweet potato is a great way to eat more vegetables, and it's a crowd-pleaser at the holidays or for a potluck.

1 medium head cauliflower, core removed, broken into florets

2 large sweet potatoes, peeled and chopped into about 1" pieces

½ cup unsweetened almond milk

1 teaspoon garlic powder

½ teaspoon salt

¼ teaspoon freshly ground black pepper

1 Fill a large saucepan with about 1"–2" water and a steamer basket (make sure the water isn't touching the bottom of the basket) and set over medium-high heat. When water comes to a boil, add cauliflower and sweet potato to steamer basket. Cover and let vegetables steam until soft, about 15 minutes. Alternately, roast on a baking sheet lined with parchment paper in a 400°F oven for 20–30 minutes.

2 In a food processor, add steamed vegetables and process a minute to break up the pieces. (Or mash by hand.) Add almond milk, garlic powder, salt, and pepper, and continue to process until smooth.

3 Refrigerate leftovers in an airtight container for 3–4 days.

Vegan Cornbread

This applesauce-sweetened Vegan Cornbread is every bit as tasty as the nonvegan version and perfect served alongside a comforting chili on a cold day. If you'd like it a little sweeter, add ¼ cup coconut sugar with the dry ingredients. Enjoy with a touch of vegan honey.

2 tablespoons ground flaxseeds

6 tablespoons water

1 cup unbleached all-purpose flour

1 cup cornmeal

4 teaspoons baking powder

½ teaspoon salt

1 cup unsweetened soy milk

½ cup unsweetened applesauce

1 Preheat oven to 400°F. Spray an 8" × 8" baking dish with nonstick cooking spray or line with parchment paper.

2 In a small bowl, mix flaxseeds and water. Let sit for a few minutes while you prepare dry ingredients.

3 In a large bowl, combine flour, cornmeal, baking powder, and salt.

4 Add soy milk, applesauce, and flaxseed mixture. Stir until just moistened.

5 Pour into prepared baking dish. Bake for about 20–25 minutes, or until cornbread starts to brown and bounces back when touched on top. Be careful not to overcook, as it can become dry.

6 Refrigerate leftovers in an airtight container for up to 1 week.

SERVES 9

Per Serving:

Calories	137
Fat	1g
Sodium	302mg
Carbohydrates	27g
Fiber	2g
Sugar	2g
Protein	4g

IS HONEY VEGAN?

A vegan diet excludes honey, as it is produced by bees, making it an animal byproduct. This ethical choice is reflective of the potential harm caused to bees to harvest their honey. Some plant-based alternatives to honey include maple syrup, vegan honey, agave nectar, and date paste.

Macaroni Salad

This plant-based salad uses silken tofu to make a dairy-free, oil-free, and sugar-free homemade dressing. Tofu adds protein and offers antioxidants. Add a little sweet pickle juice to give it the tangy flavor we all love in a macaroni salad, or use dill pickles and a little of their juice, if you prefer.

Dressing

8 ounces firm silken tofu

¼ cup white wine vinegar

3 medium Medjool dates, pitted

1 tablespoon yellow mustard

1 tablespoon sweet pickle juice

1 tablespoon nutritional yeast

¼ teaspoon sriracha

¼ teaspoon garlic powder

½ teaspoon salt

¼ teaspoon freshly ground black pepper

Pasta

4½ cups cooked and cooled elbow macaroni

½ cup chopped broccoli florets

⅓ cup grated carrot

½ cup chopped celery

⅓ cup chopped green onions

½ cup sweet chopped pickles

⅓ cup chopped red bell pepper

1　In a blender, blend together all dressing ingredients until smooth.

2　In a large bowl, combine cooked macaroni with dressing. Note: Pasta will be a little sticky from the starch, but once the dressing coats the noodles, they'll be easier to stir.

3　Add broccoli, carrot, celery, green onions, pickles, and bell pepper. Stir well.

4　For best flavor, refrigerate for at least 30 minutes, or until chilled, before serving.

5　Refrigerate leftovers in an airtight container for up to 5 days.

Mashed Cauliflower

Steaming cauliflower is a fantastic way to retain all the beneficial nutrients the vegetable offers. Plus, it doesn't get much easier for meal prep than tossing ingredients in a food processor and blending! Try adding a few cloves of roasted garlic for a different variation.

1 medium head cauliflower, cored and cut into pieces

2 heaping tablespoons nutritional yeast

⅓ cup unsweetened almond milk

½ teaspoon salt

¼ teaspoon freshly ground black pepper

1 recipe Easy Gravy (see recipe in Chapter 9)

1 Fill a medium saucepan with about 1" water and a steamer basket (make sure the water isn't touching the bottom of the basket) and set over medium-high heat. When water comes to a boil, add cauliflower to steamer basket. Cover and let steam until tender, about 15 minutes.

2 In a food processor, combine cauliflower, yeast, almond milk, salt, and pepper. Process until smooth, adding more milk as needed to thin.

3 Serve gravy over mashed cauliflower.

4 Refrigerate mashed cauliflower and gravy separately in covered containers for up to 3 days.

SERVES 4

Per Serving:

Calories	92
Fat	1g
Sodium	667mg
Carbohydrates	16g
Fiber	7g
Sugar	4g
Protein	7g

PUMP UP THE FLAVOR OF YOUR DISHES

There are lots of unique ways to infuse your plant-based dishes with even more flavor. Nutritional yeast and low-sodium tamari's salty, umami flavor are two satisfying options for savory dishes. Or try miso paste, which has a healthy dose of digestive system–enhancing probiotics. Also, lemon and the liberal use of herbs and spices help add more flavor when eating a plant-based diet.

Thick-Cut Seasoned Fries with Chipotle Sauce

With thick-cut fries, you have even more potato to love, and they taste great with this dairy-free version of Chipotle Dipping Sauce made with cashews. Use russet potatoes or even sweet potatoes for a satisfying and healthy treat.

Potatoes

3 large russet potatoes, peeled and sliced into thin wedges

1 recipe Chipotle Dipping Sauce (see recipe in Chapter 9)

Seasoning Mix

1 tablespoon cornstarch

½ teaspoon salt

2 teaspoons Italian seasoning

2 teaspoons garlic powder

2 teaspoons sweet paprika

1 Preheat oven to 425°F. Line a rimmed baking sheet with parchment paper.

2 Place potato wedges into a large bowl.

3 In a small bowl, stir together all Seasoning Mix ingredients until well blended. Dust the potatoes, turning them over to make sure they're all well coated.

4 Spread seasoned wedges on prepared baking sheet, making sure there's space between each one so they will crisp.

5 Bake for 25 minutes, flipping halfway through baking time. Keep an eye on them so they don't burn. Remove and serve with Chipotle Dipping Sauce.

6 Store leftover potatoes and dipping sauce in separate airtight containers for up to 3 days. To reheat fries, place on a baking sheet in a 300°F oven for 10 minutes.

SERVES 4

Per Serving:

Calories	325
Fat	7g
Sodium	454mg
Carbohydrates	59g
Fiber	5g
Sugar	3g
Protein	9g

THE MIGHTY POTATO

Potatoes are the leading vegetable crop in the United States. More than 50 percent of potato sales go to processing plants that make French fries, chips, and other products. Some studies estimate that the average American consumes around 30 pounds of French fries per year!

Sautéed Greens

SERVES 2

Per Serving:

Calories	97
Fat	0g
Sodium	932mg
Carbohydrates	19g
Fiber	9g
Sugar	5g
Protein	9g

EAT YOUR GREENS!

Leafy greens are an excellent tool for weight loss, since they can be consumed in virtually unlimited quantities. Consuming greens can also help protect your blood vessels and may reduce the risk of diabetes. They're the most nutrient-dense of all foods: Leafy greens and green vegetables are rich in folate and calcium, and contain small amounts of omega-3 fatty acids.

These Sautéed Greens are a breeze to make. It may seem like a lot of leaves for one pan, but the leaves will cook down quickly. Start with a handful at a time and add more as they begin to wilt. It's just that easy to have a super-nutritious side dish with a wonderful depth of flavor.

2 medium bunches Swiss chard, stems removed (reserve stems)

3 medium cloves garlic, peeled and chopped

¼ cup water

2 teaspoons low-sodium tamari soy sauce

1 Roughly chop Swiss chard leaves and stems separately.

2 In a large nonstick skillet over medium heat, add garlic and water, and sauté for 1 minute. Add Swiss chard stems and continue to sauté for 3 minutes.

3 Add Swiss chard leaves and tamari, and continue to sauté until softened, another 5 minutes, turning frequently. Add more water if necessary.

4 Refrigerate in an airtight container for up to 3 days.

Sweet Potatoes with Swiss Chard

Serve these Sweet Potatoes with Swiss Chard as a cold salad in the summer or as a warm, comforting lunch or side dish in the colder months. It's a powerful combination of nutritious food coated in a tangy mustard dressing.

Vegetables

1 medium red onion, peeled and chopped

½ cup water, divided

2 medium cloves garlic, peeled and diced

2 medium sweet potatoes, peeled and sliced into ¼" wedges or coins

1 medium bunch Swiss chard, tough stems removed, then chopped

½ cup toasted pecans

Dressing

1 tablespoon grainy Dijon mustard

2 tablespoons red wine vinegar

1 teaspoon maple syrup

½ teaspoon salt

¼ teaspoon freshly ground black pepper

1. Heat a large nonstick skillet over medium heat. Add onion and ¼ cup water, and sauté for 5 minutes. Add garlic and sauté for 1 more minute.
2. Add sweet potatoes and continue to sauté until almost soft, about 5 minutes.
3. Add Swiss chard with remaining ¼ cup water and cover skillet. Steam until tender, about 5 minutes.
4. Meanwhile, to make dressing, in a small bowl, whisk all dressing ingredients to combine.
5. When chard and sweet potatoes are tender, transfer them to a bowl and pour dressing over. Stir to combine.
6. Serve warm or cold topped with pecans.
7. Refrigerate in an airtight container for up to 3 days.

SERVES 4

Per Serving:

Calories	193
Fat	10g
Sodium	603mg
Carbohydrates	23g
Fiber	6g
Sugar	7g
Protein	5g

SWISS CHARD IS A POWERHOUSE OF NUTRITION

Swiss chard is a fantastic source of potassium, magnesium, and calcium. It helps reduce high blood pressure and lower cholesterol, and it's considered one of the best vegetables for diabetics. In addition to hot dishes and salad, you can also add it to smoothies.

Creamed Corn

SERVES 6

Per Serving:

Calories	93
Fat	1g
Sodium	220mg
Carbohydrates	20g
Fiber	2g
Sugar	2g
Protein	4g

This rich and creamy recipe replaces the dairy, oil, and fat with plant-based goodness. You'll be surprised how quickly it becomes a favorite addition to your meal plan. If you want your corn a little sweeter, add a couple of teaspoons of maple syrup.

1 small yellow onion, peeled and diced

¼ cup water

2 teaspoons minced garlic

1 (16-ounce) bag frozen corn kernels, thawed

4 tablespoons nutritional yeast

½ cup plus 2 tablespoons unsweetened almond milk

1½ tablespoons unbleached all-purpose flour

1 tablespoon chopped fresh thyme

½ teaspoon salt

⅛ teaspoon freshly ground black pepper

1 Heat a medium nonstick skillet over medium-high heat. Add onion and water, and sauté until soft, about 5–7 minutes. Add a little more water if it starts to dry out. Add garlic, corn, and yeast.

2 In a separate small bowl, whisk together almond milk and flour, and add to skillet. Stir to combine and let cook until thickened and the corn is cooked, about 7–9 minutes. Add more almond milk if it seems too thick.

3 Sprinkle with thyme, salt, and pepper, and stir.

4 Refrigerate leftovers in a sealed container for 3–4 days. To reheat, place in a saucepan with a couple of tablespoons almond milk and heat, stirring, over medium-low heat for about 5 minutes.

Balsamic-Roasted Vegetables

You can use different vegetables for this dish depending on the season or what you have in the refrigerator. For example, try root vegetables like sweet potato in the winter, asparagus and broccoli in the spring, red pepper or zucchini in the summer, or squash and onion in the fall. For meal prep, you can eat these for lunch over grains or a bed of lettuce.

Balsamic Marinade

3 tablespoons balsamic vinegar

1 tablespoon maple syrup

2 tablespoons low-sodium soy sauce

½ tablespoon Dijon mustard

½ teaspoon dried thyme

½ teaspoon salt

¼ teaspoon freshly ground black pepper

Vegetables

2 large carrots, peeled and cut into 1" pieces

½ medium head broccoli, trimmed and cut into 1" pieces

½ medium head cauliflower, cut into 1" pieces

1 large red onion, peeled and cut into 1" pieces

1 Preheat oven to 400°F. Line two rimmed baking sheets with parchment paper.

2 In a small bowl, combine vinegar, maple syrup, soy sauce, mustard, thyme, salt, and pepper.

3 Divide the chopped vegetables evenly among the two baking sheets. Pour marinade over the vegetables and mix. Bake for about 25 minutes, until the vegetables are crisp-tender, stirring halfway through baking.

4 Refrigerate leftovers in an airtight container for up to 3 days.

SERVES 4	
Per Serving:	
Calories	94
Fat	1g
Sodium	670mg
Carbohydrates	19g
Fiber	5g
Sugar	9g
Protein	5g

WHY FIBER IS GOOD FOR YOU

Fewer than 3 percent of Americans get the recommended daily intake of fiber, which is 31.5 grams for men and 25 grams for women. Fiber benefits your digestion, reduces chronic disease, and helps control weight, so be sure you're getting enough! Eating a plant-based diet will help.

Oil-Free Potato Salad

SERVES 6

Per Serving:

Calories	196
Fat	1g
Sodium	492mg
Carbohydrates	40g
Fiber	6g
Sugar	4g
Protein	6g

ADD MORE PROTEIN TO YOUR RECIPES

As you may have discovered, beans are a great source of fiber and protein. And they're a great way to add protein to a dish that doesn't have much. For example, in this Oil-Free Potato Salad, including a can of rinsed chickpeas adds about 20 grams of protein! Other places to add protein are in fresh green salads or in a stew or soup.

Fresh herbs and a delicious tangy dressing make this salad sing without added oil or mayonnaise. You can use different fresh herbs and dill pickles instead of sweet ones if you prefer. You may also want to add a little pickle juice.

Salad

2 pounds small red potatoes, peeled and sliced into coins

1 cup diced celery

5 medium whole sweet pickles, diced

¼ cup sliced green onions

½ cup sliced red onions

2 tablespoons chopped fresh dill

2 tablespoons chopped fresh parsley

Dressing

1 (15-ounce) can low-sodium cannellini beans, drained

⅓ cup unsweetened almond milk

⅓ cup red wine vinegar

2 tablespoons grainy mustard

½ teaspoon garlic powder

½ teaspoon salt

¼ teaspoon freshly ground black pepper

1 Fill a large pot with about 1" water and a steamer basket (make sure the water isn't touching the bottom of the basket) and set over medium-high heat. When water comes to a boil, add potatoes to basket. Cover and let potatoes steam until tender, about 20 minutes.

2 Transfer potatoes to a large bowl and allow to cool. Add remaining salad ingredients.

3 In a blender, combine all dressing ingredients and blend until smooth. Adjust seasonings to your taste. Pour over salad and stir carefully, so as not to break up the potatoes. Chill before serving.

4 Refrigerate in an airtight container for up to 4 days.

Broccoli–Red Pepper Stir-Fry

SERVES 4

Per Serving:

Calories	313
Fat	17g
Sodium	1,109mg
Carbohydrates	32g
Fiber	8g
Sugar	17g
Protein	15g

A stir-fry recipe is a great addition to a meal prep schedule. It can be divided into individual servings and kept in the refrigerator all week. Serve it over brown rice to add a grain if you like. To lower the sodium amount, simply use only half a recipe of Peanut Dipping Sauce.

1 medium head broccoli, trimmed and cut into 1" pieces
¼ cup water
2 medium red bell peppers, seeded and cut into 1" pieces
1 recipe Peanut Dipping Sauce (see recipe in Chapter 9)

1 Heat a large nonstick skillet or wok over medium-high heat. Add broccoli and water, and stir-fry for 1 minute. Add peppers and steam until vegetables just start to become soft, about 5 minutes.

2 Add Peanut Dipping Sauce and stir to combine. Continue cooking until broccoli is crisp-tender, another 2 minutes.

3 Refrigerate leftovers in an airtight container for up to 4 days, or freeze (after cooling) in a freezer-safe container for up to 3 months. Reheat in a skillet on medium heat until heated through or in the microwave.

Cabbage Carrot Slaw

Cabbage slaw is a dish that can be easily thrown together and made with a variety of crunchy vegetables, not just the ones listed here. Feel free to add chopped broccoli, radishes, or even cauliflower. In addition, if you prefer a slaw that's not creamy, you can leave out the white beans and proceed with the recipe.

Salad

3 cups sliced green cabbage

3 cups sliced red cabbage

2 cups chopped kale

1 cup grated carrots

1 cup grated beets

½ cup chopped fresh cilantro

¼ cup unsalted shelled pumpkin seeds

Dressing

3 tablespoons Cashew-Tofu Mayonnaise (see recipe in Chapter 9)

3 tablespoons apple cider vinegar

1 tablespoon maple syrup

¼ teaspoon salt

¼ teaspoon freshly ground black pepper

1 In a large bowl, combine all salad ingredients. In a separate small bowl, whisk together all dressing ingredients.

2 Toss salad with dressing.

3 Refrigerate leftovers in an airtight container for 2–3 days.

SERVES 6	
Per Serving:	
Calories	95
Fat	3g
Sodium	194mg
Carbohydrates	14g
Fiber	4g
Sugar	7g
Protein	4g

Mushroom-Farro Pilaf

SERVES 4

Per Serving:

Calories	302
Fat	5g
Sodium	419mg
Carbohydrates	52g
Fiber	12g
Sugar	9g
Protein	13g

WHAT ABOUT INTESTINAL DISTRESS?

If you're new to eating a plant-based diet, you may discover that you experience more gas than usual. This is common and most likely temporary. It's caused by the increase in fiber in your diet. Fiber promotes a healthy gut, but your body may feel overwhelmed by the additional fiber at first, so start more slowly with raw vegetables and drink plenty of water.

Farro is a high-fiber and high-protein whole grain that becomes a bit chewy when cooked. It comes in pearled (the most common) and more intact grain varieties, so be sure to check your package for cooking times. Make plenty on your meal prep day, and use leftovers tossed in a salad or divide into containers with vegetables and a sauce for use throughout the week.

¾ cup dry-packaged sun-dried tomatoes

2½ cups One-Pot Vegetable Broth (see recipe in Chapter 5), divided

1 medium yellow onion, peeled and chopped

3 medium cloves garlic, peeled and minced

4 ounces sliced button mushrooms

1 cup uncooked farro

1 cup frozen green peas

⅓ cup slivered almonds

1 tablespoon finely chopped fresh thyme

½ teaspoon salt

¼ teaspoon freshly ground black pepper

½ cup chopped fresh flat-leaf parsley

1 In a small bowl with hot water to cover, soak sun-dried tomatoes for 10 minutes to soften, then drain and slice. Set aside.

2 Heat a large nonstick skillet over medium heat. Add ¼ cup broth and onion, and sauté until soft, about 5–7 minutes. Add garlic, then cook 5 minutes more.

3 Add mushrooms and sauté 5 minutes, adding a little extra broth or water if the pan gets too dry, until mostly cooked through.

4 Add farro and remaining 2¼ cups broth, and bring to a boil. Reduce heat to low and cover. Simmer until liquid is absorbed, about 35–40 minutes. Note: Times may vary depending on the type of farro you have, so check the directions on the package.

5 Add the peas during the last few minutes of cooking along with sun-dried tomatoes, almonds, thyme, salt, and pepper. Stir to combine.

6 Serve garnished with parsley.

7 Refrigerate leftover cooked farro in an airtight container for up to 3 days.

Roasted Beets

Roasted Beets are tasty in many types of recipes, such as Roasted Beet and Mushroom Tacos (see recipe in Chapter 7), Beet Hummus (see recipe in Chapter 3), or beet soup. They're also great tossed on top of salads or even in smoothies for a burst of flavor and healthy nutrition. Once you've roasted them here, simply chop or slice as needed for your recipe.

3 large beets, ends trimmed

3 tablespoons water

1 Preheat oven to 400°F.
2 Place beets and water in a medium-sized baking dish and cover with foil. Roast beets for 50–60 minutes, until soft when poked with a knife. Let beets cool about 5–10 minutes. Once beets are cool enough to handle, peel using the backside of a paring knife. This can be a messy job, so use gloves.
3 Once roasted, beets can be refrigerated whole or sliced and kept in an airtight container for up to 1 week.

SERVES 6

Per Serving:

Calories	42
Fat	0g
Sodium	74mg
Carbohydrates	10g
Fiber	2g
Sugar	8g
Protein	2g

Spiced Baked Sweet Potato Fries

SERVES 4

Per Serving:

Calories	164
Fat	7g
Sodium	476mg
Carbohydrates	22g
Fiber	3g
Sugar	5g
Protein	4g

Fries are such a treat! I don't know anyone who can resist them, so finding a way to make them healthier is a noble goal. Because sweet potatoes can be tricky to make crisp, they are kept thin in this recipe. The Chipotle Dipping Sauce adds a burst of creamy flavor.

Seasonings

½ tablespoon sweet paprika

1 teaspoon brown sugar

½ teaspoon salt

¼ teaspoon freshly ground black pepper

¼ teaspoon onion powder

¼ teaspoon garlic powder

⅛ teaspoon cayenne pepper

Potatoes

1 tablespoon cornstarch

2 large sweet potatoes, peeled and cut into ¼" wedges

1 recipe Chipotle Dipping Sauce (see recipe in Chapter 9)

1 Preheat oven to 425°F. Line 2 baking sheets with parchment paper.

2 In a small bowl, stir to combine all Seasonings ingredients.

3 Fill a large saucepan with water and bring to a boil over high heat. Prepare a large bowl of ice water. Drop cut potatoes into boiling water and boil for 2 minutes. Remove and transfer immediately into ice water. Leave in ice water for several minutes, up to 20 minutes for crispier fries.

4 Blot fries dry. In a large sealable plastic bag or in a large bowl, add cornstarch and then potatoes. Shake or stir to completely dust potatoes with cornstarch, making sure all potatoes are covered.

5 Place sweet potatoes on baking sheets and sprinkle with Seasonings mixture, making sure they're evenly coated. Spread out evenly so there's space between each one. This will help them crisp.

6 Bake for 30 minutes, flipping halfway through baking time. Keep an eye on them so they don't burn.

7 Refrigerate fries in an airtight container for up to 3 days, or freeze in a freezer-safe container or bag for 3–5 months. To reheat, bake in a 400°F oven for 20 minutes.

Sweet Potato–Zucchini Gratin

This dish is easy to prep and quick to make. Save any leftover cheese sauce for Easy Italian Pita Pizzas (see recipe in Chapter 6).

1 large sweet potato, peeled, cut in half lengthwise, and sliced

1 large or 3 small zucchini, trimmed, cut in half lengthwise, and sliced

½ teaspoon salt

¼ teaspoon freshly ground black pepper

1 recipe Blender "Cheese" Sauce (see recipe in Chapter 9)

1 Preheat oven to 375°F. In an 8" × 8" baking dish, layer half of the sweet potato and zucchini. Season with ¼ teaspoon salt and ⅛ teaspoon pepper. Pour over half of the Blender "Cheese" Sauce. Repeat layers for remaining vegetables, seasonings, and sauce.

2 Cover with foil and bake for 30 minutes or until the potatoes are soft.

3 Refrigerate leftovers in an airtight container for 3–4 days. Save leftover Blender "Cheese" Sauce for another recipe.

SERVES 6	
Per Serving:	
Calories	186
Fat	7g
Sodium	530mg
Carbohydrates	24g
Fiber	5g
Sugar	6g
Protein	7g

Loaded Tahini-Spiced Potato Skins

Piled high with fluffy tahini mashed potatoes and deliciously spiced chickpeas, this recipe is a crowd-pleaser and perfect for lunch or dinner.

Potatoes

4 medium russet potatoes

1 (15-ounce) can low-sodium chickpeas, drained and rinsed

½ medium head of broccoli, trimmed and cut into bite-sized pieces

Double recipe Quick Tahini Sauce (see recipe in Chapter 9)

¼ teaspoon salt

¼ teaspoon freshly ground black pepper

¼ cup chopped fresh cilantro

Spice Blend

½ teaspoon cardamom

1 teaspoon coriander

1 teaspoon ground cumin

1 teaspoon garlic powder

1 teaspoon onion powder

½ teaspoon cinnamon

½ teaspoon salt

SERVES 4

Per Serving:

Calories	586
Fat	26g
Sodium	926mg
Carbohydrates	76g
Fiber	12g
Sugar	12g
Protein	19g

HOW IMPORTANT IS IT TO EAT ORGANIC?

Some foods are better eaten organic because it's difficult to wash off pesticides. Others aren't as bad. If you can afford organic, it's a good choice, but if not, stick with following the suggestions for the Dirty Dozen and the Clean Fifteen. You can find these listed in Chapter 1.

1 Preheat oven to 400°F. Line two large rimmed baking sheets with parchment paper.
2 Pierce potatoes a few times with a knife to allow steam to escape. Place directly on oven rack and bake for 45 minutes, until tender. Remove from oven and let sit until cool enough to handle.
3 In a small bowl, stir to combine all spice blend ingredients.
4 In a medium bowl, combine chickpeas and one-third of the spice blend. Stir to coat completely. Remove chickpeas and place on one of the prepared baking sheets.
5 Add broccoli to the same bowl and season with enough spice blend to cover. Remove broccoli and place on second prepared baking sheet. Place both baking sheets into oven.

continued

Loaded Tahini-Spiced Potato Skins—continued

6   Bake broccoli for 15 minutes, or until crisp-tender. Remove from oven and set aside. Stir chickpeas and continue to bake for about another 15 minutes, until golden brown and crispy. Check frequently to make sure they're not getting too brown. Remove from oven and set aside.

7   Slice potatoes in half lengthwise. Scoop flesh out of potato halves, leaving ½" layer inside skins. Transfer potato flesh to a large bowl. Using a fork, mash potatoes with half of the Quick Tahini Sauce, ¼ teaspoon salt, and ¼ teaspoon pepper.

8   Spoon mashed potatoes back into potato skins. Top with chickpeas, broccoli, and more Quick Tahini Sauce. Sprinkle each potato with cilantro.

9   Store in a covered container and refrigerate up to 3 days. Reheat on baking sheet in 350°F oven for about 10–15 minutes until heated through.

Instant Pot® Pinto Beans

Beans are a great way to add fiber and protein to your diet. They even help control your cholesterol and are full of excellent nutrition! Pinto beans are easy to make in a pressure cooker or on the stove-top. The bouillon vegetable base recommended has salt in it, so if you prefer to control your salt, you can use low-sodium vegetable broth or water instead.

1 pound dry pinto beans, rinsed and debris removed, soaked at least 6 hours

6 cups water, divided

1 tablespoon low-sodium vegetable bouillon paste (like Organic Reduced Sodium Better Than Bouillon Seasoned Vegetable Base brand)

3 medium cloves garlic, peeled and minced

2 medium bay leaves

SERVES 6	
Per Serving:	
Calories	265
Fat	1g
Sodium	267mg
Carbohydrates	48g
Fiber	12g
Sugar	2g
Protein	16g

1 Drain soaked beans and place them into an Instant Pot®.

2 Add 5 cups water. Mix bouillon into remaining 1 cup water and microwave for 40 seconds to combine. Stir and add to Instant Pot® along with garlic and bay leaves.

3 Seal Instant Pot® and make sure the vent is set to close. Push "manual" button and move time down to 20 minutes. When done, allow steam to slow release. Remove the bay leaves before serving.

4 Store beans in a covered container for 5 days or freeze (after cooling) in smaller freezer-safe containers for up to 3 months.

Vegetable Fried Rice

SERVES 4

Per Serving:

Calories	163
Fat	1g
Sodium	415mg
Carbohydrates	35g
Fiber	8g
Sugar	12g
Protein	5g

EAT YOUR CRUCIFEROUS VEGETABLES

Cabbage and kale are part of the cruciferous vegetable family, which also includes cauliflower, Brussels sprouts, broccoli, radishes, Napa cabbage, bok choy, and arugula. They have cancer-fighting properties, are low in calories, and are chock-full of nutrients. Be sure to include cruciferous vegetables in your recommended 5 servings a day.

Cooked rice is an excellent staple to keep on hand, so it'll be ready to add to vegetable grain bowls, stir-fries, soups, and wraps. This recipe is beautiful with all the different-colored vegetables.

1 medium carrot, peeled and diced
1 cup diced yellow onion
¼ cup water
1 medium red bell pepper, seeded and diced
1 cup diced red cabbage
1 cup diced broccoli
1 cup brown rice, cooked according to package directions
2 tablespoons low-sodium soy sauce

1 Heat a large nonstick skillet over medium-high heat. Add carrot, onion, and water. Sauté about 3 minutes. Add pepper, cabbage, and broccoli, and continue to sauté until they are crisp-tender, about 5 more minutes.

2 Add cooked rice and soy sauce to vegetables and stir to combine and heat through, about 5 minutes.

3 Refrigerate leftovers in an airtight container for 3–4 days, or freeze (after cooling) in a freezer-safe container for up to 3 months. To reheat, thaw overnight in the refrigerator and reheat over medium heat on the stovetop with a couple of tablespoons of water or in the microwave.

CHAPTER 9
Sauces and Condiments

Whipped Aquafaba

MAKES 4 CUPS

Per Serving (¼ cup):

Calories	9
Fat	0g
Sodium	1mg
Carbohydrates	2g
Fiber	0g
Sugar	2g
Protein	0g

The juice from chickpeas is filled with proteins that, when whipped, behave similarly to whipped cream. Adding a stabilizing agent helps form stiffer peaks. It can then be used in different recipes that call for whipping "cream." (For a sugar-free version, use stevia instead of maple syrup.) It can also be used as an egg replacement. Two tablespoons Whipped Aquafaba are equal to 1 egg white, and 3 tablespoons are equal to 1 egg.

⅔ cup aquafaba (liquid from a can of chickpeas)

¼ teaspoon cream of tartar

½ teaspoon vanilla extract

2 tablespoons maple syrup

1 In a medium bowl, combine aquafaba, cream of tartar, maple syrup, and vanilla. Using either a stand mixer or hand mixer, beat on high speed for about 10 minutes for soft peaks. For stiff peaks, beat for about 15 minutes.

2 Check for sweetness and add more maple syrup to your liking. Be careful because the aquafaba will deflate if overbeaten.

3 Whipped aquafaba has a tendency to separate, so use it as soon as you can. Extra (unwhipped) aquafaba can be frozen in ice cube trays for later use. Once frozen, transfer cubes to a freezer-safe container or freezer bag.

Basil Marinara

This sauce can be used with anything that calls for a basic marinara sauce, such as lasagna, stuffed peppers, or even as a topping for baked potatoes.

1 medium yellow onion, peeled and diced

¼ cup water

4 medium cloves garlic, peeled and minced

1 medium carrot, peeled and diced

1 teaspoon dried basil

¼ teaspoon crushed red pepper flakes

1 (28-ounce) can low-sodium crushed tomatoes

2 teaspoons maple syrup

½ teaspoon salt

¼ teaspoon freshly ground black pepper

10 medium leaves fresh basil, julienned

1 Heat a medium nonstick skillet over medium-high heat. Add onion and water, and sauté for 5 minutes. Add garlic and carrot, and continue to cook until onion is translucent and soft, about another 2 minutes.

2 Add dried basil, red pepper flakes, and tomatoes.

3 Add maple syrup, salt, and black pepper. Reduce heat to low and simmer for 30 minutes.

4 Add fresh basil and stir. Taste and adjust seasonings.

5 Refrigerate in an airtight container for up to 7 days, or freeze (after cooling) in a freezer-safe container for up to 3 months. Thaw overnight in the refrigerator and reheat over medium heat on the stovetop or in the microwave.

SERVES 4

Per Serving:

Calories	39
Fat	0g
Sodium	121mg
Carbohydrates	7g
Fiber	2g
Sugar	4g
Protein	2g

BASIL CAN BOOST YOUR IMMUNE SYSTEM

Basil is an herb that people love for its fragrance and flavor, but did you know that consuming basil also offers an immune-system-protecting punch? Plus, it fights cancer, combats stress and depression, and acts as an antimicrobial and antiviral.

Blender "Cheese" Sauce

MAKES 2 CUPS

Per Serving (¼ cup):

Calories	102
Fat	4g
Sodium	202mg
Carbohydrates	12g
Fiber	2g
Sugar	2g
Protein	5g

This is a quick and easy sauce to keep on hand to use on roasted vegetables or a baked potato, or to use in recipes that call for a cheese sauce, such as the Fiesta Mac and "Cheese" (see recipe in Chapter 7). It can all be made in one container, making cleanup easier.

½ cup unsalted raw cashews

1 cup unsweetened almond milk

1 cup One-Pot Vegetable Broth (see recipe in Chapter 5)

⅓ cup rolled oats

½ cup roughly chopped yellow onion

½ cup chopped red bell pepper

⅓ cup nutritional yeast

2 tablespoons cornstarch

4 tablespoons fresh lemon juice

1 tablespoon onion powder

1 tablespoon garlic powder

½ teaspoon salt

1 In a high-powered blender, add cashews. If you do not have a high-powered blender, quick-soak the cashews by pouring boiling water (enough to cover) over cashews in a small bowl. Let stand for 30 minutes, then transfer to a regular blender.

2 Add remaining ingredients to blender. Blend on high speed for 4–5 minutes. It will get hot and cook to thicken sauce.

3 If it doesn't seem to thicken or you don't have a blender that will get hot, pour sauce into a medium saucepan over medium heat and heat until it thickens, about 5–7 minutes.

4 Pour sauce into a container, cover, and refrigerate for up to 5 days, or freeze (after cooling) in a freezer-safe container for up to 2 months. Thaw overnight in the refrigerator and when defrosted, blend it with a little water to thin if needed.

Cashew-Tofu Mayonnaise

Keep this staple on hand for dressings or to use on sandwiches or in sauces. Naturally lower in fat than traditional mayonnaise and full of flavor, this version also has more nutritional value. It's best to use a small high-powered blender such as a NutriBullet for this job.

½ (14-ounce) container firm organic tofu, drained and rinsed

¼ cup unsalted raw cashews, soaked and drained (see Chapter 1 for soaking instructions)

2 tablespoons apple cider vinegar

2 teaspoons date syrup

1 teaspoon onion powder

1 tablespoon spicy mustard

½ teaspoon salt

1–2 tablespoons unsweetened almond milk to thin if needed

1 In a high-powered blender, combine all ingredients.

2 Blend, scraping sides of blender occasionally, until mayonnaise is smooth and creamy. Add up to a couple of tablespoons more of almond milk to thin to your desired consistency.

3 Adjust seasonings to your liking.

4 Refrigerate mayonnaise in an airtight container for 3–5 days.

MAKES 2 CUPS

Per Serving (1 tablespoon):

Calories	13
Fat	1g
Sodium	49mg
Carbohydrates	1g
Fiber	0g
Sugar	0g
Protein	1g

THE AMAZING CASHEW

Cashews are packed full of nutritious plant-based goodness. They're rich in heart-healthy fatty acids and protein and are an excellent source of antioxidants. They make the perfect base for creamy sauces and dips with their buttery sweet flavor, and they can be used to make plant-based cheese or milk, or to thicken soup.

Blueberry–Chia Seed Jam

MAKES 2 CUPS

Per Serving (1 tablespoon):

Calories	15
Fat	0g
Sodium	0mg
Carbohydrates	3g
Fiber	1g
Sugar	2g
Protein	0g

This quick chia seed jam is versatile and easy to make on your stove. Other fruits like strawberries, raspberries, and cherries also work well in this recipe.

1 (12-ounce) bag frozen or 1½ cups fresh blueberries

2 tablespoons maple syrup

¼ cup chia seeds

1 tablespoon fresh lemon juice

1. In a medium saucepan over medium heat, add blueberries and cook until berries start to break down, about 5–10 minutes.
2. Mash fruit with the back of a spatula, leaving some blueberries whole.
3. Remove from heat and stir in maple syrup. Taste and add more, as needed, for desired sweetness.
4. Add chia seeds and lemon juice, and stir to combine. Cool to room temperature, then transfer to a Mason jar. Cover and put in the refrigerator until thickened, about 1 hour.
5. Refrigerate for up to 2 weeks, or freeze in a freezer-safe container for up to 3 months.

Chipotle Dipping Sauce

MAKES ¾ CUP

Per Serving (2 tablespoons):

Calories	31
Fat	2g
Sodium	49mg
Carbohydrates	2g
Fiber	0g
Sugar	0g
Protein	1g

If you double this sauce, it's much easier to make it in a regular-sized blender—and you'll have plenty on hand for dipping vegetables and fries, topping tacos and burgers, and spreading inside quesadillas. For a single batch, a small blender will work fine.

½ cup unsalted raw cashews, soaked and drained (see Chapter 1 for soaking instructions)

¼ cup plus 2 tablespoons water

¼ teaspoon chipotle chili powder (or more for a spicier dip)

1 medium clove garlic, peeled

1 tablespoon fresh lime juice

¼ teaspoon salt

1 In a small, high-powered blender, combine cashews and water. Blend until smooth. It may take several minutes.

2 Add remaining ingredients and blend again until smooth, adding 2 tablespoons more water to thin as necessary. Taste and adjust seasonings. If you like it spicier, carefully add more chipotle chili powder, as it can be very spicy.

3 Store in a small airtight container and refrigerate for up to 4 days.

Peanut Dipping Sauce

This versatile recipe can be used on a salad or as a dipping sauce for Fresh Spring Rolls with Two Dipping Sauces (see recipe in Chapter 3), lettuce wraps, Baked Tofu (see recipe in Chapter 7), or with sliced vegetables. You can use ordinary soy sauce instead of the tamari if that's what you have in your pantry.

½ cup all-natural peanut butter

⅓ cup low-sodium tamari soy sauce

4 tablespoons rice vinegar

1 tablespoon chili garlic sauce

2 tablespoons maple syrup

2 tablespoons minced ginger

In a small bowl, whisk all ingredients together until well combined. Refrigerate in a glass container for up to 1 week.

MAKES 1 CUP	
Per Serving (2 tablespoons):	
Calories	122
Fat	8g
Sodium	313mg
Carbohydrates	9g
Fiber	1g
Sugar	6g
Protein	5g

Tartar Sauce

This Tartar Sauce is made with tofu, making it a perfect accompaniment to your favorite vegan dishes. The flavor is perfectly tangy and tart and it's super easy to make.

½ (14-ounce) container firm organic tofu, drained, rinsed, and pressed for 30 minutes (see Chapter 1 for pressing instructions)

2 tablespoons fresh lemon juice

1 tablespoon yellow mustard

2 tablespoons minced red onion

½ teaspoon horseradish

½ tablespoon minced fresh dill

2 tablespoons minced sweet or dill pickles

In a small bowl, add tofu and mash with a fork. Add remaining ingredients and mix. Refrigerate in an airtight container until ready to use, up to 3–5 days.

MAKES 1 CUP	
Per Serving (2 tablespoons):	
Calories	122
Fat	8g
Sodium	530mg
Carbohydrates	9g
Fiber	1g
Sugar	6g
Protein	5g

Quick Tahini Sauce

Tahini is a creamy sauce made from ground sesame seeds. The addition of garlic and lemon makes it the perfect topping for a salad, falafel, burger, or Buddha bowl (a tasty meal of grains, greens, and protein served in a single bowl topped with a sauce).

¼ cup plus 2 tablespoons tahini paste

¼ cup water (or more for consistency)

2 medium cloves garlic, peeled and minced

¼ cup fresh lemon juice

1 tablespoon maple syrup

¼ teaspoon salt

In a small bowl, whisk all ingredients together until sauce is creamy and smooth. If it seems too thick, add water, 1 tablespoon at a time. Transfer to an airtight container and refrigerate for up to 1 week.

Cannellini Bean Cream Sauce

This simple and versatile recipe can be made from a variety of healthful bases, such as cashews, tofu, beans, nuts, or unsweetened plant milk of your choice. Toss it with your favorite whole-grain pasta or vegetable noodles along with chopped fresh herbs such as dill or basil.

1 (15-ounce) can low-sodium cannellini beans, drained and rinsed (or 2 cups cooked from scratch)

¾ cup unsweetened almond milk

Juice of ½ medium lemon

2 medium cloves garlic, peeled and crushed

2 tablespoons nutritional yeast

¼ teaspoon salt

1 In a blender, combine all ingredients and blend until smooth, about 3 minutes.

2 Add to a saucepan over medium heat and whisk slowly until heated through, about 3 minutes. Adjust consistency with additional vegetable stock or water, if needed.

Tomatillo Sauce

Tomatillos come with a papery outer skin and are sticky to the touch. They should be easy to find in the produce section. Once the skin is removed and the tomatillos are washed, they're ready to use. Roasting the ingredients in the oven gives this salsa a wonderful smoky flavor.

12 medium tomatillos, peeled

1 medium yellow onion, peeled and cut in half

1 medium jalapeño pepper, seeded and cut in half

3 medium cloves garlic, peeled

1 small bunch fresh cilantro

1½ tablespoons chopped fresh oregano

⅓ cup water

½ teaspoon salt

¼ teaspoon freshly ground black pepper

1. Adjust oven rack to 4" below broiler unit. Preheat broiler on high and line a baking sheet with parchment paper.
2. Place tomatillos, onion, and jalapeño (cut sides down) on prepared baking sheet. Broil until slightly charred, about 5 minutes. Cool slightly before transferring to a blender or food processor.
3. Add garlic, cilantro, oregano, water, salt, and black pepper to blender and blend for 30 seconds. Continue to blend until ingredients are combined but still chunky and not overprocessed.
4. Refrigerate in an airtight container for up to 1 week.

SERVES 10	
Per Serving:	
Calories	20
Fat	0g
Sodium	118mg
Carbohydrates	4g
Fiber	1g
Sugar	2g
Protein	1g

Avocado Cream Sauce

Quick and easy to make, this sauce is just the right topping for tacos, burritos, or quesadillas. It makes a great dip for cut-up fresh vegetables as well.

2 medium avocados, peeled and seeded

1 (5.3-ounce) container unsweetened plain plant yogurt

1 cup chopped fresh cilantro (leaves and stems)

Juice of 1 medium lime

½ teaspoon ground cumin

2 medium cloves garlic, peeled and roughly cut

1–2 tablespoons water

¼ teaspoon salt

1 In a food processor, combine all ingredients and process until cilantro is finely minced.
2 To thin sauce, if needed, add 2–4 tablespoons more water.
3 Refrigerate in an airtight container for up to 7 days.

MAKES 3 CUPS	
Per Serving (2 tablespoons):	
Calories	35
Fat	3g
Sodium	29mg
Carbohydrates	2g
Fiber	1g
Sugar	0g
Protein	0g

Almond Ricotta

Although you can purchase store-bought almond ricotta, it's very easy to make in a high-powered blender. You'll find lots of uses for it, such as in sandwiches, on pizza, in lasagna, and in salads. Slivered almonds do not need to be soaked, so you can whip up this recipe in minutes.

2 cups slivered almonds

2½ tablespoons fresh lemon juice

1 cup water

1½ tablespoons nutritional yeast

1 medium clove garlic, peeled

¼ teaspoon salt

1. In a blender, combine all ingredients. Blend at low speed, adding more water if it becomes too thick. Scrape down sides of blender as needed. Turn speed to high and continue to blend until almonds are smooth with a tiny bit of texture. Be careful not to overblend or you'll get almond butter.
2. Refrigerate in an airtight container for up to 7 days.

Date Paste

You'll be happy to have date paste in your cupboard because it's a time saver and the perfect substitute for sugar in most recipes. Dates are a nutrient-dense, high-fiber whole food that are easy to make into a paste if you have a blender. If you don't need to add dates to a recipe, just pop them right in your mouth for a tasty sweet treat.

2 cups pitted medium Medjool dates

Up to 1 cup water

1. In a medium bowl, cover dates with boiling filtered water and allow to sit for 30 minutes.
2. Drain, reserving 1 cup of the soaking water.
3. In a high-powered blender, blend dates and ½ cup of the soaking water on high for about 1 minute, until it becomes a paste. Add more water if it's too thick. You want a thick but pliable paste.
4. Refrigerate paste in an airtight container for up to 3 months.

Basic Barbecue Sauce

People often have very specific tastes when it comes to barbecue sauce. Making it at home is a great way to customize it to your liking! This simple barbecue recipe is an easy place to start. Add more heat, sweetness, or herbs and spices to fit your fancy.

2 (6-ounce) cans no-salt-added tomato paste

3 tablespoons apple cider vinegar

½ cup water

1 tablespoon garlic powder

2 tablespoons yellow mustard

3 tablespoons maple syrup

3 tablespoons balsamic vinegar

3 tablespoon molasses

2 tablespoons vegan Worcestershire sauce

½ teaspoon salt

½ teaspoon cayenne pepper

MAKES 3¼ CUPS	
Per Serving (2 tablespoons):	
Calories	28
Fat	0g
Sodium	81mg
Carbohydrates	7g
Fiber	1g
Sugar	5g
Protein	1g

1 Add all ingredients to a bowl and whisk until combined.
2 Refrigerate in an airtight container for up to 1 week.

Homemade Ketchup

It's so easy to make ketchup at home and store it in a safe glass container, so why bother purchasing at the store in plastic? This maple syrup–sweetened version fits right in with your healthy plant-based lifestyle. If you'd like to try a sugar substitute, use monk fruit. Or leave out the sweetener completely; your choice.

1 (6-ounce) can no-salt-added tomato paste

2 tablespoons water

1 tablespoon maple syrup

2 tablespoons apple cider vinegar

⅛ teaspoon ground allspice

½ teaspoon onion powder

¼ teaspoon garlic powder

¼ teaspoon salt

MAKES ½ CUP	
Per Serving (1 tablespoon):	
Calories	25
Fat	0g
Sodium	86mg
Carbohydrates	6g
Fiber	1g
Sugar	4g
Protein	1g

In a small bowl, whisk all ingredients together until smooth.

Cashew Cream

Cashew Cream is a great staple to have on hand. It adds creaminess to any dish and can be made either savory or sweet. This recipe makes a savory version that works well in dips and soups, but you could add 1½ tablespoons maple syrup to make a sweetened version. That is a great choice for desserts such as Baked Apples with Cashew Cream (see recipe in Chapter 10) or as an addition to dressings.

MAKES 2¼ CUPS

Per Serving (2 tablespoons):

Calories	135
Fat	11g
Sodium	41mg
Carbohydrates	7g
Fiber	1g
Sugar	1g
Protein	4g

MAKE YOUR OWN VEGAN CREAMERS

Yes, there are a lot of store-bought vegan choices when it comes to creamer, but not many of them are also whole-food choices. Make your own healthier creamer using raw cashews. It's basically a thinner version of Cashew Cream. Use a lower cashew-to-water ratio of ½ cup cashews to 1½ cups water for an unsweetened creamer. Add a little maple syrup and vanilla, or other flavors, if you like.

1½ cups unsalted raw cashews, soaked and drained (see Chapter 1 for soaking instructions)

1½ cups water

1 medium clove garlic, peeled

⅛ teaspoon salt

1 Using a blender or a good-quality food processor, blend cashews, water, and other ingredients for either a sweet or savory cream until smooth and creamy. Scrape down sides with a spatula. Adjust seasonings to your taste.

2 Refrigerate Cashew Cream in an airtight container for up to 1 week. It can also be frozen in small portions. Spoon into ice cube trays and, once frozen, pop the cubes into a freezer bag, seal tightly, and freeze for up to 3 months. You can use frozen Cashew Cream cubes in your smoothies for extra creaminess.

Tofu Feta

In this recipe, tofu is cubed and marinated to create a tangy feta-like "cheese" that's perfect for lettuce or grain salads and in wraps.

3 medium cloves garlic, peeled and minced

2 tablespoons light miso

1½ teaspoons dried oregano

¼ cup fresh lemon juice

⅓ cup red wine vinegar

½ teaspoon salt

½ (14-ounce) container firm organic tofu, drained, rinsed, pressed for 30 minutes, and diced into ½" squares (see Chapter 1 for pressing instructions)

SERVES 4	
Per Serving:	
Calories	67
Fat	3g
Sodium	665mg
Carbohydrates	5g
Fiber	1g
Sugar	2g
Protein	6g

1 In a large bowl, combine garlic, miso, oregano, lemon juice, vinegar, and salt.

2 Add tofu to bowl. Stir carefully to coat tofu with marinade. Cover and refrigerate for at least 30 minutes before serving. Refrigerate leftovers in an airtight container for 2–3 days.

Easy Gravy

There's no need to feel guilty eating this fat-free vegan gravy. You can use a combination of broth and almond milk for more creaminess.

¼ cup whole-wheat all-purpose flour

½ teaspoon onion powder

2 heaping tablespoons nutritional yeast

2 cups One-Pot Vegetable Broth (see recipe in Chapter 5)

2 teaspoons low-sodium tamari soy sauce

¼ teaspoon salt

¼ teaspoon freshly ground black pepper

MAKES 2 CUPS	
Per Serving (⅓ cup):	
Calories	30
Fat	0g
Sodium	209mg
Carbohydrates	5g
Fiber	2g
Sugar	1g
Protein	2g

1 In a medium skillet over medium heat, combine flour, onion powder, and yeast. Add broth, whisking constantly to keep it from clumping. Add tamari. Stir until thickened, about 3–4 minutes, and season with salt and pepper.

2 Refrigerate in an airtight container for up to 3 days.

Oil-Free Basil Pesto

MAKES 1 CUP

Per Serving (2 tablespoons):

Calories	28
Fat	2g
Sodium	96mg
Carbohydrates	2g
Fiber	1g
Sugar	0g
Protein	2g

This pesto is super tasty without the addition of cheese or oil. It uses miso paste to give it a tangy, umami flavor. Use with cooked noodles, on roasted potatoes, or as a pizza sauce.

2 tablespoons pine nuts

2 cups tightly packed basil

3 medium cloves garlic, peeled

1 tablespoon light miso

3 tablespoons nutritional yeast

2 tablespoons fresh lemon juice

2–4 tablespoons water (depending on desired consistency)

1 In a small skillet over medium heat, stir pine nuts frequently for about 3 minutes, until toasted and golden.

2 Transfer pine nuts to a food processor. Add basil, garlic, miso, yeast, and lemon juice.

3 Begin to process. While machine is running, slowly drizzle in water to desired consistency.

4 Refrigerate pesto in an airtight container for up to 1 week.

Plant-Based Sour Cream

MAKES 1½ CUPS

Per Serving (2 tablespoons):

Calories	11
Fat	0g
Sodium	4mg
Carbohydrates	1g
Fiber	0g
Sugar	0g
Protein	1g

You don't need dairy to enjoy sour cream–like flavor. This plant-based version is perfect for topping baked potatoes, tacos, or burritos, or used in creamy dressings.

½ **(14-ounce) package firm organic silken tofu, drained**

Juice of 1 medium lemon

2 tablespoons apple cider vinegar

1 medium clove garlic, peeled and minced

3 tablespoons almond milk

1 In a blender, combine all ingredients. Blend, scraping sides of blender occasionally, until creamy. Add more almond milk if needed to thin.

2 Refrigerate in an airtight container for up to 5 days.

Tzatziki

MAKES 3 CUPS

Per Serving (¼ cup):

Calories	59
Fat	4g
Sodium	50mg
Carbohydrates	3g
Fiber	0g
Sugar	1g
Protein	3g

This light and refreshing Middle Eastern condiment is best served cold as a dip for vegetables, to top falafels, or in the Mushroom Pita Pockets (see recipe in Chapter 6).

2 cups Greek-style unsweetened plain plant yogurt

2 cups diced cucumber

2 medium cloves garlic, peeled and minced

1½ tablespoons fresh lemon juice

1 tablespoon chopped fresh mint

1 tablespoon chopped fresh dill

¼ **teaspoon salt**

1 In a large bowl, combine all ingredients and stir to mix well. Taste and add more lemon or herbs to your liking.

2 Refrigerate in an airtight container for 3–4 days. Stir before serving if the yogurt has separated.

CHAPTER 10

Desserts

Cinnamon-Apple Yogurt Parfait

SERVES 4

Per Serving:

Calories	322
Fat	13g
Sodium	65mg
Carbohydrates	52g
Fiber	7g
Sugar	28g
Protein	4g

This is a delicious and elegant dessert that comes together quickly, especially if you've made the granola and apples ahead of time. (It also makes a great breakfast!)

1 recipe Baked Cinnamon-Apple Slices (see recipe in this chapter)

3 (6-ounce) containers unsweetened plain plant yogurt

1 cup Pumpkin Cinnamon Nut Granola (see recipe in Chapter 2)

1 For each parfait, add 1 cup Baked Cinnamon-Apple Slices to a parfait glass.

2 Add one-fourth of the yogurt on top of apples. Top with 2 tablespoons granola. Repeat the yogurt, apple, and granola layers.

3 Refrigerate leftovers in a covered container for up to 1 day. Or store Baked Cinnamon-Apple Slices and granola separately in covered containers for up to 5 days.

Chocolate Chip Cookie Dough Hummus

SERVES 4

Per Serving:

Calories	275
Fat	11g
Sodium	309mg
Carbohydrates	39g
Fiber	6g
Sugar	22g
Protein	8g

This unusual, sweet, guilt-free, plant-based treat pairs well with fresh sliced apples, baked pita chips, or spread on toast with sliced bananas.

1 (15-ounce) can low-sodium chickpeas, drained and rinsed

¼ cup maple syrup

2 tablespoons almond butter

¼ teaspoon vanilla extract

¼ teaspoon salt

2–3 tablespoons unsweetened soy milk

¼ cup vegan mini chocolate chips

1 In a food processor, combine chickpeas, maple syrup, almond butter, vanilla, and salt. Pulse a few times and scrape down sides of bowl. Add soy milk until hummus is the consistency you like. Remove to a bowl.

2 Fold chocolate chips in by hand and garnish with additional chips.

3 Refrigerate leftovers in an airtight container for up to 5 days, or freeze in a freezer-safe container for 3–4 months.

Avocado Brownies

These deliciously rich Avocado Brownies are sure to satisfy your chocolate craving—and you won't even taste the healthy avocado in them. You can add up to ½ teaspoon liquid stevia for sweeter brownies, if you prefer. Or pump them up a notch by adding vegan chocolate chips.

1 medium avocado, peeled, seeded, and roughly chopped

½ medium banana, peeled and mashed

1 cup unsweetened soy milk

¼ cup maple syrup

¼ cup date sugar

1 cup whole-wheat all-purpose flour

½ cup unsweetened cocoa powder or cacao powder

1 teaspoon baking soda

¼ teaspoon salt

1 Preheat oven to 350°F. Lightly spray an 8" × 8" baking dish with nonstick cooking spray.

2 In a food processor, combine avocado, banana, soy milk, maple syrup, and date sugar. Blend until smooth.

3 In a large bowl, combine flour, cocoa powder, baking soda, and salt. Stir to combine. Add avocado mixture and stir to mix well.

4 Scrape batter into prepared baking dish. Bake for 20 minutes and check for doneness; a fork stuck in the center should come out clean. If not, bake for 7–8 minutes more, or until set.

5 Cool for at least 15 minutes before serving.

6 Store leftovers in an airtight container at room temperature for 2 days or refrigerate for up to 5 days. You can also wrap brownies with plastic, place in a freezer-safe container, and freeze for up to 4 months.

SERVES 8

Per Serving:

Calories	161
Fat	5g
Sodium	245mg
Carbohydrates	29g
Fiber	6g
Sugar	12g
Protein	4g

WHAT'S THE DIFFERENCE BETWEEN CACAO AND COCOA?

Cacao is less processed because it's made from unroasted cold-pressed cacao beans, and it's also high in fiber and antioxidants. Cocoa, while less expensive than cacao, is roasted at high temperatures and will have fewer nutrients. You can use either in most recipes that call for cacao or cocoa powder.

Carrot–Chocolate Chip Cookies

This tastes like carrot cake in cookie form—but it has lots of great protein from quinoa. These cookies are slightly sweet without being overwhelmed by sugary flavor. For variety, add 2 tablespoons unsalted pumpkin or sunflower seeds.

3 tablespoons ground flaxseeds

5 tablespoons water

½ cup cooked quinoa

1 cup rolled oats

1 cup unbleached all-purpose flour

1 teaspoon baking powder

1 teaspoon baking soda

½ teaspoon salt

½ teaspoon cinnamon

1 large very ripe banana, peeled and mashed

½ cup unsweetened applesauce

½ cup almond butter

1 cup finely grated carrots

½ cup coconut sugar or date sugar

1 teaspoon vanilla extract

½ cup mini vegan chocolate chips

½ cup walnuts

1 Preheat oven to 350°F. Lightly spray a baking sheet with non-stick cooking spray or line with parchment paper.

2 In a small bowl, combine flaxseeds and water, and let sit for 10 minutes.

3 In a medium bowl, combine quinoa, oats, flour, baking powder, baking soda, salt, and cinnamon. Stir to mix well.

4 In a separate large bowl, combine banana, applesauce, almond butter, carrots, coconut sugar, vanilla, and flaxseed mixture.

5 Add quinoa mixture to banana mixture and combine thoroughly.

6 Fold in chocolate chips and nuts.

7 Drop by large spoonfuls about 2" apart onto prepared baking sheet.

8 Bake for 20–25 minutes, until they are golden, checking to make sure they don't brown too much on the bottom. These will be soft but if you like them a little browner and crispier, bake a little longer.

9 Cover and refrigerate leftovers for up to 7 days. Or wrap in plastic wrap and foil and freeze for up to 2 months.

MAKES 30 COOKIES

Per Serving (2 cookies):

Calories	225
Fat	11g
Sodium	215mg
Carbohydrates	28g
Fiber	4g
Sugar	11g
Protein	5g

ANTI-INFLAMMATORY BENEFITS OF CAROTENOIDS

Carotenoids are fat-soluble yellow, orange, and red plant pigments found in carrots, certain squashes and fruits, and other yellow, orange, or red plant foods. Both carotenoids and flavo-noids reduce inflam-mation by affecting the inflammation-promoting communications within our bodies.

Baked Apples with Cashew Cream

SERVES 4

Per Serving:

Calories	297
Fat	12g
Sodium	24mg
Carbohydrates	48g
Fiber	7g
Sugar	32g
Protein	5g

WALNUTS: THE SUPERNUT

If you eat nuts, walnuts are a great choice because they have the best heart-healthy profile. Although high in fat, they're also high in healthy omega-3s, vitamins, fiber, and plant sterols, which are anti-inflammatory and help lower cholesterol, among other things. There's evidence that people who eat nuts live longer, healthier lives than people who don't eat nuts. Moderation is the key.

Apples are a common staple in most households, so this Baked Apples with Cashew Cream recipe is a great go-to in a pinch. As an added bonus, the delightful smell of cinnamon will fill your house. Choose your favorite apple variety or Honeycrisp, as suggested. You'll use a Cashew Cream, something you can meal prep, for the topping. If you want the topping to taste sweeter, simply add 2 teaspoons maple syrup to the Cashew Cream recipe. Any extra Cashew Cream can be stored in the freezer.

4 large Honeycrisp apples, cored

2 tablespoons maple syrup

½ teaspoon cinnamon

⅓ cup chopped unsalted walnuts

¼ cup water

½ cup Cashew Cream (see recipe in Chapter 9)

½ cup Pumpkin Cinnamon Nut Granola (see recipe in Chapter 2)

1 Preheat oven to 400°F.
2 Peel just the top 1½" of skin from each apple.
3 Place apples in an 8"–9" baking dish. If apples don't stand up, trim a small slice from the bottom of each.
4 Drizzle apples with 2 tablespoons maple syrup and sprinkle with cinnamon. Stuff the centers with a few walnuts.
5 Pour ¼ cup water into bottom of baking dish, cover with foil, and bake for about 30–45 minutes, until apples are tender.
6 Uncover and bake another 10 minutes.
7 Before serving, top each apple with 2 tablespoons chilled Cashew Cream and 2 tablespoons Pumpkin Cinnamon Nut Granola.
8 Refrigerate leftovers in an airtight container for up to 4 days.

Chocolate-Cinnamon Ice Cream

It's incredibly easy to still have ice cream–like desserts without dairy. Frozen bananas and cashews give this dessert a creamy texture, and the cinnamon wonderfully complements and deepens the flavor of the chocolate. To freeze bananas for this recipe, peel and cut them into 1" chunks. Freeze on a flat surface before storing in a freezer-safe bag or container. Top finished ice cream with your favorite plant-based additions, such as fresh raspberries.

½ cup unsalted raw cashews, soaked overnight or at least a few hours and drained (see Chapter 1 for soaking instructions)

8 large bananas, peeled, cut into chunks, and frozen

8 medium Medjool dates, pitted and roughly chopped

½ cup unsweetened soy milk

1 teaspoon cinnamon

½ cup unsweetened cacao or cocoa powder

1 In a high-powered blender, combine cashews, bananas, dates, soy milk, cinnamon, and cacao. Blend until smooth, scraping down sides of blender as needed. Add more soy milk if needed to help facilitate blending.

2 Serve immediately in individual bowls. If saving for later, freeze ice cream in a freezer-safe container. When you're ready to eat, let ice cream sit at room temperature for about 20 minutes to soften, as it will harden when completely frozen. Freeze for up to 3 months in a freezer-safe container.

SERVES 6

Per Serving:

Calories	334
Fat	7g
Sodium	12mg
Carbohydrates	74g
Fiber	10g
Sugar	44g
Protein	7g

THERE ARE DIFFERENT TYPES OF CINNAMON

Cassia cinnamon, the most common form of cinnamon available, contains high levels of coumarin, a naturally occurring substance that has the potential to cause liver damage when used in high doses. If possible, choose Ceylon cinnamon, which contains only trace amounts of coumarin and has a sweeter, more delicate flavor.

Banana Bread with Maple Glaze

This traditional banana bread recipe has been revamped into a delicious, plant-based, healthy treat.

Wet Ingredients

½ cup plus 2 tablespoons unsweetened soy milk

1 teaspoon apple cider vinegar

3 tablespoons almond butter

2 medium bananas, peeled and mashed

3 teaspoons vanilla extract

⅓ cup maple syrup

½ teaspoon cinnamon

½ teaspoon salt

Dry Ingredients

½ cup old-fashioned oats

¾ cup unbleached all-purpose flour

1½ teaspoons baking powder

½ teaspoon baking soda

½ cup mini vegan chocolate chips

¼ cup chopped unsalted walnuts

Maple Glaze

6 tablespoons confectioners' sugar

½ teaspoon cinnamon

2 tablespoons maple syrup

1 Preheat oven to 350°F. Line a 9" × 5" × 3" loaf pan with parchment paper, leaving a 2" overhang on all sides.

2 In a small bowl, whisk together soy milk and vinegar. Set aside for at least 5 minutes, until it curdles.

3 In a large bowl, combine curdled soy milk, almond butter, bananas, vanilla, maple syrup, cinnamon, and salt. Stir well to combine.

4 In a separate medium bowl, whisk together all dry ingredients. Add dry ingredients to wet ingredients, and stir to combine. Fold in the chocolate chips and walnuts.

5 Pour batter into prepared loaf pan. Bake for about 25 minutes, or until an inserted toothpick comes out clean.

6 In a small bowl, sift confectioners' sugar with cinnamon. Add maple syrup and whisk until smooth. Drizzle over top of bread.

7 Store covered at room temperature or refrigerate in an airtight container for 3–4 days. Or wrap individual slices in plastic wrap, place in a freezer-safe container, and freeze for up to 2 months.

Chocolate-Orange Zucchini Cake

This is an indulgent, rich cake that's moist and delicious even without oil! It's also a sneaky way to eat more vegetables, heart-healthy chocolate, and a touch of vitamin C.

Cake

½ cup whole-wheat all-purpose flour

1½ cups unbleached all-purpose flour

½ cup unsweetened cacao or cocoa powder

1 teaspoon baking soda

1½ teaspoons baking powder

¼ teaspoon salt

¾ cup coconut sugar

½ cup unsweetened orange juice

½ cup unsweetened applesauce

1 teaspoon vanilla extract

1¾ cups shredded zucchini

Glaze

3 tablespoons maple syrup

¼ cup unsweetened orange juice

1 Preheat oven to 350°F. Spray an 8" × 8" baking pan with nonstick cooking spray.

2 In a medium bowl, combine whole-wheat flour, unbleached flour, cacao powder, baking soda, baking powder, salt, and coconut sugar.

3 In a large bowl, mix orange juice, applesauce, vanilla, and zucchini.

4 Add the flour mixture to the zucchini mixture and stir until just combined. Don't overmix, or the cake will be tough. Keep in mind that the zucchini will release a lot of moisture.

5 Scrape batter into the prepared pan and bake 45 minutes, or until a toothpick inserted in the center comes out clean.

6 While the cake is cooling, prepare the glaze. In a small bowl, whisk together maple syrup and orange juice until combined. While the cake is still warm, poke a few holes in it with a fork and drizzle glaze over cake.

7 Let cake cool thoroughly before slicing and serving. Refrigerate leftovers in an airtight container for up to 7 days.

8 To freeze, wrap cake tightly in parchment paper and then plastic wrap. Put it into a freezer bag and freeze for up to 3 months. Allow to come to room temperature in the refrigerator before eating.

Lemon Cake with Vanilla Frosting

Per Serving:

Calories	246
Fat	9g
Sodium	206mg
Carbohydrates	38g
Fiber	3g
Sugar	18g
Protein	6g

MAKING PARCHMENT PAPER EASY TO USE

Parchment paper can easily slip right out of your pan, but the secret to making it stay in place is to first crumple it completely with your hands. Then open and smooth it out again. This will make it easy to mold to your pan.

The addition of whole-wheat pastry flour helps to keep this moist lemon cake lighter while still being a whole-grain food. The tofu frosting is a game changer and will fool even the most discerning taste buds.

Wet Ingredients

½ cup maple syrup

⅓ cup plus 2 tablespoons fresh lemon juice

¼ cup unsweetened applesauce

¼ cup unsweetened soy milk

½ teaspoon vanilla extract

1 tablespoon chia seeds

Dry Ingredients

½ cup whole-wheat all-purpose flour

¾ cup whole-wheat pastry flour

¾ cup blanched almond flour

1 teaspoon baking powder

¾ teaspoon baking soda

⅛ teaspoon salt

¼ teaspoon ground turmeric

Zest of 1 medium lemon

Frosting

4 ounces extra-firm silken tofu, drained and rinsed

¼ cup raw cashew butter

¼ cup maple syrup

2 tablespoons fresh lemon juice

½ teaspoon vanilla

1 Preheat oven to 350°F. Line an 8" × 8" baking pan with parchment paper or spray lightly with nonstick cooking spray.

2 In a large bowl, combine wet ingredients and stir until well combined.

3 In a separate bowl, whisk together dry ingredients.

4 Add dry ingredients to wet ingredients and mix well.

5 Pour batter into prepared baking pan and spread evenly with a spatula. Bake for 25 minutes or until a toothpick inserted into center comes out clean. Cool completely before frosting.

6 To make frosting, in a small bowl or with an immersion blender, combine all frosting ingredients until smooth. Place frosting in refrigerator for 2 hours to thicken slightly.

7 When cake is cooled and frosting is chilled, spread frosting evenly on cake. Slice and serve.

Peach Crisp with Oats

THE MANY VARIETIES OF OATS

You can find many different types of oats: quick, old-fashioned, rolled, steel-cut, groats, and even oat flour. The more whole the oat is, the longer they'll take to digest, keeping you full longer as well. Steel-cut are great for breakfast, and oat groats are even delicious in savory dishes.

Ripe, delicious peaches are the star of this dish—and unlike in some traditional crisps, they retain their health benefits in this version! If you have an abundance of fresh peaches, it's easy to freeze them for later by slicing and placing separately on a baking sheet in the freezer until frozen. Then gather up the peaches and transfer to a freezer-safe container.

Peaches

5 large peaches, peeled, pitted, and sliced

3 tablespoons chia seeds

1 tablespoon fresh lemon juice

2 teaspoons cinnamon

2 tablespoons date sugar

Topping

1 cup old-fashioned oats

¼ cup oat flour

1 tablespoon maple syrup

½ cup date sugar

3 heaping tablespoons almond butter

1 teaspoon cinnamon

⅛ teaspoon nutmeg

1 Preheat oven to 350°F. Spray a 9" × 11" baking dish with nonstick cooking spray.

2 Put peaches in a large bowl. Sprinkle with chia seeds, lemon juice, and cinnamon, and stir to coat. Add date sugar if your peaches don't seem sweet enough. Depending on how much juice your peaches are giving off, you might need to add a little more or fewer chia seeds.

3 Let peaches stand for about 15 minutes to thicken up. Scrape into prepared baking dish.

4 In the same bowl, combine all topping ingredients. Mix until it's a crumbly texture. It should not be too wet or too dry.

5 Evenly sprinkle topping over peaches.

6 Bake for 30 minutes or until topping starts to brown. If it doesn't seem to be browning, turn on broiler for a few minutes and watch carefully. Cool slightly before serving.

7 Refrigerate toppings and peaches separately in airtight containers for up to 4 days.

Gluten-Free Pumpkin Spice Cake

This delightfully scrumptious cake is great for fall (or any time of the year, really) and is easily made with canned pumpkin puree. You could try it with sweet potato puree too! This recipe is gluten-free as written. One brand of gluten-free flour is Bob's Red Mill, which makes a combination of bean and gluten-free flours. This cake can also be made with a combination of whole-wheat plus all-purpose flours just as well.

Wet Ingredients

¾ cup pumpkin puree

¼ cup unsweetened soy milk

1 teaspoon vanilla extract

⅓ cup maple syrup

¼ cup date sugar

2 teaspoons apple cider vinegar

Dry Ingredients

1 cup gluten-free all-purpose flour

½ cup blanched almond flour

1 tablespoon pumpkin pie spice

2 teaspoons baking powder

¼ teaspoon salt

1 Preheat oven to 350°F. Line an 8" × 8" baking dish with parchment paper or spray lightly with nonstick cooking spray.

2 In a large bowl, whisk together all wet ingredients until combined.

3 In a separate medium bowl, mix all dry ingredients together. Add to wet ingredients and stir until just combined.

4 Scrape batter into baking dish, evening out with a spatula. Bake for 30 minutes, until a toothpick inserted into the center comes out clean.

5 Refrigerate leftovers in an airtight container for up to 4 days, or freeze (after cooling) in a freezer-safe container for up to 3 months.

SERVES 9

Per Serving:

Calories	140
Fat	3g
Sodium	177mg
Carbohydrates	27g
Fiber	1g
Sugar	12g
Protein	2g

MAKE YOUR OWN PUMPKIN PUREE

You can make your own pumpkin puree in an Instant Pot® when pie pumpkins are available in the market, usually during the fall. Remove the stem and seeds and add 1 cup of water to the Instant Pot®. Place the pumpkin on the rack, set your machine on manual and high for 15 minutes, and then naturally release pressure for 5 minutes. Let cool, cut into pieces, and remove pulp from the skin.

Strawberry Bread Pudding

KEEPING BERRIES FRESH

You may have discovered that fresh berries can spoil quickly. Here's a tip to help. After removing any bad berries, place remainder in a large bowl and cover with 3 parts water to 1 part distilled white vinegar for a few minutes. Then rinse, let dry on the counter, and place in a covered airtight container with a couple of paper towels.

Use up your older stale bread (and avoid waste!) in this easy-to-make bread pudding. It's similar to strawberry shortcake with a beautiful whipped topping made from the juice of chickpeas (called aquafaba). For a sugar-free version of aquafaba, use stevia instead of maple syrup.

8 cups cubed stale whole-grain bread

½ pound fresh hulled or thawed frozen strawberries

2 cups unsweetened soy milk

⅓ cup maple syrup

2 tablespoons ground flaxseeds

2 tablespoons chia seeds

2 teaspoons vanilla extract

2 teaspoons cinnamon

1 recipe Whipped Aquafaba (see recipe in Chapter 9)

1 Preheat oven to 350°F. Spray a 9" × 13" baking dish with nonstick cooking spray.

2 Spread bread cubes in prepared baking dish and set aside.

3 In a blender, combine strawberries, soy milk, maple syrup, flaxseeds, chia seeds, vanilla, and cinnamon. Blend until smooth, about 1 minute. Pour mixture over bread, stir, and let sit for about 1 hour at room temperature.

4 Bake for 60 minutes, until bread pudding is golden brown on the outside and heated through on the inside. If pudding is getting too brown on top but needs to cook more, cover with aluminum foil.

5 Remove from oven and allow to cool slightly before serving with a dollop of Whipped Aquafaba.

6 Refrigerate bread pudding leftovers covered in refrigerator for 2–3 days or freeze in a freezer-safe container for 2–3 months.

7 Refrigerate Whipped Aquafaba in an airtight container for up to 3 days.

Baked Cinnamon-Apple Slices

If you love apple pie, you'll love this recipe, which is very versatile. Use Baked Cinnamon-Apple Slices in a parfait, over oatmeal, on a baked sweet potato for breakfast, or in the Cinnamon-Apple Crepes (see recipe in Chapter 2) for dessert. Be creative with toppings of chopped nuts, seeds, or shredded coconut.

Baked Sliced Apples

4 tart medium Granny Smith apples, peeled, cored, and sliced

1 tablespoon date syrup

½ teaspoon cinnamon

¼ teaspoon nutmeg

⅛ teaspoon allspice

1⁄16 teaspoon ground cloves

½ tablespoon cornstarch

Topping

6 tablespoons Cashew Cream (see recipe in Chapter 9) plus 2 teaspoons maple syrup

½ cup chopped unsalted walnuts

1 Preheat oven to 350°F.
2 Add sliced apples to a large baking dish. Combine date syrup, cinnamon, nutmeg, allspice, cloves, and cornstarch in a small bowl and stir to combine. Pour over apple slices and stir to coat completely.
3 Cover with foil and bake for 45 minutes, until tender.
4 On each serving, place 1 tablespoon Cashew Cream and a sprinkling of chopped walnuts.

SERVES 6	
Per Serving:	
Calories	447
Fat	35g
Sodium	38mg
Carbohydrates	32g
Fiber	6g
Sugar	15g
Protein	10g

Almond Chickpea Bars

What a surprise that chickpeas make delicious desserts! These bars have a soft, chewy texture much like brownies, and a tender butterscotch flavor, thanks to the maple syrup. To make a peanut butter version, substitute peanut butter for the almond butter.

SERVES 9

Per Serving:

Calories	311
Fat	17g
Sodium	228mg
Carbohydrates	37g
Fiber	4g
Sugar	22g
Protein	6g

Dry Ingredients

⅓ cup oat flour

2 tablespoons coconut sugar

1 teaspoon cinnamon

½ teaspoon baking powder

¼ teaspoon baking soda

¼ teaspoon salt

Wet Ingredients

1 (15-ounce) can low-sodium chickpeas, drained and rinsed (reserve liquid)

3 tablespoons aquafaba (liquid from a can of chickpeas)

½ cup almond butter

½ cup maple syrup

1 teaspoon vanilla extract

½ cup vegan chocolate chips

½ cup chopped unsalted walnuts

1 Preheat oven to 350°F. Line an 8" × 8" baking pan with parchment paper, leaving a 2" overhang on all sides.

2 In a large bowl, combine all dry ingredients until well mixed. In a food processor, combine chickpeas, aquafaba, almond butter, maple syrup, and vanilla. Process until well mixed.

3 Add wet ingredients to dry ingredients and mix until just combined. Fold in chocolate chips and walnuts, reserving a few for the top, if desired. Batter will be thick.

4 Transfer batter to the prepared pan. Smooth top with spatula, and bake for 25–30 minutes, until edges are browned and pulling away from the pan. A toothpick inserted in the center should come out with just a few crumbs.

5 Let bars cool completely, then remove from pan by lifting parchment paper. Cut into 9 squares. Store in an airtight container at room temperature for up to 3 days or freeze in a freezer-safe container for up to 3 months.

Cherry Chia Pudding

Per Serving:

Calories	294
Fat	13g
Sodium	66mg
Carbohydrates	38g
Fiber	10g
Sugar	23g
Protein	9g

Chia seeds are amazing little packages of nutrition that have unique gelatinous properties. You can use any fruit for this recipe. They're great for meal prep because they can be refrigerated in sealable glass jars. Then eat them for breakfast or a snack on the run all week long.

2 cups unsweetened soy milk, divided

½ cup chia seeds

2 tablespoons almond butter

1 teaspoon vanilla extract

¼ cup maple syrup

2 cups unsweetened fresh or thawed frozen dark sweet cherries, stems and pits removed

1 In a medium bowl, whisk together 1 cup soy milk, chia seeds, almond butter, vanilla, and maple syrup. Stir to combine completely then add the second cup of soy milk and fold in cherries.

2 Place in refrigerator for 5 minutes, then remove and stir again to mix chia seeds throughout the pudding. Stir again after about 30 minutes.

3 Chill in the refrigerator for 2–3 hours to allow the pudding to fully set.

4 Refrigerate leftovers in an airtight container for up to 5 days, or freeze in a freezer-safe container for up to 3 months. Thaw overnight in the refrigerator.

Chewy Granola Bars

These are a delicious treat for an on-the-go snack for any age or a dessert that's sure to please your sweet tooth while staying true to your plant-based diet. Add peanut butter instead of almond butter or other nuts or seeds for variety. If you don't have cacao nibs, substitute vegan chocolate chips.

⅓ cup almond butter

½ teaspoon vanilla extract

⅓ cup date syrup

⅓ cup coconut sugar

2 cups old-fashioned oats

1 cup puffed rice

¼ cup cacao nibs

⅓ cup chopped unsalted dry-roasted peanuts

1 Preheat oven to 350°F. Line an 8" × 8" baking dish with parchment paper, leaving a 2" overhang on all sides.

2 In a small microwave-safe bowl, mix almond butter with vanilla, date syrup, and coconut sugar. Microwave on high for about 20 seconds to loosen the mixture.

3 In a large bowl, combine oats, puffed rice, cacao nibs, and peanuts. Add almond butter mixture and stir with a spatula until well combined. (You may need to use your hands to combine completely.)

4 Firmly press evenly into prepared baking dish and bake for 8–10 minutes, until they are firm to the touch. Cool completely, then lift out with parchment paper and cut into 9 squares. (Be sure to cool before cutting, or bars may crumble.)

5 Store covered on the counter for up to 1 week. To freeze, wrap individual bars in parchment paper and store in a freezer-safe container for up to 3 months.

SERVES 9

Per Serving:

Calories	254
Fat	11g
Sodium	32mg
Carbohydrates	34g
Fiber	4g
Sugar	6g
Protein	7g

MORE ABOUT CACAO NIBS

Cacao nibs are a pure form of chocolate made without added sweetener or fat. They're shaped into tiny nuggets that can be added to smoothies or used in recipes to replace chocolate chips. Since they have no sugar, they are slightly bitter—but unless you eat them by themselves, they work well in most recipes. You can find them in most natural-food stores.

Chunky Yogurt Bark

SERVES 4

Per Serving:

Calories	301
Fat	14g
Sodium	16mg
Carbohydrates	39g
Fiber	5g
Sugar	24g
Protein	8g

FRESH VERSUS FROZEN FRUIT

You can usually decide whether fresh fruit or frozen is better on a case-by-case basis, depending on the recipe you're making. In this recipe, either would work, but frozen fruit can become mushy once defrosted, so use fresh if you're topping a dessert, for example. If you have too much fresh fruit, cut it up, store it in the freezer, and grab it to use in smoothies.

When it's hot out, try these cooling chunks of sweetness that set up quickly in your freezer. Mix up the topping by adding your favorite fruit and keep it on hand for that afternoon sweet-tooth craving.

2 (6-ounce) containers unsweetened plain plant yogurt (or 1½ cups homemade)

3 tablespoons maple syrup

⅓ cup slivered almonds

1 cup fresh or frozen whole unsweetened raspberries

3 tablespoons unsalted shelled pumpkin seeds

¼ cup mini vegan chocolate chips

½ cup Pumpkin Cinnamon Nut Granola (see recipe in Chapter 2)

1 Line a baking sheet that will fit in your freezer with parchment paper and set aside.

2 In a medium bowl, mix yogurt with syrup and almonds. Spread onto the parchment paper.

3 Sprinkle raspberries, pumpkin seeds, chocolate chips, and Pumpkin Cinnamon Nut Granola over the top.

4 Freeze until firm, about 2–3 hours.

5 Let sit on the counter a couple of minutes before breaking apart with your hands, or cut into serving pieces.

6 Wrap leftovers with parchment paper and store in a covered container or freezer bag in the freezer for up to 1 month.

Caramel-Oat Bites

These quick and easy bites are a great snack—they're crunchy and chewy with a touch of healthy sweetness. And you can easily make variations to fit your preferences. For example, try using peanut or almond butter, chocolate chips, coconut, or different nuts and seeds. You can't go wrong!

1 cup old-fashioned oats

½ cup unsalted walnuts

1 cup packed pitted medium Medjool dates

¼ cup unsalted crunchy all-natural peanut butter

2 tablespoons water

1   In a food processor, combine oats and walnuts. Pulse until mixture resembles a coarse meal.

2   Add dates and pulse again to incorporate. Add peanut butter and water. Pulse until mixture forms a sticky, but not completely smooth, dough. Do not overprocess—there should still be some texture.

3   Using your hands, roll about 1 tablespoon batter into a bite-sized ball. Repeat with remaining batter.

4   Refrigerate in an airtight container for 7–10 days, or freeze in a freezer-safe container for up to 6 months.

MAKES 20–24 BITES

Per Serving (2 bites):

Calories	150
Fat	8g
Sodium	2mg
Carbohydrates	19g
Fiber	3g
Sugar	10g
Protein	4g

Easy Fruit Pops

Per Serving:

Calories	45
Fat	0g
Sodium	4mg
Carbohydrates	10g
Fiber	1g
Sugar	7g
Protein	1g

These are an easy and fun way to eat more fruit. Kids especially love them. Experiment with different combinations, because any juice or frozen fruit will do. If you don't have molds, use small paper cups or ice cube trays and popsicle sticks. Put plastic wrap across the top of the tray or paper cup after filling, and then simply poke the stick through the plastic.

1½ cups unsweetened apple juice
¾ cup vanilla Greek plant yogurt
2½ cups organic frozen fruit, such as strawberries or mangoes

In a blender, combine all ingredients and blend until smooth. Pour into molds and freeze until firm, about 4–6 hours. Store in freezer for up to 6 months.

Peanut Butter Cookies

BE CHOOSY ABOUT PEANUT BUTTER

Store-bought peanut butter often has added ingredients that are not recommended on a plant-based diet. Peanut butter doesn't need added oil, sugar, or salt to be delicious. This goes for other nut butters as well. Choose only those made with one ingredient (plus maybe a little salt) and nothing else.

These Peanut Butter Cookies are soft and chewy, just like the ones you know and love—but these are a healthier option. If you prefer less sugar, substitute ½ teaspoon liquid stevia for ¼ cup of the maple syrup.

1 (15-ounce) can low-sodium chickpeas, drained and rinsed

½ cup all-natural peanut butter

½ cup maple syrup

⅓ cup oat flour

1 teaspoon vanilla extract

1 teaspoon cinnamon

2 teaspoons baking powder

½ teaspoon salt

½ cup chopped walnuts

1. Preheat oven to 350°F. Line a baking sheet with parchment paper.
2. In a food processor, combine chickpeas, peanut butter, maple syrup, flour, vanilla, cinnamon, baking powder, and salt. Process until mixture is completely smooth, scraping down the sides of the bowl as needed.
3. Scrape batter into a large bowl and stir in walnuts.
4. Drop about 2 tablespoons of batter 2" apart onto prepared baking sheet. Flatten cookies with the back of a fork. You should be able to get 20 cookies.
5. Bake for 25 minutes or until the edges turn a bit brown. The interior of the cookie will be slightly chewy.
6. Store in an airtight container at room temperature or refrigerate for up to 5 days, or freeze in an airtight container for up to 2 months.

Chocolate Hummus Pudding

This quick and easy dessert is sure to surprise your guests since it's both delicious and low-carb. Serve it by itself, topped with sliced strawberries, or use it as a dip for apple slices or pretzels.

1 (15-ounce) can low-sodium chickpeas, drained and rinsed

2 tablespoons tahini

⅓ cup cacao or cocoa powder

⅓ cup maple syrup

½ teaspoon vanilla extract

½ teaspoon cinnamon

2 tablespoons (or more) soy milk

SERVES 4	
Per Serving:	
Calories	226
Fat	7g
Sodium	150mg
Carbohydrates	39g
Fiber	7g
Sugar	19g
Protein	8g

1. In a food processor, combine all ingredients and process, stopping occasionally to scrape down sides, until mixture is smooth, about 2 minutes. Add more soy milk if it needs to be thinned.

2. Refrigerate in an airtight container for at least 2 hours to cool before serving. Refrigerate leftovers for up to 3 days.

Sautéed Bananas and Strawberries

For a quick and easy sweet treat, try sautéed fruits. They work well with the addition of Cashew Cream and granola.

2 teaspoons maple syrup

Juice of 1 medium orange

½ teaspoon cinnamon

2 medium bananas, peeled and cut in half lengthwise, then into thirds

12 medium strawberries, hulled and sliced

⅓ cup Pumpkin Cinnamon Nut Granola (see recipe in Chapter 2)

½ cup Cashew Cream (see recipe in Chapter 9) plus 2 teaspoons maple syrup

SERVES 4	
Per Serving:	
Calories	174
Fat	5g
Sodium	21mg
Carbohydrates	31g
Fiber	4g
Sugar	17g
Protein	4g

1. Heat a large nonstick skillet over medium heat. Add maple syrup, orange juice, cinnamon, and bananas. Sauté until heated through, about 3 minutes, flipping over a couple of times.

2. Add strawberries and warm for 1 minute more.

3. Serve topped with granola and cream. Refrigerate leftovers in an airtight container for 3–5 days.

2-Week Plant-Based Meal Plan

	Week 1				
	Breakfast	**Lunch**	**Snack**	**Dinner**	**Dessert**
MON	Heart-Healthy Smoothie (Chapter 2)	Tofu Eggless Salad Sandwich (Chapter 6)	High-Protein Trail Mix (Chapter 3; make enough for Wednesday's snack)	Penne Pasta with Roasted Vegetables (Chapter 7; make enough Roasted Vegetables for tacos on Tuesday and on Saturday)	Chocolate Hummus Pudding (Chapter 10; make enough for snack on Tuesday and dessert on Wednesday)
TUE	Breakfast Burrito with Tofu Scramble (Chapter 2; make enough scramble for Wednesday's Tacos and Thursday's Breakfast Tacos)	Mexican Chopped Salad (Chapter 4)	Leftover Chocolate Hummus Pudding (Chapter 10) and apple slices	Roasted Vegetable Tacos (Chapter 7; use roasted veggies from Monday's dinner)	Cinnamon-Apple Yogurt Parfait (Chapter 10; make enough apple filling for Cinnamon-Apple Crepes on Thursday)
WED	Steel-Cut Oat with Fruit and Nuts (Chapter 2; make enough for breakfast on Friday)	Scrambled Tofu Tacos (Chapter 2; use Tofu Scramble from Tuesday's Breakfast Burrito)	Leftover High-Protein Trail Mix (Chapter 3)	Falafel Burger (Chapter 7; make enough burger for Greek Spinach Salad on Thursday)	Leftover Chocolate Hummus Pudding (Chapter 10)
THU	Scrambled Tofu Tacos (Chapter 2; use Scramble from Tuesday's Breakfast Burrito)	Greek Spinach Salad with Falafel (Chapter 4; use yesterday's Falafel Burger to make Falafel Balls)	apple slices and peanut butter	Vegetable Divan with a side of brown rice (Chapter 7; make extra Vegetable Divan and rice for Friday's lunch)	Cinnamon-Apple Crepes (Chapter 2; use apple filling from Tuesday's dessert)

Week 1

	Breakfast	Lunch	Snack	Dinner	Dessert
FRI	Leftover Steel-Cut Oats with Fruit and Nuts (Chapter 2)	Leftover Vegetable Divan (Chapter 7) with a side of brown rice	plant yogurt and berries	Curried Red Lentil Soup (Chapter 5; make enough for Sunday's lunch) with a side of lettuce salad	fresh pineapple
SAT	Raspberry Chocolate Chia Smoothie (Chapter 2)	Quinoa Salad with Spinach (Chapter 4; make enough for tomorrow's snack)	Mashed avocado and Oil-Free Tortilla Chips (Chapter 3)	Roasted Vegetable Tacos (Chapter 7; use leftover roasted vegetables from Monday's dinner)	Avocado Brownies (Chapter 10; make enough for Sunday's dessert)
SUN	Country Hash Browns with Sausage Gravy (Chapter 2)	Leftover Curried Red Lentil Soup (Chapter 5)	Leftover Quinoa Salad with Spinach (Chapter 4)	Cauliflower Pasta Alfredo (Chapter 7; make enough for tomorrow's lunch)	Leftover Avocado Brownies (Chapter 10)

Week 2

	Breakfast	Lunch	Snack	Dinner	Dessert
MON	Overnight Chocolate-Chia Oats (Chapter 2; make enough for Wednesday's and Friday's breakfast)	Leftover Cauliflower Pasta Alfredo (Chapter 7)	Black Bean–Mango Salsa with Oil-Free Tortilla Chips (Chapter 3)	Pineapple Fried Rice with Baked Tofu (Chapter 7; make enough for tomorrow's lunch) with a side of green salad	Chocolate-Cinnamon Ice Cream (Chapter 10; make enough for tomorrow's snack)
TUE	Heart-Healthy Smoothie (Chapter 2; make enough for tomorrow's snack)	Leftover Pineapple Fried Rice with Baked Tofu (Chapter 7)	Leftover Chocolate-Cinnamon Ice Cream (Chapter 10)	Orzo Pasta Salad with Roasted Vegetables (Chapter 4; make enough salad for tomorrow's lunch)	Carrot-Chocolate Chip Cookies (Chapter 10)
WED	Leftover Overnight Chocolate-Chia Oats (Chapter 2)	Leftover Orzo Pasta Salad with Roasted Vegetables (Chapter 4)	Leftover Heart-Healthy Smoothie (Chapter 2)	Lasagna Soup (Chapter 5; make enough for Thursday's dinner)	Sautéed Bananas and Strawberries (Chapter 10; make enough for tomorrow's snack)
THU	Black Bean Breakfast Tacos (Chapter 2; use Black Bean–Mango Salsa from Monday's snack for the tacos)	Hummus-Vegetable Wrap (Chapter 6; make extra Beet Hummus for tomorrow's snack)	Leftover Sautéed Bananas and Strawberries (Chapter 10)	Leftover Lasagna Soup (Chapter 5)	Gluten-Free Pumpkin Spice Cake (Chapter 10; make enough for tomorrow's dessert)

Week 2

	Breakfast	Lunch	Snack	Dinner	Dessert
FRI	Leftover Overnight Chocolate-Chia Oats (Chapter 2)	Caesar Salad with Homemade Croutons (Chapter 4; make enough for tomorrow's lunch)	Leftover Beet Hummus (Chapter 3) with sliced vegetables	Tempeh Burrito Bowl (Chapter 7; make enough pinto beans for Saturday's snack and Sunday's breakfast)	Leftover Gluten-Free Pumpkin Spice Cake (Chapter 10)
SAT	Pumpkin Pancakes (Chapter 2; make enough for tomorrow's snack)	Caesar Salad Wrap with Chickpeas (Chapter 6; use salad from yesterday's lunch)	Nachos (Chapter 3; use leftover pinto beans from Friday's dinner)	Beefless Beef Stew (Chapter 5; make enough for tomorrow's lunch)	Easy Fruit Pops (Chapter 10; make enough for tomorrow's dessert)
SUN	Huevos Rancheros with Tomatillo Sauce (Chapter 2; use leftover pinto beans from Friday's dinner)	Leftover Beefless Beef Stew (Chapter 5)	Leftover Pumpkin Pancakes (Chapter 2)	Black Bean Meatloaf (Chapter 7)	Leftover Easy Fruit Pops (Chapter 10)

STANDARD **US/METRIC**
MEASUREMENT CONVERSIONS

VOLUME CONVERSIONS

US Volume Measure	Metric Equivalent
⅛ teaspoon	0.5 milliliter
¼ teaspoon	1 milliliter
½ teaspoon	2 milliliters
1 teaspoon	5 milliliters
½ tablespoon	7 milliliters
1 tablespoon (3 teaspoons)	15 milliliters
2 tablespoons (1 fluid ounce)	30 milliliters
¼ cup (4 tablespoons)	60 milliliters
⅓ cup	90 milliliters
½ cup (4 fluid ounces)	125 milliliters
⅔ cup	160 milliliters
¾ cup (6 fluid ounces)	180 milliliters
1 cup (16 tablespoons)	250 milliliters
1 pint (2 cups)	500 milliliters
1 quart (4 cups)	1 liter (about)

WEIGHT CONVERSIONS

US Weight Measure	Metric Equivalent
½ ounce	15 grams
1 ounce	30 grams
2 ounces	60 grams
3 ounces	85 grams
¼ pound (4 ounces)	115 grams
½ pound (8 ounces)	225 grams
¾ pound (12 ounces)	340 grams
1 pound (16 ounces)	454 grams

OVEN TEMPERATURE CONVERSIONS

Degrees Fahrenheit	Degrees Celsius
200 degrees F	95 degrees C
250 degrees F	120 degrees C
275 degrees F	135 degrees C
300 degrees F	150 degrees C
325 degrees F	160 degrees C
350 degrees F	180 degrees C
375 degrees F	190 degrees C
400 degrees F	205 degrees C
425 degrees F	220 degrees C
450 degrees F	230 degrees C

BAKING PAN SIZES

American	Metric
8 × 1½ inch round baking pan	20 × 4 cm cake tin
9 × 1½ inch round baking pan	23 × 3.5 cm cake tin
11 × 7 × 1½ inch baking pan	28 × 18 × 4 cm baking tin
13 × 9 × 2 inch baking pan	30 × 20 × 5 cm baking tin
2 quart rectangular baking dish	30 × 20 × 3 cm baking tin
15 × 10 × 2 inch baking pan	30 × 25 × 2 cm baking tin (Swiss roll tin)
9 inch pie plate	22 × 4 or 23 × 4 cm pie plate
7 or 8 inch springform pan	18 or 20 cm springform or loose bottom cake tin
9 × 5 × 3 inch loaf pan	23 × 13 × 7 cm or 2 lb narrow loaf or pate tin
1½ quart casserole	1.5 liter casserole
2 quart casserole	2 liter casserole

Index

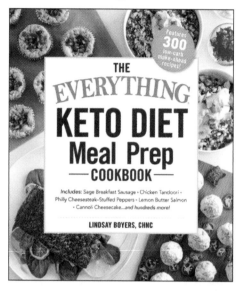